Countryside Recreation Site Management

Countryside r̲ ... .s be ... an in...asingly popular leisure activity, with rural recreation offering an escape from the stresses of life in the modern city. Consequently, the pressures on managers of countryside recreation sites are greater than ever before. This important new vocational text offers comprehensive guidance on the management of countryside sites of all types, from national parks and heritage coasts to cycle paths and tourism enterprises.

The book takes an innovative marketing-driven approach to the subject, focusing on the development of each site as a 'product' to meet the needs of the leisure 'consumer'. It offers step-by-step guidance to every management issue, from developing infrastructure to on-site health and safety, and is richly supported with diagrams, photographs, case studies and web links.

Countryside Recreation Site Management is an essential resource for all students studying recreation or tourism management, and for all professional recreation managers.

Ian Keirle is a Course Director and Lecturer at the Institute of Rural Studies, University of Wales, Aberystwyth.

Countryside Recreation Site Management
A marketing approach

Ian Keirle

London and New York

First published 2002 by Routledge
11 New Fetter Lane, London EC4P 4EE

Simultaneously published in the USA and Canada
by Routledge
29 West 35th Street, New York, NY 10001

Routledge is an imprint of the Taylor & Francis Group

Typeset in 10/12pt Sabon by Wearset Ltd, Boldon, Tyne and Wear
Printed and bound in Great Britain by TJ International Ltd, Padstow,
Cornwall

British Library Cataloguing in Publication Data
A catalogue record for this book is available from the British Library

Library of Congress Cataloging in Publication Data
A catalog record for this book has been requested

ISBN 0-415-24884-1 (hbk)
ISBN 0-415-24885-X (pbk)

Contents

Plates

Figures

Tables

Preface

The importance of recreation in the countryside is increasingly being recognised. It is of value in many ways. First, it is important for the individual. Recreating in the countryside is a form of relaxation that allows the stresses and strains of modern living to be stripped away. It provides opportunities to unwind, contemplate life, for adventure, challenge, development of fitness and social interchange between friends and families. Second it is important for rural communities. Visitors attracted into the countryside spend money on food and drink, fuel, accommodation, souvenirs and entrance fees. This directly helps the rural economy and provides much needed employment. In addition, in providing facilities for the visitor, the surrounding communities also benefit in terms of better facilities, improved access and so forth. The development of recreational opportunities within the countryside is therefore an investment in personal health and well being, and in the rural economy.

This book focuses on the management of countryside recreation sites. For the purpose of this book a countryside recreation site can be defined as any site in the countryside where provision is made for people to recreate out of doors. Such sites include national parks, country parks, heritage coasts, national trails, regional routes, cycle routes and tourism enterprises. The scale of provision can range from large sophisticated sites with high quality facilities, large visitor numbers and dedicated staff, to small-scale informal sites with very few visitors. Countryside recreation sites can be free to enter or could be of a more commercial nature with entrance charges such as gardens or wildlife parks. Therefore, if you have anything to do with the management of visitors to the countryside, the contents of this book are appropriate for you.

The book takes a marketing approach to the subject matter. This means that countryside sites are viewed as products that the consumer (the recreational visitor) makes a choice as to whether to visit or not. The development of the site product to meet the needs of the consumer is therefore what this book is all about. The book starts by outlining the subject of marketing and considers how a marketing approach can be applied to the management of countryside sites. It then considers what you need to find out about sites and site visitors, prior to planning the management of a site, and details techniques that can be used. Following this, the issues that need to be considered when managing a site are considered. Chapters on making sites more accessible, disabled access, customer care, site infrastructure (stiles, gates, paths, bins, bollards, etc.), information and interpretation, developing attractions, dealing with conflicts, health and safety and management planning, all provide practical hands-on information to aid site planning and management. Throughout the book examples and case studies are used to illustrate the points being made and extensive use is made of web links as case studies and information sources.

This practical book is written and structured in a manner to make the contents easily accessible to the reader. Photographs, diagrams and examples illustrate the text and each chapter contains an extensive reference and suggested reading list to allow the subject matter to be studied more widely.

The book is aimed at students on any course associated with the management of visitors in the countryside and as such is suited to courses in leisure, countryside management, recreation management and tourism. It will also be a useful book for anyone working within the industry.

I hope you enjoy it.

Ian Keirle

Acknowledgements

This book was inspired by the many interesting days I have had visiting countryside recreation sites around the country as a customer and as a professional visitor. My thanks therefore go to all the professionals in the industry who have developed inspiring recreational facilities that show what can be done with enthusiasm, inspiration and dedication.

Thanks also go to Mick Green and Kath Keirle for proof-reading and suggestions and to Ray Youell for advice on preparing a manuscript.

Most of all, this book is dedicated to Kath my partner and friend, for her constant support and encouragement, and to my patient children Megan and Iwan who did not see as much of me as they would have liked to have on occasions!

1 Marketing

Marketing is concerned with developing goods and services that meet the needs of the consumer. Countryside recreation sites can be considered as products that consumers make a decision to purchase or not. A marketing approach to the management of countryside recreation sites therefore, provides a framework by which decisions about site management can be made. This chapter outlines what marketing is and considers how it can be applied to the management of countryside recreation sites.

Without doubt the term 'marketing' is one that is often misused, misunderstood and seen in countryside recreation as some kind of devil to be avoided at all costs! It smacks of commercialism, salesmen and women, advertisers and worst of all the pursuit of profit. These views are based upon a lack of understanding concerning what marketing actually is. The correct use of marketing can be of considerable benefit to the recreation manager, in developing recreation facilities that match the needs of the public. As such, the use of the marketing ethic will form a backbone to this book that will be developed in all future chapters. It is the intention of this chapter to dispel some of the myths surrounding the term 'marketing', and provide the reader with an understanding of the marketing concept and how it can be applied for positive benefit in the development of high quality recreation facilities. However, marketing is a very complex subject with many high quality books written about it. This book therefore only introduces marketing and concentrates on aspects that are of particular relevance to the development of the recreational site product and site based services. For greater depth, a number of excellent texts, listed at the end of this chapter which develop the study of marketing much more profoundly are highly recommended.

What marketing is not

If you were to conduct a survey and ask the public 'What is marketing?' you could be pretty sure that the main answer would be advertising, with sales coming a close second. This is not surprising, as these are often the most visible and obvious faces of marketing. However, marketing is neither advertising nor sales. Advertising and sales may well be part of a marketing process, but marketing is much much more.

What then, is marketing?

Before talking in marketing terms about what marketing is, let us consider a friend of mine, Joe Public, waking up on a sunny Saturday morning after a stressful week in the office and a Friday night in the pub. Having heaved his tired and pale body out of his bed he looks out of the window, sees the fresh blue sky of an autumn day and decides he really ought to go out for a day in the countryside. Where should he go and what should he do? He will decide by assessing a complex set of issues that will ultimately lead to him going on a trip to a particular countryside site. Fundamentally he will have certain *needs* that he will seek to *satisfy* on his day out. For Joe on this sunny day these may be:

- the need to drive a relatively short distance
- the need for exercise, a walk perhaps – somewhere dramatic with good views, but not too steep (still feeling a bit hung over)
- a pub for lunch, with somewhere to sit outside
- a hassle and stress free day
- the need not to spend too much money
- the need to do some shopping at some time during the day.

Using the information he has to hand (his memory of past visits, other people's recommendations, perceptions of what places he has not been to may be like, a local Ordnance Survey map, a pub guide) he will make a decision about where to go. As part of this decision making process he will have to consider the *benefits* offered by one location over another. One location may have a pub where he knows he can get a good lunch; another may be close to a large supermarket. Some of the benefits offered may be in the form of *service*. Joe may have visited a site before and found that the landlord of the local pub was rude and lunch had taken over an hour to arrive and that the warden of the country park he had visited had been particularly unhelpful. Joe will make his decision about where to go based upon his knowledge of the *benefits* of the *products* and *services* offered by the different countryside *products* available to him. His ultimate choice will depend upon an evaluation of what will *satisfy* his *needs* on that particular day.

Having made his decision, Joe will have his day out and will, at the end of the day, decide whether the day's activities satisfied his needs. If the answer is yes, he is likely to return at a future date; if the answer is no he is unlikely to visit again. Thus by experience Joe is constantly updating his knowledge base upon which future decisions will be based.

In this scenario a few key concepts have been raised that will be looked at in more detail later in this chapter. In particular the words *needs*, *benefits*, *service*, *products* and *satisfy* were highlighted. These key words form the backbone of *marketing*.

Marketing as a philosophy

Marketing is a philosophy, a state of mind if you like that considers the needs of the public in making management decisions.

> The key aspect of marketing is an attitude of mind. It requires that in taking marketing decisions, the manager looks at these from the viewpoint of the consumer. These decisions will thus be driven by what the consumer needs and wants.
>
> (Mercer 1992: 11)

This concept of making management decisions by looking at the needs of the consumer is fundamental. Let us look at a fictitious example from a countryside recreation site.

An example of how not to do it!

The management of a country park outside a small suburban town decides that in order to increase the visitor numbers to the site, a new attraction needs to be developed. The wardens get together at a wardens' meeting and after a brainstorming session decide that a BMX track is required. Reports are written, budgets allocated and contractors contracted. Eventually a year later a BMX track is developed and opened. The numbers of bikers using it is monitored on a daily basis and after a few months it quickly becomes apparent that the amount of use is far less than anticipated. What has gone wrong? The wardens decide to talk to the bikers that do come to find out why it is not used more. The children tell them that BMX biking went out of fashion five years ago and that the track is boring and unexciting.

What was the mistake made by the wardens? The primary mistake was to make an assumption about what the young people coming to the park wanted. No attempt was made to survey young people to ask them about their needs. In addition, once it had been decided that a BMX track was what would be developed, no attempt was made to find out from the young people that may use it what features make a BMX track a good one.

What are the lessons from this example? The key lesson is that the needs of the consumer (the young people of the area) were not addressed. A product was developed, but it was the wrong product. This was based upon an *assumption* of what the consumer wanted rather than being based upon what was *actually* wanted. An important element of marketing is therefore developing an understanding that in developing any product, whether it be a new kitchen gadget, a swimming pool or a countryside site, the needs of the consumer are of utmost importance and must be understood. Marketing can therefore be considered to be a 'state of mind' that lies behind all decision making concerning the development of products and services.

Marketing as a management process

In the last section we looked at marketing as being a philosophy based upon an underlying belief that the needs of the consumer are important. However, marketing is also a management process. If you like, we need a methodological framework within which to assess what the needs of the consumer are, and to develop products or services that match them. This process sounds so simple. Why then are so many books published on the subject and why are so many expensive mistakes made? The answer is that like most things in life, the process, whilst being simple in concept, has hidden complexities. For example, consumers in making decisions about which products to purchase will be driven by a complex set of motives. Ask yourself the following questions:

- When you last purchased a car what were the factors that led you to buy car *x* over car *y*?
- When you last went shopping for food, why did you select a particular shop or supermarket to go shopping in and what influenced you in deciding what to put in your basket?

It is likely that some of the following issues may have been of influence:

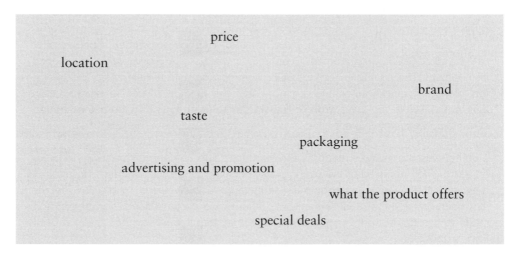

For people involved in the development of products and services these complexities need to be addressed. To help us, a number of techniques have been developed to make sense of them. The techniques are often sequential in their nature and we are therefore involved in a process. Marketing is a management process in as much as within the process, consideration will need to be made about all the above issues as well as organisational issues such as finance, staff, use of time, and so on. Some of the marketing techniques involved will be outlined in this and later chapters. Many others exist and readers should refer to mainstream marketing texts.

A definition

People are always after definitions of words. If you read through the many marketing texts on library shelves you will find a variety of definitions about what marketing is. The Chartered Institute for Marketing defines marketing as: 'The management process responsible for identifying, anticipating and satisfying customer requirements profitably' (Adcock *et al.* 1995: 3).

This encapsulates nicely the ideas outlined in the previous sections and reflects the structure of this book very well. Chapters 1 to 3 of the book will reflect issues about the management process for identifying and anticipating customer requirements and the remainder is concerned with the development of products and services that will satisfy customer requirements. The final word 'profitably' needs to be considered generically to mean more than just making money. In the context of the management of recreation sites the pursuit of financial gain may not be the prime consideration. However, ensuring that your organisation and or site profits from the benefits offered by marketing, is important.

Needs, products, benefits and satisfaction

Earlier in the chapter a description was made of Joe Public deciding to go for a day out in the countryside. It was shown that he had certain *needs* for his day out that needed to be *satisfied*. He could only satisfy them by selecting the right countryside product (a countryside site or walk). The selection process that would go on in his brain in choosing where to go involves him considering a variety of countryside *products* and the *services* that may be offered with each product and assessing the *benefits* that each may offer him, to enable his needs to be *satisfied*.

This section of the chapter will consider each of these key marketing elements in more detail.

Needs

In life we all have individual needs all of the time. The most basic needs are those concerning the servicing of the physical needs of our bodies. Every day we need to eat, drink, sleep and go to the toilet. These are our most basic needs. After this our needs become more complex. At different times we may have some of the following needs:

Physical needs	food
	drink
	exercise
	toilet
	warmth/shelter
Social/personal needs	friends
	family
	I want to be alone!
	socialise
	status in community
Emotional/spiritual needs	love
	acceptance
	confidence
	peace and quiet

In life we spend most of our time trying to satisfy these complex needs in many different ways. Indeed, the pursuit of the satisfaction of these needs is the game of life! Each individual will, at different times have an individual set of needs that require satisfaction, at any one moment in time. However, this is where the simple becomes more complex. Each individual need may be satisfied in more than one way. Let us consider one of our most basic needs, that of thirst. To quench our thirst all we have to do is drink water. However, few of us do this. Most of us drink tea, coffee, squash, fizzy drinks or beer. Normally these drinks are packaged as distinct individual products. We may choose a particular drink for one of the following reasons:

taste	image	how refreshing it is
peer group pressure	availability	price
weather	time of day	habit

We may, based upon this list, on a sunny afternoon sitting by a swimming pool, choose to drink a cola drink because we like the way it tastes; we know it will be cool and refreshing and will definitely quench our thirst. In addition, when we open the bottle we can guarantee what the drink inside will taste like. On a cold winter's evening when we come in from work, a mug of warm comforting tea may be just right to satisfy our need to drink, whilst after a stressful day a stiff gin may be required! Therefore we are led to one of the basic principles of marketing: 'There is always more than one way of satisfying a need'.

What may be the needs of a visitor, on a day out in the countryside?

Physical needs

Exercise	A walk, cycle ride, swim . . .
Challenge	Challenge walks, mountain bike tracks, distance cycled, a hard rock climb, a grade 4 rapid . . .
Shelter	Somewhere to go and something to do if it rains or gets cold.
Natural features	Mountains, cliffs, rivers, woods, lakes . . .
Accessibility	How easy is it to get somewhere?
Toilets	We've all got to go sometime.
Food/drink	Pubs, cafés, shops, picnic areas.

Social/personal needs

Socialising	Somewhere to meet and socialise with friends and family.
I want to be alone!	Don't we all sometimes, the countryside is a good place for contemplation.
Have a laugh	And what's wrong with that? Somewhere to let off steam.
Prestige	Keeping up with and doing better than the Joneses. Doing something more exciting, exclusive or exotic.
Children	Get the children out of the house, education, stop them getting bored.

Emotional needs

Love	Country walks, romantic weekends, romantic places.
Lack of hassle	Somewhere to go that will be stress free.
Confidence	A place to go where there is no danger of trespassing or any physical dangers. Somewhere where you know you are welcome.

Financial needs

Price   How much will the day cost?
Value for money   Is the expenditure incurred good value for money?

Products

To satisfy a lot of our needs we purchase *products*. What is a product?

A product is something you choose to invest in to satisfy a need, whether it is an investment of money or time. Usually a product is something that has been developed to satisfy particular needs. Normally we would consider a product to be a physical entity such as a washing machine, a car or a bar of chocolate. However, we need to take a wider view of what products are.

If we buy a package holiday to Majorca we are buying a holiday product. A package holiday is a specific product that has been developed to satisfy people's need for a couple of weeks in the sunshine of the Mediterranean. It may not be something we can put in a shopping trolley but it is nonetheless still a product. In a similar fashion, managed countryside sites can be viewed as products. For example, country parks have been specifically developed to provide informal countryside recreation opportunities. Although we may not have to actually buy the product, we still have to invest our time in it and we will have made a decision about whether to visit or not (i.e. whether to purchase the product).

In marketing the understanding of what products are, and the development of new ones is of fundamental importance. Indeed most of this book is dedicated to the development of countryside recreation 'products'. In marketing terms we divide products into the *core product*, the *tangible features of the product* and the *intangible features of the product*, which combined together, make up the *total product*. Let us consider these product elements.

Core products
The core product represents the essential service or benefit on offer that may be purchased to satisfy a need. For example, the core product from a can of baked beans are the beans themselves in tomato sauce. Similarly the core product of a car is a metal cage on wheels that can move people from A to B.

Tangible features of the product
The tangible features of a product are its physical elements that make it distinct from its competitors. In the car example tangible features may be air conditioning, ABS braking, 0 to 60 time, air bags, style, colour, radio, and so on. Each type of car on the market although being the same basic core product will be made distinct from it rivals by a unique assemblage of tangible features. For the beans, the main tangible feature will be the packaging of the can.

Intangible features of a product
These are the non-physical elements of a product and include such issues as service, delivery, image, price and brand. In the car example the intangible

features associated with a make of car are very important. Some makes are known for their style, some for their prestige, whilst others have an image of reliability. Other intangible features of a car product are likely to be warranty, credit facilities and depreciation rate. Service is often one of the biggest intangible features that surround a product. For the beans the intangible features may be the price and the brand.

The total product
The total product is a mixture of the core product, its tangible features and the intangible extras that are associated with the product. As such it is what the consumer actually considers when making a decision about which particular product will satisfy their particular needs.

Examples of core, tangible, intangible and total products can be seen in Table 1.1.

The product of the product

The above forms a good framework for considering products. However, products are even more complex than this. When considering what a product is we must view it in terms of what the consumer is actually buying when they purchase a product. This is often very different from the physical product itself.

For example, what product is a compact disc? Physically it is a small round fairly uninteresting plastic disc. Is this what we really pay our hard earned money for? No, this is definitely not the case. What we are buying when we purchase a compact disc is the music that is on it. However, it goes further than that. When we put on some music we select it according to how we feel. Sometimes we put on easy listening

Table 1.1 Core, tangible, intangible and total products: examples of the car and a countryside recreation site

	Car	*Countryside recreation site*
Core product	A vehicle to move you from A to B	A non urban area in which to recreate
Tangible product	Engine size, ABS braking, safety features, colour, style, speed . . .	The physical nature of a countryside site such as lakes, coast, hills, landscape, views, together with physical site attractions such as car parks, visitor centres, playgrounds, walks and other facilities
Intangible product	Insurance group, service, warranty, image of car, brand	Image of the site and the organisation that looks after the site, service, security, accessibility, lack of hassle, site ambience
Total product	The total car product made up of a combination of the physical products and intangible products	The total product made up of a combination of the physical products and intangible products

Table 1.2 What are we really buying? The product of the product

Product	The physical product	The product of the product
CD	A small plastic disc	Music, relaxation, feelings, party
A drill bit	A piece of metal with a spiral	A hole
Shampoo	White slimy stuff in a bottle	Beauty, attractiveness, hope
A novel	Lots of paper with words on it	Relaxation, excitement, romance
A car	A metal cage on four wheels	Journeys, flexibility, independence

music, sometimes moody music and sometimes we just want to party. The music has the power to make you feel sad, happy, want to dance, and so on. Therefore when buying a compact disc we not only buy a piece of plastic and the music contained on it but we are also buying relaxation, mood and feelings. This extra element to a product is termed the *product of the product*. Table 1.2 shows some everyday products and suggests what the product of the product may be for in each one.

Viewing products from this dimension gives them an entirely different feel and it is essential when considering products to look at them from this perspective. Always ask yourself what is it that the consumer is *actually* buying when they select your product. For countryside sites this is particularly pertinent since when you visit a site you cannot 'consume' the site product, but gain the benefits from what the product offers you.

So what is a countryside recreation product?

First it has to be said that each location in the countryside is unique and has its own characteristics. As such, each countryside recreation site is its own unique product. However, various surveys show that certain aspects of the countryside are particularly sought after when deciding to go on a visit to the countryside. Let us take an example of such a survey. The 1996–7 Pembrokeshire Coast Path user survey asked visitors what had attracted them to the trail. Table 1.3 shows the results of the survey.

The answers to this question are typical of many other surveys about visitors' reasons for visiting the countryside. Note that some of the answers revolve around

Table 1.3 Factors that influenced visitors to use the Pembrokeshire Coast Path

Long distance users (visitors using the path for more than one day)		Short distance users (visitors using the path for less than one day)	
Scenery/landscape	91%	Scenery/landscape	55%
Good walking	81%	Relaxation	7%
Good exercise	70%	Nature/birds/wildlife	7%
Nature/birds/wildlife	73%	Good walking	4%
Relaxation/peace and quiet	72%	Live nearby	4%
Get away from it all	57%	Countryside	3%
Countryside	50%		
Standard of path	36%		
Keen walker	36%		

Source: Pembrokeshire Coast National Park 1998: 3.

the core product (scenery/landscape); some are concerned with the tangible product (standard of path), whilst many are concerned with the intangible product (relaxation, peace and quiet, getting away from it all). Also note that there is a difference between the short-distance and the long-distance walkers in terms of what attracted them to the trail.

Benefits

In the section above we saw how a product is made up of many elements ranging from the physical product itself to the intangible benefits associated with it. When making a decision whether to purchase a product the consumer will view the products on offer in relation to their needs at the time. In particular a decision will be made about the benefits offered by one product over another.

For example, there are many makes of cola drinks that you can buy. The first choice you make as a consumer is that a Coke is the product that will satisfy a particular need you have at the time. If you buy your Coke from a bar by the swimming pool there will probably only be one make available so the choice will be easy. If you are in a supermarket you will be confronted with a wide variety of cola products, manufactured by different companies. Why do we choose one variety rather than another? After all, blind tasting has often shown that people find it difficult to differentiate between the makes. In making this second-level choice we are likely to be influenced by:

> habit (what we normally buy)   peer group pressure (what your friends buy)
>
> packaging   the image associated with the product   price
>
> special deals   taste

So in choosing a cola drink from a supermarket you may choose brand X because you *think* it tastes better than brand Y. You like the packaging, and it has an image associated with young people doing exciting things such as throwing themselves off bridges and snowboarding. Another person may be more influenced by the price and perceived value for money. In making the choice of brand X over brand Y the *perceived benefits* offered by the product will be of major importance in decision making.

In the cola example above, product X will be chosen over product Y because X offers benefits over Y. We call the difference between the two products *the differential advantage* of the product. In terms of countryside recreation sites, what might the issues be, that give one site a differential advantage over another, in attracting people to it? Some of the issues may be:

- site attractions
- price
- scenery/views
- refreshments
- parking

- indoor facilities
- accessibility
- crowded/uncrowded
- perceived quality of product
- disabled facilities
- quality of information
- organisation managing the site.

In a commercial world developing a differential advantage over your competitors with your product is vital, as it is this that draws customers to purchase your product over that of your competitors. Similarly in a countryside recreation setting, developing your site product to have a differential advantage over your competitors will lead to more people visiting your site. It is therefore good practice to keep a constant eye on your competitors' products and to consider constantly how your product matches up. This of course should be done through the eyes of the customer.

Service

A service can be defined as any task carried out for a customer (Jobber 1998: 693). In marketing terms a service or 'service' is one of the intangible elements of a product. The concept of service is a broad one and covers such areas as how promptly you are served, how helpful a shop assistant is, whether an enquiry is answered quickly and how knowledgeable the staff in a tourist information centre are.

For many products service is a largely unimportant element of a product. For example, in buying a can of baked beans the service surrounding the can is of little importance. However, for some products service is of utmost importance. In the restaurant trade the way in which the waiters deal with the needs of the customer is a critical element of running a successful restaurant business. In this example the core product will be the food on the plate and one of the intangible products will be the service of the waiters. The leisure and tourism industry is often referred to as a 'service industry' indicating the importance of service to these industries. The management of countryside recreation sites could also be said to fall under this umbrella. The development of high quality service at countryside sites is therefore crucial to success. A customer that has received poor service will be disgruntled and will soon spread the word about your product. Horowitz (in Seaton and Bennett 1996: 448) considers that a disgruntled customer will tell eleven people about their experience, whilst a satisfied customer will tell only three. The truth is bad news travels fast and is remembered for a long time. To this end, an important chapter of this text is Chapter 8 on customer care.

Satisfaction

So far in this chapter we have established that we all have needs that require satisfaction and that we do this by the selection of suitable products and services. So, what do we mean by satisfaction?

Let us explore this through the use of some examples. If we are thirsty we have a need for liquid. If we have a drink this need will be satisfied. At a more complex level, we may need to go for a walk in the countryside for exercise and relaxation. A very enjoyable walk along a beautiful path will satisfy this. However, we may go on a walk that turns out to be muddy, goes through a field with a bull in it and requires you to climb over three barbed wire fences ripping your trousers in the process. In both cases the physical need of a walk may have been satisfied but in the second walk the whole experience will not have been satisfactory. In making a future decision about where to walk you are likely to return to the first walk and give the second wide berth.

Satisfaction therefore relates to how we consider a product after we have consumed it. If a product has satisfied a need it is very likely that it will be purchased again; whereas if it falls below expectation, it is unlikely to be purchased a second time.

It is therefore important in developing countryside recreation products that we satisfy customers' needs. This of course implies that we must know what their needs are!

Markets and market segmentation

The market for a product is the people who represent the actual or potential demand for a product. Kotler (1997: 13) considers a market to 'consist of all the potential customers sharing a particular need or want who might be willing and able to engage in exchange to satisfy a need or want'. A market can therefore be defined as: the people who represent the actual or potential demand for a product.

Let us illustrate this with some examples. The market for a shop selling wedding dresses will be fairly small and will be limited to women about to get married. The market for wedding dresses is therefore easily definable. Similarly the market for lawnmowers is composed of people who need to cut lawns! Some products are more complex than this and the markets for these products are correspondingly more complex. Take for example holidays. There are many types of holiday that people choose to take, ranging from seaside holidays with the children to treks in Nepal. Each type of holiday can be considered to be a different product appealing to a different market. However, even the same type of holiday (and therefore the same product) will appeal to different people. A package tour for two weeks to a Greek island may appeal to very different groups of people. Some people will go for sun, sangria and sex, others for the chance of romance. Families may go for the beaches and clean seas whilst others will wish to view archaeological ruins. For the same product therefore there may be many different groups of people interested in it and therefore the product can be said to appeal to more than one market.

In the example of tourists going to Greece, the people interested in the product were broken up into different groups. Let us remind ourselves of who they were and attempt to add a few characteristics to them.

Reason for choosing holiday	*Characteristics*
sun, sangria and sex	young people 18–30 years
romance	single people
beaches and clean seas	family groups
archaeology	people interested in archaeology with no children or retired

Undoubtedly this is a simplistic picture. However, it illustrates well that the same product will appeal to many different markets each with their own distinct identity. In marketing terms we call this *market segmentation*. Market segmentation can be defined as: 'the process of dividing the total market into homogeneous groupings or segments' (Jobber 1998: 693).

Markets can be segmented in many ways. The following are some of the many cited in marketing texts that are commonly used:

Profile

Age	under 12, 12–18, 19–25, 26–35, 36–49, 50–64, 65+
Gender	male, female
Lifestyle	young single, young couples, young parents, middle-aged, empty nesters, retired
Social class	upper middle, middle, skilled working, unwaged
Income	affluent, tight-budgeters
Geographic	country, region, urban/rural
Geodemographic	upwardly mobile young families living in larger owner-occupied houses, older people living in small houses

Physiographic profile

Lifestyle	trendsetters, conservatives, sophisticates
Personality	extroverts, introverts, aggressive, submissive

Behavioural

Benefits sought	convenience, status, performance
Purchase occasion	self-buy, gift
Purchase behaviour	buyer of new products, brand loyal, experimenter
Usage	heavy, light
Perceptions and beliefs	favourable, unfavourable

(Jobber 1998: 175)

The segmentation of a market is very useful in that it allows us to identify groupings of people who may be interested in purchasing a product. As such, it allows us to target resources at this grouping so as to influence their purchasing behaviour. These segments are therefore often referred to as *target markets*.

Let us take an easy example from a countryside recreation setting. A new mountain bike trail has been developed in a forest park. What market segment from the total population is likely to use such a facility? First, it can be assumed that the principal market will be people who use mountain bikes. However, this facility is unlikely to appeal to every mountain biker in the world! Therefore we can define the market segment more tightly. It is likely to be mountain bikers from within an area of 50 miles of the facility and those mountain bikers who are holidaying in the area. This knowledge can then be used to identify where to contact this specific market segment to let them know about the new facility. To do this you have to think about things this group all have in common. The first things are bikes! At some point most mountain bikers will use their local bike shop for repairs, spares and new kit. Local bike shops may therefore be a good place to communicate with this grouping. In addition mountain bikers are likely to read one of the many mountain bike magazines on offer in newsagents. Advertisements or articles in these publications are therefore likely to be read by a significant proportion of this market segment. Finally there may be local mountain bike clubs who will communicate with their members.

Market segmentation and advertising

Market segmentation is very important when it comes to advertising a product. In deciding how best to get customers to purchase a particular product, marketers first of all consider who has a need to buy the product. Undoubtedly the product will have been designed to meet a very particular need and so the market for that product will be specific and definable. The product will therefore have its own market segment. Advertisements can then be designed to appeal directly to that market segment to encourage people to buy the product designed to fit their particular needs.

This may explain why so often when you watch television, you feel the advertising has not been effective in making you buy a product. The advert was probably not aimed at you, but geared to a very specific market segment. This affects not only the design of the advert but also when the advert is shown. Not surprisingly adverts for children's toys are shown in amongst children's cartoons and are designed specifically at a market segment of children.

Next time you watch television consider the target markets that adverts for the following products are aimed at:

- Carling Black Label
- Tampax sanitary protection
- McDonald's hamburgers.

Market segmentation in a countryside recreation setting – a case study of a sand dune nature reserve

Sand dunes will appeal to different groups of people for different reasons. How can we divide up these visitors into market segments and what do they come to the site for? Here are some suggestions.

Market segment	Reasons for visiting the site
education groups	to study the site's ecology and geomorphology
bird watchers	to view the birds on the site
local people	exercise dogs, evening walks, read the Sunday paper, learn to drive on the beach, swim, sunbathe
holidaymakers	walk, play, swim, sunbathe
families	play, swim, socialise, learn
young people	space to run around, windsurfing, jet skiing
older people	tranquillity, peace, easy to use paths, toilets

Sometimes these market segments cross over. For example, you may find a family on holiday that goes bird watching. This indicates the potential complexity of segregating a market for a product. However, it is a very useful framework for developing an understanding of the different types of people who visit a recreational site and why they visit. Products and services can then be developed and targeted at particular groups for maximum effectiveness. This is done through the development of an appropriate *marketing mix*.

The marketing mix

There are many elements that relate to a particular market for a product that we have little control over. An example of this may be how fluctuations in the value of the pound influence how many people visit Britain for a holiday. There are however, many areas over which we do have control. These areas of decision making are a backbone of marketing and are known collectively as the marketing mix. Kotler (1997: 92) defines the marketing mix as: 'The set of marketing tools that the firm uses to pursue its marketing objectives in the target markets'.

The marketing tools referred to by Kotler are numerous but can be conveniently grouped together into four categories known as the four Ps. These are:

- *p*roduct
- *p*rice
- *p*lace
- *p*romotion.

A range of marketing tools can be gathered under each of the Ps. Each one can be used in combination, to influence the decision making of consumers. The key tools grouped under each P can be seen in Figure 1.1.

The marketing tools in Figure 1.1 relate to marketing in general, but many of them can be directly applied to a countryside recreation setting. Indeed, it is these tools that most of this book is concerned with. Each will be covered in greater depth in later chapters. However, Figure 1.2 illustrates some of the possible tools available to the countryside recreation site manager in developing a marketing mix.

The four Ps relate directly to issues that are under the control of the site manager. However, we have to remember that marketing is concerned with the customer. It is therefore important to view the development of products and services through the eyes of potential customers. As people involved with the development and management of products and services we will know a great deal about them, but does the customer? To make a decision as to whether to purchase a product or

The marketing mix

Product	*Price*	*Place*	*Promotion*
features	cost of product	distribution	advertising
design	discounts	coverage	sales
quality	value for money	location	publicity
branding	credit	accessibility	merchandising
variety			public relations
presentation			information
benefits			
service			

Figure 1.1 The marketing mix

Possible tools in a countryside site marketing mix

Product	*Price*	*Place*	*Promotion*
landscape	parking fees	location	advertising
site features	entrance fees	accessibility	information
site attractions	refreshments	public transport	guidebooks
site facilities	discounts		word of mouth
name of site	season tickets		open days
image of site	value for money		media
customer care			entrance signs
site quality			
management			
infrastructure			
interpretation			

Figure 1.2 Possible tools in a countryside recreation site marketing mix

service customers need to know some key information. In particular they need to know:

- that the product or service exists
- where it can be purchased
- that it is affordable
- that it will meet their individual needs.

These can be translated into the four As of marketing

- awareness
- availability
- affordability
- acceptability.

It can be readily seen that these mirror directly the components of the four Ps of the marketing mix.

> *Awareness* relates to *promotion*.
> *Availability* relates to *place*.
> *Affordability* is a function of *price*.
> *Acceptability* relates to the *product* on offer.

However, as, managers, when we consider the marketing mix of the four Ps we tend to start our thinking with a consideration of the product and then work down through price and place and consider as a last step how we may promote a product or service. From a consumer's point of view the opposite normally applies. The consumer often will start by being aware of a product or service, considering its availability, affordability and finally acceptability. It is therefore vital in marketing terms to consider the four Ps and the four As together, reflecting the needs of the customer at the same time as considering the needs of the organisation you are working for in relation to a product or service. It is also clear that in deciding on any marketing mix for a product or service that the market segment is always considered in taking any marketing decision.

Market research

Throughout this chapter we have considered that marketing is concerned with making decisions about the development of products and services so as to satisfy the needs of the customer. To do this effectively it is essential that we know who our customers are and what their needs are, together with developing a clear understanding of our product or service. We do this through market research. Market research can be defined as: 'The use of scientific methods to collect information relevant to the marketing of products and services' (Hill 1989: 71).

What is relevant information? We could easily spend most of our working lives gathering information. What do we really need to know? The types of information that can be gathered can be broken down into:

- product/services information
- customer information
- competitor information.

Let us examine each of these in turn.

Product/services information

The function of research concerning products and services is to gain a clear understanding of what a product or service actually is. A large part of this will be gaining an understanding of the physical nature of the product (the core product and the tangible product), but will also entail researching the intangible elements of the product or service. As such researching the product often involves researching the customer as well. Chapter 2 of this book looks at some of the methods available to the countryside recreation manager to research the recreational site 'product' and the services associated with it.

Customer information

The function of research concerning the customers of a site and the potential customers of a site is to develop an understanding of the market for the product. Who at present purchases the product? What are their needs and how do they feel about the product? In addition, it is concerned with identifying potential new markets for products and identifying trends in customer behaviour that will aid the development of new products and services. Chapter 3 of this book details the methods available to the countryside recreation manager to find out more about the customer.

Competitor information

Carrying out research about your competitors in a market is an essential element of any commercial marketing. What products and services are your competitors offering, at what price and how are they promoted? What new products are coming onto the market in your product area? What are the differential advantages between you and your competitor? Countryside recreation sites are often seen as being a service to the public and not in competition with one another. However, keeping an eye on the competition will aid the continuing development and management of any recreation site, and will ensure that the highest quality products and services can be delivered to the public.

In developing any product or service, market research is an essential precursor to making any decision about the product. Chapters 2 and 3 of this book consider some of the techniques that can be used to find out more about the site product and the consumers of the product.

References and further reading

Adcock, D., Bradfield, R., Halborg, A. and Ross, C. (1995) *Marketing Principles and Practice*, London: Pitman Publishing.

Baker, M. J. (1998) *The Marketing Manual*, Oxford: Butterworth-Heinemann.

Cannon, T. (1996) *Basic Marketing*, London: Cassell.

Hill, N. (1989) *Introduction to Marketing*, Sunderland: Business Education Publishers Ltd.

Holloway, J. C. (1995) *Marketing for Tourism*, Harlow: Longman.

Horowitz, J. (1990) *How to Win Customers: Using Customer Service for a Competitive Edge*, London: Pitman.

Jobber, D. (1998) *Principles and Practice of Marketing*, Maidenhead: McGraw-Hill.

Kotler, P. (1997) *Marketing Management; Analysis, Planning, Implementation and Control*, New Jersey: Prentice Hall International.

Mercer, D. (1992) *Marketing*, Oxford: Blackwell.

Middleton, V. T. C. (1998) *Marketing in Travel and Tourism*, Oxford: Butterworth-Heinemann.

O'Sullivan, E. L. (1991) *Marketing for Parks, Recreation, and Leisure*, PA: Venture Publishing Inc.

Pembrokeshire Coast National Park (1998) *Pembrokeshire Coast Path: National Trail User Survey 1996–1997*, Pembrokeshire Coast National Park, Countryside Council for Wales.

Seaton, A. V. and Bennett, M. M. (1996) *Marketing Tourism Products*, London: Thompson Business Press.

Swarbrooke, J. and Horner, S. (1999) *Consumer Behaviour in Tourism*, Oxford: Butterworth-Heinemann.

2 Finding out about your site

Every individual site is different in its nature. There will be differences in issues such as size, topography, habitat and wildlife interest, history and land use. To help with the decision-making process for site management, it is essential that a full knowledge of all aspects of a site be developed. Information to help us with this will come from a wide variety of sources including documentation, maps, surveys and audits. This chapter considers the type of knowledge that is needed in order to manage a site and the potential sources of, and methods for, obtaining the required information.

Why do we need to carry out research about recreation sites?

Before we can plan any management of a recreation site it is essential that full understanding is gained of the site itself. This will not only help us to establish the opportunities that the site offers, but will also inform us about the many factors that may constrain what we are able to do. It is particularly pertinent to the management of recreational sites in that whilst recreation may be a key objective of the site, other factors such as conservation, landscape, archaeology and community issues need to be considered in making decisions about development. The following examples illustrate how individual site issues may affect its management.

Example 1 – archaeology affecting site management

A recreation site may contain an important archaeological feature such as an Iron Age hill fort, protected by being designated as a Scheduled Ancient Monument (SAM). This may well be an opportunity to attract visitors to the site and to tell them about its history. However, it will also influence the management of the site. It may mean that to protect the archaeology the number of people visiting the site may need to be limited, or directed more carefully than would otherwise be the case. The designation of Scheduled Ancient Monument may also constrain the management. Permission will need to be obtained from English Heritage (in England) or CADW (in Wales) to carry out work on the monument and it may not be possible for example, to build paths where you would wish, or dig holes to place signposts. In this example, knowledge of the archaeology, the designation carried by the site, and the impact that these have on management is fundamental to ensuring that the archaeology is protected whilst managing the site for a recreational purpose.

> *Example 2 – habitat affecting site management*
>
> A recreation site may contain an area of bog, that has been recognised as a site of national importance for conservation following survey work. As such, it has been designated as a Site of Special Scientific Interest (SSSI). This will certainly affect the management of the site. In this case the conservation interests of the bog must take priority over recreation in terms of management. Bogs are easily damaged through people walking on them, so a prime consideration will be to keep people off the area. It may be that visitors need to be diverted away from the area through developing other attractions elsewhere on the site, or by careful signposting and path management. It may be that a boardwalk should be erected across a small area of the bog for educational and interpretive purposes to let the visitor know why the bog is important and what is special about it. Whatever management is decided upon, monitoring of the conservation interests of the bog will be an important, if not the primary management task.

In addition, to assessing the issues that affect recreation sites it is also important to consider the present management of the site for recreation. This will include considering what the site product is, assessing the present infrastructure of the site, its staffing and organisational structure, its accessibility, the information provided about the site, as well as considering how user friendly and welcoming the site is to the first-time visitor. Consideration of these issues will enable us to assess the good points and bad points of present site management and will help us to plan improvements.

The assessment of a site needs to be carried out in a systematic manner. Indeed, within the management planning process this initial site assessment is usually broken down into a series of headings under which details about the site are inserted. Different management planning models use different headings, but overall the areas that need to be covered are the same. This chapter therefore considers the issues that need to be considered when assessing a site and outlines some of the methods available for gathering relevant information. The following will be outlined:

General site information

This consists of policy framework, maps, photographs, published materials, land tenure, designations, staffing, management and outside links.

The site environment

This covers the physical, biological, historical, landscape and land use of the site.

The recreational environment

This comprises of access to the site and on the site, information provision, site features, site product assessment, interpretation and environmental education, infrastructure and condition of paths, provision for the disabled, welcoming nature of the site and service quality.

General site information

Policy framework

Few sites exist as self-contained islands with no outside influences having a bearing upon them. The reality is that most recreational sites will lie within a range of policy and planning documentation produced by a variety of organisations. Before any planning can be carried out on any site it is therefore imperative that an understanding is gained of the policy framework within which the site lies. This will be different for every site and requires a systematic desktop survey in order to identify and locate documentation relevant to the individual site. The type of documentation that should be searched for includes:

- Countryside Agency, Countryside Council for Wales, English Nature and Scottish Natural Heritage policy documents
- local authority development planning documentation – structure plans, local plans and unitary development plans
- national park, heritage coast, areas of outstanding natural beauty and national trail plans
- tourism planning documentation, such as regional tourism strategies and tourism development action plans
- local authority recreation plans and strategies
- interpretation plans and area interpretation strategies
- previous site management plans.

This list is by no means exhaustive. However, it does show the plethora of planning documentation that may have an influence on the development of a site. Having gained access to all relevant documentation, consideration needs to be given as to how to pull it all together into something that is meaningful and usable.

The first stage is to read through each document page by page and identify and mark the sections that have an impact on your recreation site. These can then be identified, summarised and presented in a systematic way within a site management plan. Finally when all relevant documentation has been considered, the implications on the management of the site need to be outlined to ensure that the boundaries within which you can operate are clearly defined and understood.

Maps

Maps are useful. They provide us with a great deal of detail about our sites and provide templates upon which the development of a site can be planned. Maps can have the following uses for us:

- They can act as base maps and as templates for planning purposes. Maps can provide the spatial framework upon which site planning can occur. If you like we can draw on them to plan trails, record site infrastructure, locate important features and so forth.
- They can provide us with interesting information of a historical nature.

- They can inform us about the geology and soils of our sites.
- They can be valuable sources of information for the visitor.
- They can provide us with details of land ownership, administrative boundaries and designations.

The collection of maps of your site and the surrounding area is therefore a good use of time. The following map types should be sought out:

- Ordnance Survey maps – variety of scales including 1:50,000, 1:25,000, and 1:10,000
- British Geological Survey maps
- Soil Survey maps
- historical maps.

In addition, there may be other maps that can be of use to a site manager. For example, maps showing the location and boundaries of designations, agricultural land classification maps or phase one habitat survey maps are all useful. Once collected the maps should be located in one place and catalogued within a site management plan.

Photographs

The development of a collection of photographs of a site is a useful exercise. Photographs can be in the form of prints, slides or these days electronic digital images and can be in colour or black and white. There may also be aerial photographs that cover the site taken on a variety of dates. Photographs have many uses. Those from the past can show us graphically how a site has changed over time and as such, are very useful for interpretation and education purposes. They can be used to aid the promotion of the site within publicity material such as leaflets or media articles. They are also useful for slide shows given to education and local community groups. At most sites there are large numbers of images of the site taken over long periods of time by a variety of people. As such, photographs are often scattered in many locations. To be useful they need to be brought together into one central resource that can be used in the management of the site.

Published material

Most sites will have had material published about them in a variety of forms. This may be in the form of academic papers, surveys, books, magazine articles and student projects. All of these may be of use in developing knowledge and understanding of a site. Such information should be brought together in one location and catalogued to enable relevant information to be found easily.

Land tenure

To manage a site it is essential to have a full understanding of the ownership of the land and issues relating to ownership. The first stage in this process is to locate all legal documentation (such as deeds and management agreements) relating to the site.

Legal documents are normally written in such a way as to make them difficult for the person not trained in legal matters to interpret. Often they need to be translated into everyday language to establish what they really mean. Legal expertise may well be required here. In particular the following issues need to be investigated and recorded:

- Who owns the land that makes up a site?
- Is the land leased, purchased outright or held by agreement?
- What was the date of acquisition or the start of the lease or agreement?
- If land is leased or managed by agreement, when was the start date and when does the lease or agreement end?
- What areas of the site do individual purchase agreements or leases cover?
- What legal rights of access exist on the site?
- Are there any conditions stated in the purchase, lease or agreement documentation?
- Do any common rights exist on the land and what are they?

Some sites are very complex when it comes to land tenure with different sections of the site purchased or leased at various times and with different conditions attached. It is therefore important to record accurately all legal details relating to the site. It is useful to gather copies of all legal documentation relating to a site and to record the location of original documentation. It is essential that when discussing any issue relating to the tenure of a site, that reference be made to the original legal documents.

Designations

It is essential for site management to know all of the designations that a site may carry, the boundaries of the designations, and the implications that designation may have for the management of the site. The following are some of the possible designations that may impact upon recreation sites:

national park   heritage coast

area of outstanding natural beauty (AONB)   national trail

environmentally sensitive area (ESA)   local nature reserve (LNR)

site of special scientific interest (SSSI)   ramsar site

special protection area (SPA)   special area of conservation (SAC)

national nature reserve (NNR)   scheduled ancient monument (SAM)

listed building   local conservation area

It is not within the scope of this text to review the implications of each type of designation. Indeed, the management implications of the differing designations are normally specific to each individual site designation. It is therefore important to find the designations that apply to your specific site and to locate the documentation associated with any designation, so as to ascertain the implications for its management. This is best carried out by checking with the nearest regional office of the statutory agencies responsible for the designations such as English Nature, English Heritage, CADW, the Countryside Agency, the Countryside Council for Wales and Scottish Natural Heritage.

Example designation: site of special scientific interest

Sites of special scientific interest (SSSI) are designated in England by English Nature (EN), in Wales by the Countryside Council for Wales (CCW) and in Scotland by Scottish Natural Heritage (SNH). SSSIs are designated as a result of their importance to conservation. Having been identified as a site of conservation merit each SSSI is documented. This will include a schedule that contains a map showing the boundary of the SSSI, a description of the site describing why it is important and most crucially for site management, a considered list of operations that will detrimentally damage the conservation interest. These may be such things as application of fertiliser, mowing and grazing, drainage, burning, felling or introduction of new species. Obviously having an understanding of such issues will have an impact on site management and these clearly need to be understood before planning the management of a site.

Staffing, management and outside links

One of the often forgotten site resources is the staff who work on the site. To gain an understanding of the site as a resource, an assessment of the staff and how they are organised is required. The first stage of this is to list all of the staff employed who manage the site and to consider what each staff member is responsible for. This will inform you clearly as to who does what on the site. The second stage is to consider the organisation of the staff on the site. If you consider who is accountable to whom, you will have an idea of the managerial structure of the site. In considering the staffing on recreation sites we must view staff in the widest context. Contractors and volunteers carry out much valuable work on sites. The work that these people do and how they are organised will play a central part of any staffing appraisal.

Another way that staff can be viewed to assess their potential in relation to the development of the site, is to carry out a skills audit. This involves individual staff listing the skills they possess that may be of benefit to the management and development of the site. These skills may be anything from practical estate skills, information technology skills, photography, graphic and artistic skills to languages. Audits such as these often identify skills within staff that have not been utilised to their full potential. It will also help in assessing who is the best person to carry out particular tasks and identify training needs.

The links that a site has with other organisations also need to be considered. These may be links with local authorities, 'quangos' such as English Nature or the

Countryside Agency, charitable organisations such as the National Trust, the Royal Society for the Protection of Birds, county wildlife trusts or local community groups. Links with such agencies may be formalised into committees, access groups and steering groups or may be on a more informal basis.

The site environment

Why collect environmental information?

To manage our sites effectively an understanding of the site and its surrounding environment is essential. This is to enable us to maximise the potential of the site whilst safeguarding the site's individual special interests. Without sufficient information we may well 'be flying in the dark' and cause unintentional harm to important features, species or habitats.

What sort of information do we need to find out?

The environment can be broken into a number of key areas. These are:

> *The physical environment*: the geology, geomorphology, soils, climate, hydrology and topography of the site.
> *The biological environment*: all living things such as birds, mammals and plants but also the communities of living things and the habitat types found on the site.
> *The historical environment*: the remains of past use of the site.
> *The landscape*: the landscape types found on the site.
> *The land use of the site*: the differing uses made of the site.

Let us look at each of these areas in turn and consider the type of information that is required. What will be outlined is the ideal situation in which large amounts of information are available about the environment. The 'ideal' is not the usual and in most cases there will be significant gaps in knowledge about the site environment. However, a systematic review of the current state of knowledge will help us to identify what is known about the site. It is equally important, that we are aware of the gaps in our knowledge about the site environment. This will aid us in planning any future survey work.

There are a huge number of survey techniques that can be used to investigate these issues. In fact there are far too many to be addressed in this book. The references and further reading section at the end of this chapter lists some of the major texts in this area.

What sort of information do we need to know? The following is a broad and by no means exhaustive checklist of key areas that need to be investigated. Each site is different with an individual assemblage of biological, historical, landscape and land use issues. As such the importance of carrying out specific investigations will vary from site to site. It is unlikely, due to resource constraints, that all areas can be investigated at once. Prioritisation will therefore be required.

The physical environment

Geology	• the rock types present at the site
	• any outcrops on the site
	• mines and quarries
	• geological features of special scientific interest.
Geomorphology/landform	• geomorphological features present on the site
	• geomorphological features of special scientific interest
	• nature of site topography/altitude/aspect.
Soils	• soil types present on the site
	• soil characteristics.
Climate	• temperature, rainfall, wind, relative humidity, sunshine, snow
	• records from nearest weather stations.
Hydrology	• water features on the site such as ponds, rivers and bogs
	• drainage characteristics of the site.

The biological environment

Flora and fauna	• species present:
	vascular plants
	bryophytes
	fungi
	lichen
	mammals
	birds
	reptiles
	amphibians
	fish
	• endangered species
	• species requiring particular management
	• pest and invasive species
	• species accorded legal protection
	• significant surveys and monitoring projects.
Communities	• national vegetation classification by compartments
	• significant habitat features.

The historical environment

Land use and landscape	• features from past land use and landscaping.
Archaeology	• archaeological and historic remains on the site
	• features afforded legal protection.
Buildings	• buildings of importance on the site
	• buildings with listed status and management implications.
Culture	• cultural associations with the site.

The landscape

Landscape	• objective description of landscape
	• notable landscape features
	• features detracting from the landscape.

The land use of the site

Present land use	• agricultural systems present
	• land grades
	• sporting usage
	• recreational usage
	• other land uses.

The recreational environment

Why collect recreation information?

Before the provision of recreation on a site can be planned it is important to have a full understanding of the provision that already exists on the site. Much of the information that is required such as auditing where the signposts and benches are, will seem very obvious to staff working on a site. However, there are sound reasons for 'stepping back' for a while and taking a systematic approach to reviewing the recreational provision already present there. These reasons are:

1 Staff often know their own sites too well

The approach to this book is one of considering recreational site management through a marketing perspective. In Chapter 1 we considered that 'in taking marketing decisions, the manager looks at these from the viewpoint of the consumer'

(Mercer 1992: 11). A very real problem for site managers is that often they know their own sites too well to do this, and find it hard to appreciate what it would be like as a customer, visiting a site for the first time. Familiarity with a site can create blinkers that hamper good site management. As an example, site managers may consider the signposting on a site to be adequate because they already know their way around and may consider that some routes do not need to be signposted because it is obvious where to go. A person visiting for the first time may view the site very differently and will be confused as to where to go, leading to dissatisfaction.

2 *To allow rational decisions to be made about site management*

Decisions made based upon little or partial information are normally bad decisions. Stepping back and systematically reviewing the recreational provision on a site will lead to better quality decisions being made. For example, after reviewing the recreational provision at a site, a large amount of maintenance and development work may be identified and new attractions proposed. With limited budgets what are the priorities? Which projects need to be carried out in year 1, which in year 2 and so on? Systematically reviewing the recreational provision will assist considerably in making these decisions.

3 *To avoid 'fire fighting'*

Fire fighting is a management approach that involves doing little until something goes wrong and then dealing with it. Often this leads to a culture of crisis management. This approach normally means that sites do not meet their full potential. A systematic survey of recreational provision will allow programmes of work to be drawn up and even better, for maintenance to be planned. Would you fly on an aircraft that was maintained through a system of waiting for the plane to break down and then fixing it? The maintenance of planes is carefully planned and programmed, giving the consumer confidence to fly on them. A similar approach to the development of a recreation site will increase the quality of the site management and the quality of the site product, and hence improve the visitors' experience whilst at the site.

4 *To create an empirical basis for resource bids*

In bidding for new money to maintain and develop a site it is helpful to base bids on numeric data obtained from systematic survey work. This approach to developing a bid for resources will demonstrate that you have done your homework in preparing the bid and that the work that you propose to carry out has been soundly researched and is not just a wish list based upon the whim of the site manager. As an example, an audit of the recreational infrastructure will create a list of repair and maintenance work that needs to be carried out and will help in identifying new infrastructure requirements. A total costed work programme can then be developed into a bid application with a higher chance of succeeding in obtaining the required funding.

5 To help identification and development of site products and services

In Chapter 1 in the section on market research, it was considered that in order to make sound marketing decisions, market research was required. This was split into researching product and services, customers and competitors. A systematic review of the recreational provision on the site will help the manager to gain a greater understanding of the site products (both the core and the tangible), and will assist in identifying and assessing the quality of the services provided on site.

6 Creation of base lines

In management terms a base line is a benchmark upon which you can check performance. For example, a survey may be carried out on the condition of the recreational infrastructure of a site in year x. This may be followed by a similar survey being carried out in year y two years later. A comparison can then be made between the two surveys to check if the quality of the recreational infrastructure has improved or deteriorated. In this case the results of the first survey act as a base line upon which the second survey could be compared. This approach allows the management performance of the site to be monitored.

What sort of information do we need to find out?

There is a wide variety of information that can be collected about the recreational provision on a site. As with researching the environmental aspects of the site, the list below of possible areas of research is an ideal scenario and it may not be possible or indeed required that every aspect will always be covered. The individual site characteristics will determine the priorities of carrying out different surveys. However, by working through the list the key requirements for an individual site can be identified and action taken. The following are areas where research is desirable:

- the accessibility of the site
- the actual site features that may draw people to the site
- the information about the site provided externally to the site
- the information about the site provided within the site
- the interpretation and environmental education provided on the site
- the recreational infrastructure provided at the site such as seats, playgrounds, toilets, car parks and refreshments
- the provision made at the site for disabled visitors
- how welcoming the site is to visitors
- the quality of service provided by staff at the site.

To gather this information we need techniques that are easy to use, do not take up large amounts of time and money, and will provide us with reliable and accurate information. The rest of this chapter considers some of the techniques that can be used in these research areas.

Accessibility of the site

Accessibility is a term that describes how easy it is for the public to gain access to a site. It is vital when considering accessibility to always consider it from the point of view of the visitor. There are a number of aspects to accessibility that need to be considered:

> *Physical accessibility* – this relates to how physically accessible the site is. This will largely be determined by the location of the site in relation to the road network. Sites situated on major A roads in close proximity to motorways are easily reached, whereas sites that require the motorist to drive large distances on more minor roads with many route finding decisions to be made, will be considered less accessible. In addition, physical accessibility may be linked to how easy a site is to get to using public transport. Some sites have no public transport links and can therefore be considered to be inaccessible by public transport. Others will have good public transport links with buses running regularly to the site from major public transport nodes. Finally is the site accessible on foot and cycle to the surrounding communities?
>
> *Psychological accessibility* – this relates to visitors' perception of how accessible a site is. If you like it is the 'hassle factor'. How much 'hassle' is it to get to your site? A site that is no hassle to get to may be perceived as more easily accessible than a site that involves a lot. One interesting area is the relationship between distance and perceived accessibility. Time is often seen as being more important in terms of accessibility than distance. As an example, it is quicker (and probably a lot less hassle) to fly from London to Corfu than it is to drive from London to Cornwall. It could therefore be said that Corfu is more accessible than Cornwall, from London.
>
> *How easy the site is to find?* – this will be determined by the complexity of the transport network surrounding the site and the quality and quantity of signposting relating to the site.

Many of the factors that relate to accessibility as outlined above, are not within the control of the site manager. For example, the site manager cannot move a recreation site nearer to a centre of population or get a motorway built to the site entrance. However, there are some areas that can be influenced. These include public transport and signposting external to the site. How to do this will be outlined in Chapter 4. It is in these areas that survey work can be carried out to assess objectively what the current state of play is.

Public transport	– research the types of public transport that can be used to access the site and the locations of stops and stations.
	– research the timetables for public transport.
Signposting to the site	– record the location and information contained on all signposts directing visitors to the site.

Developing an understanding of what makes sites accessible to the visitor will also be of help in locating new recreational sites and in the strategic identification of areas which have limited access to recreational opportunities.

Access within the site

What do we mean by access? A dictionary definition is 'the right to enter'. Therefore access within a recreation site is concerned with the places that the public have access to, either by legal entitlement or through agreement and the areas that the public do not have access to. This can be divided into three basic categories:

1 Legal linear access routes – public rights of way (footpaths, bridleways, roads byways open to all traffic (BOATs), permissive paths and highways, restricted byways)
2 Open access areas – areas where the public can wander at will by right, tradition or agreement
3 Closed areas – areas where the public is not permitted to go or are only allowed where permission is granted, for example by permit.

Although these categories may seem simple, it is important to check carefully what exactly are the access rights on a site? There are no simple guidelines for what access is permitted where. Every site is different, and frequently the access rights confirmed on areas of land will differ depending on the exact wording on any relevant legal documentation. It is therefore vital to find all legal documentation relating to access on a site and establish precisely what rights exist where. This is best documented onto a map base for clarity. The following sources of documentation should be consulted:

1 The definitive map – under the National Parks and Access to the Countryside Act (1949), every local authority is obliged to record on a map all public rights of way within their boundaries. This map (entitled the definitive map) and the legal statements attached to it, forms conclusive evidence to the existence, exact locations and type of access accorded to public rights of way. Access routes are defined as footpath, bridleway, road used as public path (RUPP) and byways open to all traffic (BOAT). Copies of definitive maps are held within local authorities.
2 Access agreements and access orders – an access agreement is an agreement drawn up between a landowner and a local authority to secure access for the public to open land (under the National Parks and Access to the Countryside Act 1949). Orders are where access to open land has been gained through compulsion (under the National Parks and Access to the Countryside Act 1949). The documentation concerning agreements and orders will be held within local authorities.
3 Open access area is defined under the Countryside and Rights of Way Act (2000). Under this legislation, areas of mountain, moor, heathland, downland and common land may be designated as open access areas, that the public have a right of access to. Local authorities and statutory agencies such as the Countryside Agency and the Countryside Council for Wales will hold details of such areas.
4 Bylaws – local authorities and government agencies are able to create bylaws for areas of land, to cater for the individual needs of an area. These can cover issues relating to access. Details of the bylaws relating to a site should be displayed there and will be held by the agency responsible for producing them.
5 Common land register – under the Common Land Registration Act (1965), local

authorities are required to map and record all commons within their boundaries and the rights that exist of these commons, including access rights.

6   Management plans and site specific documentation – local access arrangements such as restrictions to access and access accorded to specific groups to specific areas, should be recorded in any site management plan (if one exists), or within specific site related documentation.

In addition to considering the legal components of access it is also important to consider the physical access offered within the site. This can be done best by mapping all of the paths and trails within a site and considering what type of access they offer. What access is available for the walker, the horse rider or the cyclist? In addition, an assessment can be made of the nature of individual paths and trails and whom they are suitable for. Some routes will be level with a wide, even surface suitable for disabled visitors and prams whilst other areas will be steep, muddy and require a level of fitness and agility to use (for example a specialised mountain bike trail). In Chapter 6 methods of assessing paths for their suitability for the disabled visitor will be discussed. A consideration of the location and nature of all access routes on a site may draw attention to lack of provision in some areas and the potential of others for improvement.

Site features list

From a marketing perspective it is very important to establish what the 'products' of a site are. On first view these will seem obvious, but in Chapter 1 it was established that products are complex and need to be viewed from a number of perspectives. Stepping back and reviewing the products of your site from these differing perspectives may change the way your site is viewed and develop a greater understanding of what your site really represents. The questions we need to ask are:

*   What are the site features that attract people to it?
*   What is it about these features that really attract people to them?
*   What is the *real* product that people are purchasing?

By asking these questions we are establishing what the core product is, what the tangible and intangible features of the product are and considering what the product of the product is. Let us remind ourselves what these marketing concepts are (for more detail you should refer back to Chapter 1).

> *The core product* – the essential services or benefits on offer that may be purchased to satisfy a need.
>
> *The tangible features of the product* – the physical elements of a product that make a core product distinct from its competitors.
>
> *The intangible features of the product* – the non-physical elements of a product such as service, price, image and brand.
>
> *The total product* – the combination of the core product with the tangible and intangible features of the product.
>
> *The product of the product* – what the consumer is actually purchasing when deciding to purchase a product.

In reviewing your site in these terms the first step is to draw up a site features list. This is just a list of all features on your site that you consider attract people to it. There will be a wide variety of features that do this. It must be remembered that an individual's decision to visit a site will normally be based upon a combination of site features that meet their particular needs at that moment in time. Examples of the types of features that may be listed in a site features list include:

viewpoint	visitor centre	castle	river
trails	bird hides	sculpture trail	scenery
children's playground		free car park	refreshments
watersports facilities		natural history	craft centre

Whilst this is a useful exercise we need to take the process further and consider in more detail what these products really are and what it is that consumers are purchasing when visiting these features. It is therefore useful to consider each feature in terms of what the *core product* is, what the *tangible* and *intangible* features of the product are and what the *product of the product* is. Tables 2.1 and 2.2 illustrate the ways in which products such as a children's playground and a waymarked walk can be considered.

Viewing the site features as products in this way is extremely helpful in thinking about site development. In particular the consideration of what the product of the product is, aids us in viewing sites from the perspective of the visitor, (remember the key element of marketing is making decisions based upon what it is that the consumer needs and wants).

Table 2.1 The potential products of a children's playground

Core product	Tangible features of the product	Intangible features of the product	The product of the product
Swings, slides, climbing apparatus	Style of play equipment	Free	For children
		Safety	Excitement
	Age range the equipment is designed for	Image (boring/exciting)	Adventure
		Close to refreshments and toilets	Exercise
	Surroundings		Fun
	Range of activities		For adults
	Materials the equipment is made from		Relaxation
			Bonding
	Seating for parents		Safe bet
	Safety surfacing		

Table 2.2 The potential products of a waymarked walk

Core product	Tangible features of the product	Intangible features of the product	The product of the product
Waymarked circular footpath on a heritage coast	Length of walk	Free	Relaxation
	Well signposted (easy to follow)	Expectations created by walk title	Exercise
			Social opportunity
	Easy, non-muddy surface	Image of route	Spiritual renewal
		Guarantee of quality	
	Views		Lack of hassle (few decisions to be made)
	No steep gradients		
	The variety of habitats the walk encompasses		
	Features seen on the walk		
	Easy parking		

Site infrastructure audits

The word audit means 'to examine'. Infrastructure refers to all of the physical elements of a site that have been put in place to manage and assist the visitor. This would include such items as paths, seats, car parks, gates, signposts and litter bins. An audit of site infrastructure is therefore an examination of all items of site infrastructure. This needs to be carried out in a systematic manner that will allow consistent and high quality information to be collected and then analysed. Often the end point for such information is a database such that analysis of the data is simplified. The data can also be added into a geographical information system (GIS).

How can we carry out such a survey? The initial stage is to decide what we need to record and then we need to decide how to record it. A suggested list of what we need to record includes:

- the items of infrastructure found on the site
- the exact location of each item of site infrastructure
- a full description of each item
- the state of repair of each item.

To record this kind of information we need to use a large-scale map of the site (preferably a 1:10,000 Ordnance Survey map) and a recording form. Alternatively, as the end point of information collected is likely to be a computer database, a pre-programmed, hand-held, computer could be used instead of a form. This has the advantage that the data can be downloaded straight onto a computer. Once a base map and forms have been produced, a full field survey can be conducted that will record details about all items of infrastructure found on a site. Let us look at what we need to record in more detail.

1 The items of infrastructure found on the site

What items of site infrastructure do we need to record? The type of items recorded can be split into several categories:

> *Boundaries* – this category includes all boundary infrastructure such as fences, walls and hedges.
> *Crossing point infrastructure* – these items of infrastructure refer to items used to cross over or through boundaries such as fences, walls, rivers, streams and ditches. This will include such items as stiles, gates and bridges.
> *On site information and interpretation* – such as signposts, waymarkers, entrance signs, orientation boards, and interpretive panels.
> *Miscellaneous infrastructure* – such as litter bins, seats and benches, toilets, car parks, bollards and bike racks.

For ease of recording a code can be assigned to each type of infrastructure. So for example, a code of *S* may be allocated to a stile. However, there are many types of stile, for example, wooden stiles, ladder stiles and squeeze stiles. These can be separately coded to provide more specific information. For example a wooden stile can be given the code *WS*, a ladder stile *LS* and a stone stile *SS*. There is no national guidance regarding coding of infrastructure items so you can decide on your own site codings as appropriate. The following codes should only therefore be seen as examples to illustrate the type of codes that can be used. It must be remembered that the purpose of the codes is to save time recording the information, but they will also prove useful in analysing the data on a database.

Boundary codes

F	fence
PRF	post and rail fence
PWF	post and wire fence
RF	rabbit fencing
DF	deer fencing
HTWF	high tensile wire fence
CPF	chestnut paling fencing
WD	dry stone wall
H	hedge
HB	hedge bank

Optional boundary sub codes

P	pig netting
B	barbed
HT	high tensile
CL	chain link

On site information and interpretation

ES	entrance sign
RS	road sign
IP	interpretive panel
FP	fingerpost

Crossing point codes

G	gap
GK	kissing gate
GW	wicket gate
FG	field gate
GN	gateway, no gate
CG	cattle grid
STS	stepping stones
LS	ladder stile
SS	step stile
SQS	squeeze stile
SWS	stone wall stile
WB	wooden bridge
MB	metal bridge
O	path obstructed

Miscellaneous infrastructure

CR	cycle rack
CP	car park
TO	toilets
PB	picnic bench

W	waymark	MB	metal bench
P	painted	WB	wooden bench
R	routed	PG	playground
A	national trail acorn	LB	litter bin
D	destination included	L	light
M	distance included		
N	non-directional marker (post, cairn . . .)		

In order to identify each item uniquely, a number needs to be added to a code. For example the first wooden stile recorded on a site infrastructure audit might be recorded as WS1 and the second wooden stile WS2. Once an item has a unique code additional information can be added to it to provide greater detail.

2 The exact location of each item of site infrastructure

The location of each item of infrastructure needs to be recorded precisely onto a base map. This is best done by drawing a line from the item to the outside of the map and marking on the end of the line the code that you have decided upon that will uniquely identify that specific item of infrastructure. An example of how to do this can be found in Figure 2.1. In addition, you may wish to record a six-figure grid reference for each item.

3 A full description of each item

This will provide more information than the identification code. For example, for a wooden fingerpost you may also wish to record that it is routed with a symbol for a footpath (a walking man), and also states 'Dingforth Village 2 miles'. For greater detail you may wish to record the exact direction the fingerpost is pointing in. Similarly for gates, the size, any specific details regarding design, the type of catch used and details of the hanging and clapper posts should all be recorded. The purpose of all of this detail is that it may well save you having to revisit the site at a future date. People's memories are generally poor and it is surprising how easily details of even familiar things are forgotten. It is better to systematically record as much detail as possible on the initial survey. Links to photographs of an item can also be made.

4 The state of repair of each item

One of the major reasons for carrying out a site infrastructure audit is to improve the quality of the management of your site. This is achieved by identifying the items of infrastructure that need to be replaced, those that are in need of repair or maintenance and those that are in good condition. The survey therefore needs to record systematically the condition of each item. This can again be done in the form of a code. Suggested codes are:

1	first class condition	5	new work required
2	satisfactory	6	redundant/derelict.
3	deteriorating		
4	poor, requires immediate attention		

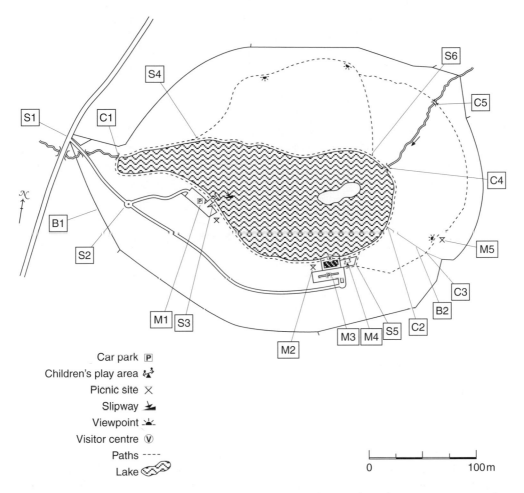

Figure 2.1 An example of a completed infrastructure audit map for a fictitious country park

As well as recording a code for the condition of each item you will need to record exactly what needs to be done if an item is coded 3, 4 or 5. Again by recording enough detail you may well save yourself having to go back and investigate what the problem is.

An example of a complete map and form can be seen in Figures 2.1 and 2.2.

Path audits

Path audits follow the same principles as infrastructure audits. However, the only aspect looked at is the surfacing and the condition of linear access routes. It is sensible to do a path audit at the same time as an infrastructure audit. Detailed audits of national trails such as the Pennine Way and the Cleveland Way have been carried out (Bate 1995), and the audit methodology outlined here is adapted from this work. In addition, much work has been carried out surveying the condition of

Boundary number	Boundary type	Condition	Crossing number	Crossing type	Condition	Signpost number	Signpost type	Condition	Miscellaneous number	Miscellaneous type	Condition	Comments
B1	WD	3				S1	ES	1				White on brown sign – Knobbly Bottom Country Park
												Dry stone wall – 4 gaps approx. 40m of repair needed
			C1	WB	1							7m bridge – stone abutments
									M1	CP		Car park for 35 cars. Tarmac surface
						S2	RS	1				Road sign. 1 Car park 2 Visitor centre/parking
						S3	IP	3				Orientation panel – badly weathered/vandalised
						S4	FP	1				2 way fingerpost 1 Scenic path 2 Lakeside walk
									M2	PB	2	3 Picnic benches – Starting to weather
			C2	GK	1							Wooden kissing gate
B2	H	3										Hedge in need of laying/some gapping up
			C3	SS	2							Wooden step stile – tread broken. Repair stile
						S5	FP	1				3 way fingerpost 1 Car park 2 Lakeside walk 3 Scenic path
									M3	CP		Car park for 40 cars. Tarmac surface
									M4	PG	1	Children's playground – swing, slide, see-saw
									M5	PB	2	1 Picnic bench – weathering
			C4	WB	1							5m bridge – stone abutments
			C5	WB	1							5m bridge – stone abutments
						S6	FP	4				3 way fingerpost 1 & 2 Lakeside walk 3 Broken. Replace broken fingerpost

Site: Knobbly Bottom Country Park   Surveyor: Mr D Light   Date: 26th May 2000

Figure 2.2 An example of a completed infrastructure audit form for a fictitious country park

upland paths and descriptions of methodologies used here can be found in Davies *et al.* (1996).

In a similar vein to infrastructure audits the information collected during survey work needs to be recorded onto maps and forms. How do we record such information? The first stage is to map the linear access routes of a site onto a high-scale base map. Each separate linear access route then needs to be allocated a unique reference code. It is useful if this code corresponds to the link number for the path found on the definitive map and definitive map statements. You can then go out and carry out your survey. What do you need to do?

Divide the linear access routes into unique lengths

A single path link may be quite long and there will be much variation in path surfacing and path characteristics along its length. It is therefore necessary to subdivide the path into sections of similar type. To do this we need to look for changes in the nature of the route. The following are reasons to make a division:

- when a crossing point is reached
- when the surfacing of the path changes
- when the condition of the path surface changes
- when the path changes in its width
- where the gradient changes.

The boundary between one subsection and another can be delineated by a line across the path on the map and each subsection given a unique coding.

Record the surfacing type of the path

As with the infrastructure audit it is useful to use codes for the differing types of path surface encountered on your site. Example codes include (after Bate 1995):

A	aggregate	GT	grass track
T	tarmacadam	SP	stone pitching
SF	stone flags	C	concrete
FB	forest bark	BW	boardwalk
TS	timber steps	SS	stone steps

These codes can be used on the recording form as a form of shorthand. An example map and form can be seen in Figures 2.3 and 2.4.

Record the width of your path

It is useful to record the width of paths. For surfaced paths such as aggregate or tarmac only the width of the path needs to be recorded. For non-surfaced paths there are two types of path width that can be recorded.

Worn width – the length across the path where the vegetation is still intact but shows visible signs of being trampled.

Bare width – the width of the path where there is no vegetation cover.

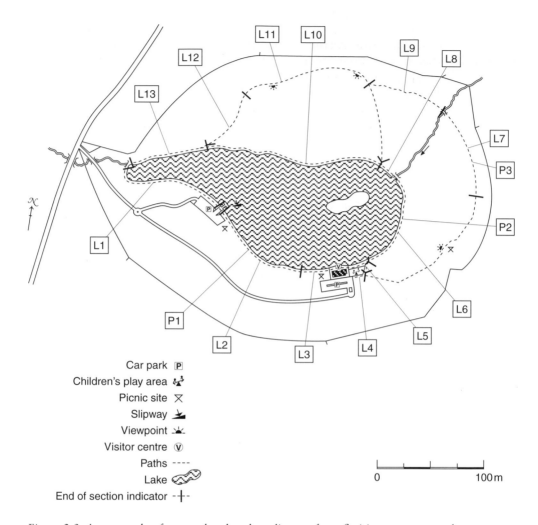

Figure 2.3 An example of a completed path audit map for a fictitious country park

Average widths for path sections should be estimated to the nearest 10 centimetres. The purpose of taking these measurements is to quantify how damaged the paths are and to act as a base line against which the future condition of the path can be compared. Figure 2.5 shows a cross section of a path and demonstrates what is to be measured when assessing path widths.

Cause of damage

One of the reasons for carrying out a path audit is to quantify the condition of the paths on a site. However, the purpose of a path audit goes further than this. It can also be used to identify the locations where restoration and maintenance work is needed and highlight the cause of any erosion on a path. The following codes are suggested for use on the recording form:

O	no damage apparent	VC	motorcycle damage
VF	farm vehicle damage	VM	4 × 4 vehicle damage
C	bicycles on path	H	horses on path
A	poaching by animal	RB	river bank collapse
LS	landslip	SW	standing water
OF	overland flow	WD	walker damage
CW	contained width (width restrictions increasing pressure on surface)		
OT	other		

Link number	Surface type	Surface path width (cm)	Average worn width (cm)	Average bare width (cm)	Cause of damage	Misalignment?	Photograph number	Comments
L1	A	180	–	–	O	No	–	
L2	A	200	–	–	O	No	P1	
L3	T	150	–	–	O	No	–	
L4	T	150	–	–	O	No	–	
L5	T	160	–	–	O	No	–	
L6	A	180	–	–	SW	No	P2	Aggregate path breaking up – puddles
L7	GT	–	40	120	WD	YES	P3	Path line does not match d. map
L8	A	190	–	–	O	No	-	
L9	GT	–	55	140	WD/OF	No	P4	Some damage from surface water Need to put in cross drains
L10	A	200	–	–	O	No	–	
L11	GT	–	50	100	WD	No	–	
L12	TS	–	75	90	WD	No	–	32 wooden steps in poor condition New risers and infill needed

Site: Knobbly Bottom Country Park   Surveyor: Mr D Light
Date: 26th May 2000

Figure 2.4 An example of a completed path audit form for a fictitious country park

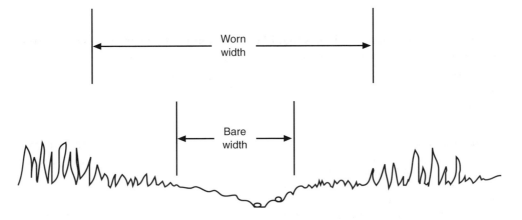

Figure 2.5 Cross-section of a path showing the worn and bare widths

Gradient

The maximum gradient for each section should be recorded in degrees over a ten-metre stretch. Gradient is very often a cause of erosion as greater foot pressure is exerted on the ground when going down a steep gradient. In addition, the gradient increases the velocity of any water flowing down a path and hence increases its power to erode the path.

Misalignment

Very often when a comparison is made between the legal line for a path shown on the definitive map and the actual line of the path on the ground, misalignments are found. If this is the case then the path on the ground may not be a legal route. There can be many reasons for this. Sometimes it is because the legal line drawn on the definitive map has been drawn in the wrong place, but more often than not it is because the path has 'migrated over time'. Misalignments found should be recorded onto the base map to highlight the misalignment as an issue. Decisions can then be made as to what to do about a misalignment.

Photographs

Whilst carrying out a path audit it is useful to take photographs of sections of path. These can be used as illustration of what the path surfacing issues are to people not familiar with the site. In addition, they act as a record of the condition of the path at a particular date. To identify the exact location of photographs taken, it is necessary to place in the photograph a board onto which is chalked a unique code that links the photo to an exact spot on the ground and the date when the photograph is taken. The location of codes given to all photographs should be recorded onto the base map.

Additional notes

As well as recording all the above it is useful to write additional notes about sections of the path that record particular issues and problems on the path. These notes should be written onto the recording form.

When should a path audit be carried out?

One of the biggest causes of path problems is water, either in the form of puddles and mud or more drastically as water flowing over the path as overland flow. It is therefore not sensible to carry out your survey on a hot day in August with the ground very dry. Many path problems may be missed if a survey is carried out in such conditions. It is better to wait and carry out an audit when the paths are wet. Therefore, it is best to survey the paths when they are in their worst state. Spring and autumn are therefore ideal times.

What do you do with all this information?

To get the most from the information collected, it is best to enter it onto a database. This will make the information more accessible and will simplify the analysis of the data. You can then use the information to draw up work programmes. For example, you can compile lists of all urgent work, maintenance and replacement work. Work on site infrastructure can then be prioritised into the urgent and less urgent jobs. It is also possible to use the information to estimate the cost of the required work. For example, if you find that five stiles need replacing and have an estimate of how much it costs to replace a stile, you can then work out the total cost of replacing them. Similarly if you work out how many paths need to be resurfaced and you have an estimate for how much the surfacing work will cost per metre, a total cost can be calculated. Do this for all items needing attention and a costed task list can be produced that can be used in the process of bidding for resources. In addition to working out the financial elements we can also use the results of the audits to estimate the number of person-days required to carry out the necessary work.

Site infrastructure audits and path audits can also be used as base lines against which managerial performance can be checked. If an audit is repeated using the same methodology three years after the initial audit and it shows that the infrastructure is in a worse condition, then you know something has gone wrong! Hopefully things will have improved. Using the audit as a base line is particularly useful if you have set management targets against which you can monitor performance. So for example, if a target was set of replacing twelve stiles on a site over a three-year period, then a second audit can be used to check if the target has been achieved.

Another area where audits prove useful, is that in taking an in-depth review of the infrastructure it often becomes apparent that new infrastructure may be required, for example new benches and signs. In reviewing the infrastructure you take a new and practical view of the whole site.

Disabled access audits

The needs of people with disabilities on recreation sites are often very different from those of able-bodied people. As such, it is necessary to carry out a separate audit of site facilities to consider them against the needs of disabled people. Chapter 6 considers the needs of the disabled on recreation sites and details a methodology that could be used in carrying out a disability access audit.

Welcome audits

Earlier in the chapter it was mentioned that site managers are often too familiar with their sites to be able to appreciate them from the point of view of the first-time visitor. Welcome audits provide us with a quick and simple method for getting around this problem. The principle of a welcome audit is to get another recreation management professional who has not visited your site before, to visit it and tell you what they think of it. To make the most of the visit, it is best to formalise the arrangement and for the site manager to draw up a series of questions that the 'visitor' can investigate and report on. The 'visitor' can then spend time looking around the site and pretending to be a visitor but recording answers to the questions as the visit progresses. The 'visitor' can then report the findings to the site manager either orally or in the form of a report. The questions can be very broad and relate to the ambience and feel of the site or be very specific such as asking how helpful the staff were or how easy it was to find the toilets. The questions for each site will be different but are likely to fall under a few key areas. Example areas and questions are listed below.

Example welcome audit questions

Signing to the site
Was the site easy to find?
Was the site clearly signed from the public highway?

Site entrances
Was the site entrance obvious?
Was the site named at the entrance?
Did the entrance create a welcoming impression?
Did the entrance signs accurately convey what the site was like?

Car parks
Was the car park easy to find?
Was it obvious where to go from the car park?
Did the information provided about the site on the orientation panel in the car park, give you enough knowledge about the site?
Did you find it easy to understand the map of the site in the car park?
Did you feel safe to leave your car in the car park?

Site ambience
What was the general 'feel' of the site?
Did you feel threatened in any way whilst on the site?
Did you feel 'welcome' whilst on the site?
Was there any sign of vandalism on the site?

Finding your way around
Did you find it easy to find the site's facilities?
Were the signposts within the site clear and easy to use?
Did the signposts contain enough information?
Was it obvious where paths led?
Was the self-guiding trail easy to follow?

Visitor facilities?
What were your impressions of the visitor centre?
What messages do you think the interpretation was trying to get across?
Were the staff in the centre friendly and helpful?
Were the staff approachable?
Were the toilets clean?
What did you think about the quality of the refreshments served in the café?
Other comments?

It can be seen that there can be a wide variety of questions that can be asked about a site. It is important therefore, to clearly identify the key issues that you wish to find out about and draft questions accordingly. One issue with welcome audits is whether to tell site staff when an audit is to be carried out. If site staff know the day an audit is to be carried out they may behave 'better' and give an unrealistic impression of the service provided. However, not telling staff that they are being assessed informally without their knowing can lead to some of them being very angry.

Welcome audits are quick to carry out and do not take large amounts of analysis. Quite often the best approach is to reach an arrangement with another site manager such that he/she visits your site and in return you repay the favour and visit their site. In this way costs are kept to a minimum. Welcome audits are particularly valuable as they take a marketing approach and view sites from the perspective of the visitor.

Information audit

An information audit is an examination of the information provided about a site both internally and externally. The following are some of the forms of information we may find:

leaflets	posters	signposts
visitor centres	Internet sites	books
timetables	sandwich boards	notice boards
interpretive panels	staff	orientation panels

In an information audit the first stage is to list all items of information relating to a site. An evaluation can then be made of their effectiveness in getting the required information across to the visitor. The best way to do this is to 'step back' from the information provided and draw up a checklist of what we want the visitor to know from differing items of information and also to consider who the target audience is. A comparison can then be made between what is required, and what is provided. This may well reveal gaps in the information provision.

As well as checking the provision of information it may be useful to audit the interpretation provided on the site. At this stage a listing of all items of interpretation and what the purpose of each item is, may be all that is required. In Chapter 9 more specific methods of evaluating the effectiveness of individual items of interpretation will be discussed.

References and further reading

Bate, J. H. (1995) *Condition Survey Methodology*, Report for the Countryside Commission, Manchester: Manchester Metropolitan University.
Beer, A. R. (1998) *Environmental Planning for Site Development*, London: E. & F.N. Spon.
Bibby, C. J., Burgess, N. D. and Hill, D. A. (1992) *Bird Census Techniques*, London: Poyser.
Bromley, P. (1990) *Countryside Management*, London: E. & F.N. Spon.

Countryside Commission (1995) *The Visitor Welcome Initiative*, Cheltenham: Countryside Commission.

Countryside Commission (1998) *Site Management Planning: A Guide*, Cheltenham: Countryside Commission.

Causton, D. R. (1988) *An Introduction to Vegetation Analysis: Principles, Practice and Interpretation*, London: Unwin Hyman.

Davies, D., Loxham, J. and Huggon, G. (1996) *Repairing Upland Path Erosion: A Best Practice Guide*, Lake District National Park, National Trust, English Nature.

Garner, J. F. (1997) *Countryside Law*, Kent: Shaw and Sons Limited.

Goldsmith, F. B. (ed.) (1991) *Monitoring for Conservation and Ecology*, London: Chapman and Hall.

Mercer, D. (1992) *Marketing*, Oxford: Blackwell.

Mynors, C. (1999) *Listed Buildings, Conservation Areas and Monuments*, London: Sweet and Maxwell.

Spellerberg, I. F. (1991) *Monitoring Ecological Change*, Cambridge: Cambridge University Press.

Spellerberg, I. F. (1992) *Evaluation and Assessment for Conservation*, London: Chapman and Hall.

Sutherland, W. J. (1996) *Ecological Census Techniques: A Handbook*, Cambridge: Cambridge University Press.

Web links

CADW homepage   http://www.cadw.wales.gov.uk/
Countryside Council for Wales   http://www.ccw.gov.uk/
English Heritage   http://www.english-heritage.org.uk/
English Nature   http://www.english-nature.org.uk/
The Countryside Agency   http://www.countryside.gov.uk/
Scottish Natural Heritage   http://www.snh.org.uk/

3 Finding out about your visitor

If we are to manage a site effectively using a marketing approach, it is important to develop a clear understanding to the 'consumer' of the site. This means gathering information on such issues, as visitor numbers, profiles, needs, attitudes, activities and trends. In marketing terms we call this market research. This chapter details the research methodologies available to the site manager to discover more about visitors to a site.

Why do we need to find out about the visitor?

The philosophy of this book is to view the management of recreation sites using a marketing approach. This means viewing sites from the perspective of the visitor. A full understanding of the visitor is therefore needed. This chapter considers the principal market research methods available to the site manager to find out about the site visitor. The intention of this chapter is to draw attention to the types of method that are available and highlight the key issues associated with each method. However, there is not enough space within one chapter to cover each method in the full depth it deserves. Indeed, there is a number of high quality texts available that cover nothing but the market research methods in the leisure and tourism areas. For greater detail the reader is therefore directed to consult these texts, details of which appear in the references and further reading section at the end of the chapter.

In carrying out any market research about site visitors, the question must always be asked as to what is the purpose of collecting the information. The following are some of the key reasons why market research on visitors is important. It will help us to:

- plan the development of the site as a product
- identify market segments for promotional purposes
- identify new markets for products
- identify trends in visitor behaviour
- monitor management performance
- prioritise resource allocation
- develop site policy.

Each separate method available to carry out market research will gather different types of information. It is therefore vital to consider what information needs to be collected to address the needs of a site and to identify what use the information will be put to. The correct method or range of methods to collect the required information can then be identified and developed.

What information do we need to find out about our visitors?

In considering carrying out market research on site visitors the following areas of research should be taken into account:

Table 3.1 Typical research questions for countryside recreation sites and the types of information that the questions will address

Research question	Type of information
How many people visit a site?	Visitor numbers
When do people visit a site?	Distribution of visitors over time
Who are the visitors to a site?	Visitor profiles
Where do the visitors come from?	Catchment area
What do the visitors do when on a site?	Activities
Where do they go whilst on a site?	Distribution of visitors over site
What are their views about a site?	Attitudes/motivation
How much money do the visitors spend?	Visitor expenditure
What changes are occurring over time?	Trends

What are the methods available to find out about visitors to countryside recreation sites?

There are a large number of market research methods available to find out information about visitors. The methods fall into two key areas.

> *Quantitative* research – concerned with collecting numeric data that can be analysed statistically.
> *Qualitative* research – concerned with gathering non-numerical information.

Let us outline the key techniques that will be covered within this chapter that fall under each of these categories.

Quantitative research methods

> *Questionnaire* – involves the gathering of data by asking specific questions to a sample of the population. The same questions are asked to each individual sampled and thus the researcher is able to analyse the data using quantitative statistical methods.
> *Observation* – involves the systematic observation and recording of individuals to establish their numbers, behaviour and distribution.
> *Visitor count* – involves the use of mechanical counters, spot counts, or other mechanisms to count visitor numbers.
> *Secondary data* – involves using data that has already been gathered for a different purpose, but that can be used in a different manner by a secondary user.

Qualitative research methods

> *In-depth interviews* – interviews with a small number of individuals on a one-to-one basis, that are less structured than questionnaires and allow the interviewer a chance to probe issues in greater depth.
>
> *Focus groups* – structured discussions with groups of people that allow for issues to be discussed and probed. In this type of survey the questioner acts as a facilitator in the process.

Having outlined the principal methods available in market research, we can now link them to the type of research question that they can provide answers to and the types of information that can be collected.

It can be seen from Table 3.2 that some research questions have more than one research method available, to provide answers. Different research methods are normally complimentary and the use of more than one technique addressing the same issue can increase the confidence concerning the results and highlight a wider range of issues than if only one technique is used. In addition, linking the results of different methodologies addressing differing research questions can build a bigger picture of the visitor and how they use a site. For example, linking visitor counts to questionnaire data on the expenditure of visitors can provide us with useful figures for the total amount of money that visitors spend on the site and in the surrounding communities, over a period of time.

The survey design process

The choice of survey technique, the development of appropriate methodology and the correct analysis of results is a complex and difficult task. Along the way, many

Table 3.2 Research questions and the type of information that different survey methods can address

Research question	Type of information to be collected	Survey type that can be used
How many people visit a site?	Visitor numbers	Visitor counts/ observation/secondary data
When do people visit a site?	Distribution of visitors over time	Visitor counts/questionnaires/ observation
Who are the visitors to a site?	Visitor profiles	Questionnaires
Where do the visitors come from?	Catchment area	Questionnaires
What do the visitors do when on a site?	Activities	Questionnaires/observation
Where do visitors go whilst on a site?	Distribution of visitors over the site	Questionnaires/observation/ visitor counts
What are visitors' views about a site?	Attitudes/motivation	Questionnaires/in-depth interviews/focus groups
How much do the visitors spend?	Visitor expenditure	Questionnaires/visitor counts/secondary data
What changes are occurring over time?	Trends	Questionnaires/observation/ visitor counts/secondary data

decisions have to be made, all of which will influence the success of any given survey. To help us through this process it is important to break it down into its component parts. The individual elements can be seen by referring to Figure 3.1.

In making the decision to carry out market research it is important to establish

Management issues identified
Research questions identified
Why is the research needed and what are the key questions that need answers?

List information requirements
What do you want to find out to answer the key question?

Search for already existing data that can address the identified information requirements
What information already exists?

Identification of appropriate research method(s)
Questionnaire
Observation
Visitor counts
Focus groups
In depth interviews
Secondary data
Which technique(s) will provide the answers to your research question?

Establish details of the survey methodology
How will you carry out the survey?

Pilot test survey
Check if your survey methodology works

Refine survey based upon findings from pilot testing
Make changes

Implement the survey
Time to actually do it!

Analyse results
What do the results mean?

Write up findings
Makes the findings available to others

Consider implications for site management
What do the findings mean for site management?

Figure 3.1 The survey design process

exactly *why* you are doing it in the first place. This should come from identifying the key management issues relating to a site that require information to help in making decisions about site management. Having identified the key management issues, research questions can then be formulated. Examples of research questions that could be asked on recreation sites have already been highlighted in Table 3.1. Having decided upon the research questions, a list of information requirements can be drawn up. This will be based upon our research questions but will consider more specifically what information needs to be gathered to answer the research questions. For example, if one of our research questions is 'Who visits our site?', then a list of the information requirements that will answer this question can be drawn up. In this example we may consider that we need to find out:

- where visitors to our site come from (locals, tourists, day visitors)
- the age profile of site visitors
- the socio-economic profile of site visitors.

It is only now that we know what information needs to be gathered, that we can consider which is the most appropriate research method to use to gather the required information. A big mistake that occurs in many surveys is not getting these first stages in survey design established clearly enough and jumping straight into survey design. For example, people often decide a questionnaire survey is required and actively start to write questions without having clearly established why the survey is required in the first place and what the information requirements are. This usually leads to research work that is unfocused, difficult to analyse and interpret and that fails to answer the real management needs of a site. Establish what you want to find out – then survey!

Table 3.2 earlier in this chapter provides a good starting point for linking research questions and the type for information to be collected, with the appropriate survey method. Choosing the right method is important, as we need to gather the required information as efficiently, effectively and as accurately as is possible. Having established the most appropriate survey method to use, the next stage is to establish the precise details of how you will carry out a survey using that methodology. This may include such issues as sampling procedures, writing questionnaires or deciding who sits on a focus group. Once details of the survey methodology have been established, the next step is to pilot-test the methodology. This means doing a test run to check for any problems and to consider any improvements that can be made.

Having piloted and improved the methodology the real survey can take place. Once completed, the data collected can be analysed to gain as much information as possible from it. This can involve calculations and statistical analysis to enable conclusions to be drawn. Survey results should always be written up so that they can be communicated to other people and to allow people in the future to use the results. It is only now, at the end of the survey that its implications can be considered for the management of the site, which after all is the reason for the survey in the first place.

Research methods

Visitor counts

Visitor counts are used to establish the number of people who visit sites. What sort of information might we want to find out about visitor numbers?

• the total number of visits a site receives over a one-year period
• when visitors visit a site (seasonal, weekly and daily patterns)
• the distribution of visitors over a site
• trends in visitor numbers over time.

Counting visitors at countryside sites is problematic. This is because there are several entrances on most sites and people arrive in cars, on bikes, on coaches and on foot. In addition, most countryside sites are free and have open access so that visitors do not have to register on arrival. Because of the difficulties most visitor counts are estimates of numbers. What we need to do is try to make these estimates as accurate and reliable as possible.

Methods of counting visitors

The methods that can be used to count visitors can be grouped into three areas:

• management data
• manual counts
• automatic counts.

Let us look into each of these methods.

Management data

In the course of normal management activities we often systematically record information. What do we collect information on which could be of use in estimating visitor numbers?

• car park tickets sold
• permits issued
• educational bookings
• till transactions
• bicycle hire.

Whilst all of these will record some information about visitor numbers they all have inherent weaknesses within them in terms of gaining reliable and accurate results. Several of the sources of information above are specific to small groupings of visitors such as school groups, anglers, or people hiring bikes. In addition, how many people are honest enough to buy a pay-and-display parking ticket at a remote countryside site? For any type of management information collected we have to question how representative is it of the total population of visitors to our site. The answer is normally that it is not representative at all. This does not mean it has no value. Information about the number of school groups visiting a site or the number of fishing permits issued, provides us with very useful information about schools or anglers. For accurate estimates of visitor numbers for a whole site we need to collect data in a more specific and systematic manner.

Manual observation

Manual observations of visitor numbers can be carried out in several ways. The basic principle is that visitors are counted at specific locations at individual points in time. Based upon these counts an estimate can be made about the total number of visitors over a longer period of time. As an example, if we wanted to find out how many people were using a particular path we could manually count visitors using that path over a period of several hours. We could repeat this manual count at various times of the year, at various times of the week and at various times of the day. These counts are called *spot counts*. Based upon our totals for each observation period we could extrapolate the data by estimating how many people use the path over a day, a week, a month or a full year. Visitor numbers based upon such a method can only be estimates of reality as there are so many factors that may influence the reliability of the data collected. On an observation day, specific factors may have an influence on visitor numbers such as the weather and if there were any major sporting occasions, or local events that may make that particular count untypical of the whole year. The more spot counts that are carried out the greater the confidence in the accuracy of our data. In addition, deciding when to carry out our spot counts based upon sampling theory (covered in the questionnaire section of this chapter), will also aid the confidence we can have in the data.

Manual counts therefore are fairly straightforward and cheap to carry out but can only ever give an estimate of visitor numbers. To obtain more accurate data we need to use mechanical counting methods.

Automatic counters

To count visitors to our sites using automatic counters we need a counter mechanism that will record the passing of a vehicle, bike or person and a means of recording the data. The data collected will then represent the total number of vehicles, bikes or cars that passed the counter mechanism over the period of time that the data was being recorded. Figure 3.2 shows the process behind automatic count mechanisms.

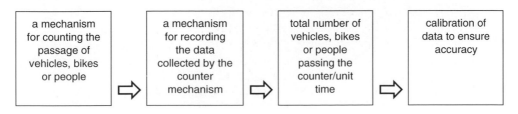

Figure 3.2 The process involved in the automatic counting of vehicles, bikes and people

Counter mechanisms

Counting equipment has improved considerably in recent years and there is now a wide variety of counters available that are both reliable and accurate. These counters can be classified by the means by which they count. Each type of counter will have its strengths and weaknesses and many are designed for specific purposes. It is important to select the most appropriate counter for your specific requirements. Often the best advice will come from the equipment manufacturers (a list of contacts can be found in the Scottish Natural Heritage (http://www.snh.org.uk), visitor monitoring handbook, details of which appear in the further reading list at the end of this chapter). The basic counter types can be broken down into those that count vehicles, and those that count people. A summary of the types of counter available, what they count, where they can be used and their relative strengths and weaknesses can be seen in Table 3.3. An example of a counter can be seen in Plate 3.1.

Collecting the data

Data produced from counters is normally in an electrical form and needs to be recorded using some form of data logger. These devices can record data in two ways:

> *Cumulative totals* – the total number of counts from when the count started to the time the counter is read. This will only record a *total count* and will provide no detail about *when* people are counted.
> *Time and date totals* – counts divided into subdivisions of minutes, hours or days for increased information about when people are counted.

Plate 3.1 A micro switch operated stile counter with an automatic data logger

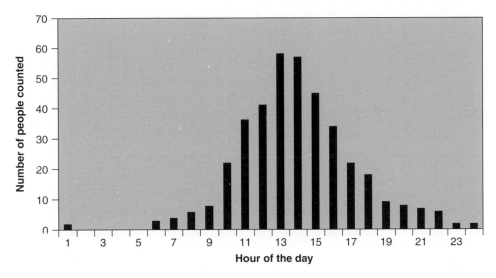

Figure 3.3 Average counts on an hour-by-hour basis for people passing along an entrance path at a countryside recreation site (fictitious data)

The output of cumulative data is normally just a single number. Time and date outputs are more complex with counts being recorded for the time intervals set on the data logger (minutes, hours, days). Often this type of data can be downloaded onto a computer for further analysis and graphical display. Figure 3.3 above shows the kind of graphic output that can be derived from time and date counts.

Calibration

To calibrate means to fix or correct. This is exactly what we do when we calibrate data collected on visitor numbers. The reason why we have to calibrate is that no matter how hard we try, the data collected by automatic counting mechanisms will always be inaccurate. This does not matter, but what does matter is that we know how inaccurate the data is. If we know this, we can correct the collected data to give us a more accurate estimate of visitor numbers.

The basic principle of calibration is to count manually the number of people or vehicles that pass a counter over a given period of time and to then compare this figure (which we know to be 100 per cent accurate because we have observed it), with the figure recorded by the counter. If the counter is inaccurate it will have recorded more or less counts than what was observed. The actual observed count and the count recorded by the automatic counter can then be used to calculate a calibration factor. The following equation can be used:

$$\text{calibration factor} = \frac{\text{actual observed count}}{\text{count recorded by automatic counter}}$$

Let us take an example. If the actual observed count is 100 and the count recorded by the automatic counter is 94 then the following calculation can be made.

Table 3.3 Counter mechanisms for recording visitor, vehicle and bike numbers

Counter type	What can be counted	How the counter works	Where it can be used	Strengths	Weaknesses
Inductive loop (uses a metal wire buried under a road or path)	Vehicles	Uses the same technology as metal detectors to record metal objects passing over it	Buried under road or path	Robust, reliable	Only records metal objects Normally not sensitive enough to record bikes Will not record walkers Cannot be moved once installed
Pneumatic tubes (stretched across road or path surface)	Vehicles	Vehicles passing over the tube creates a pulse of air which triggers a counter	On road or track surfaces	Can be moved from location to location	Counts number of axles not number of vehicles Often will not record slow moving vehicles Often will not record bikes
Pressure sensitive pads (buried under tracks and paths or hidden in stile treads)	People/bikes	Detects changes in weight above the pads	Under tracks and paths	Can be moved from location to location Not easy for visitors to detect	Will record any weight passing over it including livestock and wild animals Will record as one, two people treading on the pad at the same time
Break beam counters (located by side of track or path)	People/bikes	Count is triggered when a beam is broken. Detected by a receiver separate from source of beam	Across roads, tracks and paths	Can be moved from location to location	Requires people to be separated from one another for accuracy Will record livestock and wild animals
Passive infra-red (located by the side of track or path)	People/bikes	Detects the passive infra-red given off by people passing by	Across roads, tracks and paths	Sensitivity can be adjusted Can be moved from location to location	Requires people to be separated from one another for accuracy Can be affected by weather and ambient temperatures Will record livestock and wild animals

| Target reflection infra-red (located by side of track or path) | People/bikes | Bounces an intense pulse of invisible infra-red (non laser) light off a moving target and detects it. Analogous to a pseudo radar | Across roads, tracks and paths | Less obvious than break beam counters as it requires no separate receiver. Can be moved from location to location. Unaffected by weather and ambient temperatures | Requires people to be separated from one another for accuracy. Will record livestock and wild animals |
| Micro switches/ switches (located in stile treads of gates) | People | Mechanical switches activated by movement | Hidden in stiles and gates | Cheap. Can be moved from location to location | Mechanical, therefore prone to failure in hostile conditions. Can make a click or cause stile to bounce making it detectable by visitors |

$$\text{calibration factor} = \frac{100}{94} = 1.06$$

How do we use this to correct our overall counts? For the sake of our example let us say that the path where this calibration is taking place has an automatic counter that has recorded 23,677 visitors over a one-year period. To correct this figure we need to use the following equation:

$$\text{estimated number of visitors} = \text{counter reading} \times \text{calibration factor}$$
$$\text{along the path}$$

Therefore in this example the estimated number of visitors along the path in a one-year period $= 23,677 \times 1.06 = 25,097$.

What else do we need to think about when calibrating data?

When we are gathering data on visitor numbers we often want to know more than just the number of visitors. Whilst observing people during the calibration process we can record details of the visitors being observed. What sort of things can we record? If we are recording on a path then we could record:

- the number of people passing the counter who are walkers, cyclists or horse riders
- the direction of travel
- the number of walkers who have dogs.

If we are observing cars to calibrate a car counter it will also be important to record:

- the number of people in a vehicle (to work out an average number per vehicle)
- the direction of travel of the vehicles
- the number of axles that pass over the counter
- the proportion of vehicles that enter a car park, turn around and leave without staying
- the proportion of vehicles that belong to staff.

We can then turn such data into percentages. In our example, the following was observed:

Type of user observed	Travelling north along the path in %	Travelling south along the path in %
walker	38	49
cyclist	3	7
horse rider	1	2

We can therefore calculate yearly figures for the number of walkers, cyclists and horse riders travelling in both directions.

	Travelling north along the path in %	Travelling south along the path in %
walker	25,097/100 × 38 = 9537	25,097/100 × 49 = 12,297
cyclist	25,097/100 × 3 = 753	25,097/100 × 7 = 1757
horse rider	25,097/100 × 1 = 251	25,097/100 × 2 = 502

When do we calibrate and how often?

To gain a calibration factor that is as accurate as possible it is useful to carry out the calibration exercise more than once. To decide when to carry out a calibration exercise you need to consider over what period of time your counter is operating. If you are seeking a yearly count it may be sensible to calibrate four times say in the winter, spring, summer and autumn. If you are recording details of the number of people passing a counter who are for example walking a dog then we need to ensure that the timing of our calibration will give a fair representation of all users of the path. So, if we are interested in dogs then we will have to carry out some calibration before and after normal office hours (when people go home to walk their dogs) as well as some calibration during the day. The more often you calibrate and the larger the number of people who are observed the more confidence you can have in your calibration factor and therefore the accuracy of your data. You will normally find that each time you carry out a calibration, the calculated calibration factor will differ. To work out a calibration factor that you can use over a period of time, it is necessary to take an average of all of the calibration factors and use this average calibration factor in adjusting the overall count data.

Questionnaire surveys

Questionnaire surveys are the most common type of survey used to find out information about site visitors. The reason for their popularity is their versatility in answering a wide variety of research questions. In addition, as a quantitative method, questionnaires yield numeric data that is easy to analyse, present and draw conclusions from. However, questionnaire surveys are often poorly carried out and as such can provide less than satisfactory information about site visitors. It is therefore vital to fully understand all aspects of designing, implementing and evaluating questionnaire surveys. This section on questionnaires outlines the issues and techniques that need to be considered and understood to produce results that can be relied upon for making management decisions. Greater detail concerning the design and analysis of questionnaires can be found in texts listed in the bibliography.

Sampling

Of great importance to the design of a questionnaire survey is the concept of sampling. What is sampling? A dictionary definition of the word sample is 'a part, piece or item that shows what the whole thing or group is like'. Sampling is therefore the process of selecting a part, piece or item to show what the whole thing or group is like. Let us make this clearer by an example.

> **Sampling from a fruit cake**
>
> In front of you is a nice looking fruit cake. How can we tell what it tastes like? Well of course we have to eat a bit of it. Do you have to eat the whole cake to tell what it tastes like? Whilst this may be desirable (it is a nice cake), it is not necessary. Providing the cake is well mixed and all the cherries have not sunk to the bottom a small slice will tell us how good the cake is. This is because a slice should contain a selection of all of the ingredients such as currants, raisins, cherries, mixed peel, sugar, and so on that the cake is made from. To be most accurate you would cut a slice such that it would contain all the ingredients in the same proportions as is present in the whole cake. The slice could then be considered to be *representative* of the whole cake. If however, you only take out of the cake cherries to taste (you like cherries), you may consider that the cake tastes of cherries. If you only select currants to taste you may consider the cake to taste of currants. This would be *biased* and would not reflect the real taste of the cake.

In this example it can be deduced that to gain an understanding of the whole cake you do not have to eat the lot. In questionnaire surveys this is also true. To find out how people would vote if there were a general election, you do not have to ask every voter in the whole country. What you do is take a *sample* from the whole *population* and ask them about their voting intentions. In most questionnaire surveys it is not possible to ask questions of the whole population. Selection of a sample of the population is therefore required. How you select your sample to ensure that it is representative of the whole population is what is important.

Gaining a representative sample

In sampling it is vital to gain a representative sample of the total population that is to be sampled from. Any survey where a representative sample is not gained must be considered to be *biased* and therefore suspect. How can we achieve a representative sample? This is normally achieved by *random sampling*. In random sampling people are selected randomly and as such every member of a population has an equal chance of being selected. So for example, if we have a population to sample of 1000 and if we randomly select 100 people to ask questions of, then each of the 1000 people will have a 1 in 10 chance of being selected. It is for this reason that the technique is often referred to as *probability sampling*, as all members of a population if randomly sampled, should have an equal probability of being selected. How can we achieve this randomness in practice? Let us consider a questionnaire survey being designed for a countryside recreation site where it is intended to question people leaving the site to ask them about their opinions concerning the site.

How could we randomly select individuals to question? We could:

Select every nth person – in this technique having finished one interview you select the nth person to pass you next. For example, you may select every fifth person.

Selection by time interval – in this technique having finished one interview you select, for example, the next person to pass you after one minute.

Selection by random number tables – in this technique having finished one interview you select the next person based upon a random number chosen from a random number table.

This sounds very simple and easy. However it is not, because unlike sampling from a fruit cake the human population is much more complex in its make up. To return to the cake analogy the human fruit is not distributed evenly around the cake. What are the key difficulties associated with randomly sampling the population on a countryside recreation site?

Where do you conduct your interviews? – different types of people will use different parts of a site. So for example, if you conduct your survey near a children's playground you are likely to sample children and families. If you interview near a watersports lake you are likely to sample people interested in watersports. In both cases if we are trying to gain an understanding of the whole site then the samples will be biased. It is therefore important to select the sites where interviews take place carefully to reflect the overall use made of the site.

When do you conduct your interviews? – at different times of the day, week or year, different types of people will use recreation sites in different ways. For example, at 7.30 in the morning the only people likely to use a site are runners and people walking their dogs. During term time you are unlikely to find school children during school hours. In the summer months a large part of the use made of a site may be from tourists whereas in the winter it may be mainly local. Therefore, when you carry out your interviews will determine the population that you are interviewing and this will vary considerably over time. It is therefore important to select the times of your interviews carefully to reflect the use made of a site over time.

What if your random selection selects a group of people? – sometimes even with careful random selection it is difficult to decide who to interview as the nth person to pass is a group of people. Does this matter? Well, yes it does. If you interview a whole group you will find that the whole group chips in with answers or will make suggestions. These group answers may differ from the answers that would have been given by any individual from within the group leading to potential bias.

How do we get around these difficulties? First it has to be said that achieving a perfect sample from a population on a countryside site is almost impossible. What we have to do is strive to achieve as perfect a sample as we can. We do this by constructing a *sample frame*.

The sample frame

Designing a sample frame in concept is very simple. What you have to do is decide:

Who you sample

Where you sample

When you sample

In considering these three areas we have to make decisions about who, where and when to sample and to make these decisions in the context of attempting to try and make the sample obtained as representative of the whole population as possible. Obviously one question that has to be asked whilst deciding on a sample frame is how many questionnaires do we need to have completed for reliable results to be obtained. This will be dealt with later in the chapter. Let us first look at the three sections of the sample frame in more detail.

Who you sample

In attempting to gain a representative sample it is important to develop a systematic method for deciding *who* you sample. As outlined above, the key way of obtaining a representative sample is through randomly selecting people to interview. The accurate administration of this process is vital, as without a random sample, potential biases will creep into the data. A specific method of randomly selecting interviewees is therefore required and this needs to be applied with rigour. This sounds easy in practice but once 'out on the street' is not always so. Several factors can make it difficult. The first is intimidation. Imagine that you are conducting a survey in your countryside recreation site and that you have randomly selected the fifth person after your last interview. In this particular instance this individual is a big, hairy and mean looking Hells Angel. Do you stop him and question him? The answer is yes you must. His opinions will be relevant and if you are intimidated and fail to stop him then you are bringing potential bias into the sample. You will also probably be surprised at his response. Although this is an extreme example it is easy for inexperienced interviewers who have been inadequately trained to quickly forget the rigour required by the random selection process and only stop people who they 'like the look of'. This is likely to be a very biased section of the population and brings into question the validity of any results.

No matter how rigorous you are at selecting interviewees and stopping them to ask questions, there will always be a proportion of people who you approach who will decline to stop. It is important to record these by ticking a non-response tick box on the front page of the questionnaire. A new questionnaire should then be used for the next interview. At the end of the survey the total number (and therefore the percentage) of non-responses can be calculated. When presenting results from questionnaire surveys it is important to present this number as it will give an indication of the confidence that can be placed in the data. For example, if only 10 per cent of people approached stopped and answered questions then the response rate will only be 10 per cent and therefore the confidence that the sample is representative of the whole population will be low. If the response rate is 95 per cent (95 per cent of people selected stopped), then confidence in how representative the sample is, will of course, be much higher.

Another problem that frequently occurs with random sampling is that of different interviewers applying the random selection process in different ways. Again this will be a source of potential bias and needs to be negated by training and spot checking of interviewers. Finally in the above section on gaining a representative selection the problem of stopping groups was outlined. How can we overcome this problem? The answer is to select someone randomly from the group to answer the questions and to ensure that that person alone provides the answers. One method of randomly selecting from a group is known as the birthday method. In this you ask the group whose birthday is it next and ask only that person the questions.

Where you sample

As stated in the section on gaining a representative sample, the exact location of *where* you stop people to ask them questions may influence the type of person you are interviewing. In deciding your sample frame, therefore, a consideration of where you take your sample from is of fundamental importance. If the intention is to gain a representative sample of all site visitors then locations where all visitors congregate need to be searched for. This may be a site entrance and/or exit, a car park, a visitor centre or an information point. Being able to stop people is obviously important and therefore it is difficult to stop cars at site entrances but you can talk to visitors on leaving their cars when parked or returning to them. Bikes are hard to stop when in full flight, so locations where bikes have to stop such as gates need to be found. On complex sites a number of separate survey locations will need to be used to cover the different possibilities. For example, the main survey of a recreation site may take place at the on-site car park but separate survey days may need to be dedicated to eliciting responses from people using pedestrian entrances and public transport. As with *who* you sample, perfection is seldom achievable, but every attempt should be made to gain the best coverage of site users whenever possible.

When you sample

The use made of a recreation site varies according to the time of day, the day of the week and the season. It is therefore important in deciding your sample frame to consider exactly *when* you sample. An ideal survey would cover a full year (therefore covering all four seasons), a representative sample of weekdays and weekend days, would sample some bank holidays and would over the year cover different times of the day from early morning to late evening. The selection of survey days will depend critically on how much money you have to undertake the survey and therefore how many survey days can be carried out. As with *who* and *where*, perfection is seldom achievable but efforts should be made to cover as representative a selection of times as possible, within the constraints of the survey budget. Even with the best planning, things can go wrong. Weather, national events such as cup finals and Christmas shopping can all affect the number and type of visitor using a site on any particular day. I know of one survey that was conducted on the day of Princess Diana's funeral. As you can guess there were very few people about! The greater the number of survey days that you have, the less difference these 'odd' days will make to the overall data.

Sample size

How big should your sample be? The important thing to understand is that it is the *absolute* size of the sample that is important in determining how much confidence can be placed in the data collected, not the sample size relative to the whole population. Therefore a sample of 500 visitors is just as valid (providing rigorous random sampling is used) for a total population visiting a recreation site of 200,000 as it is for a population of 20,000. The table on page 64 illustrates this well.

Table 3.4 Confidence intervals related to sample size (confidence interval 95%)

Sample size	Percentage found from sample ('results')					
	50%	*40 or 60%*	*30 or 70%*	*20 or 80%*	*10 or 90%*	*5 or 95%*
50	13.9	13.6	12.7	11.1	8.3	–
100	9.8	9.6	9.0	7.8	5.9	4.3
200	6.9	6.8	6.3	5.5	4.2	3.0
300	5.7	5.5	5.2	4.5	3.4	2.5
500	4.4	4.3	4.0	3.5	2.6	1.9
1000	3.1	3.0	2.8	2.5	1.9	1.3
2000	2.2	2.1	2.0	1.7	1.3	1.0
10,000	1.0	1.0	0.9	0.8	0.6	0.4

Source: Veal (1997: 211).

What does this table mean? The sample size (the left hand column of the table) is the total number of questionnaires that were completed as part of a survey. The percentage found from the sample ('results'), represents the percentage found from any question answered within a survey. So for example, in a recreation site survey 80 per cent of those questioned stated that they had arrived on site by car. It is stated as 20 per cent or 80 per cent as it could be considered that 20 per cent of those questioned did not arrive by car. The figures underneath the percentage found from the sample, represent the confidence that can be placed in the data. The confidence interval is stated as 95 per cent which means that the figures represent the confidence that can be placed in the data on 95 times out of 100 (on 95 per cent of occasions). For further details of what this means and how it is calculated, refer to Veal (1997) and Smith (1995) in the references and further reading section.

Let us take an example of how we can use this table to calculate the confidence we have in our data. In the above paragraph it was stated that in a site survey 80 per cent of those questioned stated that they had arrived by car. Two hundred people were interviewed. How much confidence can we place in our answer? If we go to the left-hand column of the table we can find the sample size of 200. We can then read across the table until we find the column representing 80 per cent. At this point in the table we find a figure of 5.5. What does this 5.5 per cent mean? It means that on 95 times out of a hundred (on 95 per cent of occasions) we can be confident that the answer will lie within 5.5 per cent of 80 per cent. Therefore on 95 times out of a 100 we can be confident that the answer is between 74.5 per cent and 85.5 per cent. It must be remembered at all times in using this table that the data in the table is based upon a perfect random sample of the population.

Let us interpret this table in terms of what it means for the sample size required for a questionnaire. In the above example 80 per cent of interviewees stated that they had arrived on site by car. What difference does sample size have on the confidence we have in this answer? From the table we can see that if the sample size was 50 then the confidence interval is 11.1 per cent. Therefore on 95 per cent of occasions we can be confident that the real answer lies between 68.9 per cent and 91.1 per cent, a range of 22.2 per cent. If our sample size had been 500 the confidence interval would have been 3.5 per cent. Therefore on 95 per cent of occasions the real answer would lie between 76.5 per cent and 83.5 per cent, a range of 7 per cent. Greater confidence could therefore be placed in this result than the sample size of 50. If we used a sample size of 1000 then the confidence interval is 2.5 per cent and the real answer would lie between 77.5 per cent and 82.5 per cent a range of 5 per cent. It can therefore be seen that the greater the sample size the greater the confidence we can have as to the accuracy of our data. However, it is a question of diminishing returns. To greatly increase the accuracy of our data we have increased significantly the sample size.

So how big should our sample be?

There is no correct single answer for how large a sample should be for a questionnaire survey. In deciding our sample size we need to consider a number of factors.

> *What is the budget for the survey?* – this is critical in deciding how many days of survey can be carried out and therefore the sample size.
>
> *What degree of accuracy is required from the data?* – is pinpoint accuracy required or is a good indication all that is needed?
>
> *Is the survey going to be repeated over time to monitor trends?* – if this is the case then a high level of accuracy is required.
>
> *On analysis will one question be compared with another?* – for example, will you question the data produced by the questionnaire to see how many local people come to the site by car (comparing a question on type of visitor with a question on how people travel to the site)? This is known as cross-referencing and will require a larger sample size.

Only when these issues have been considered can a decision be made about sample size. It will almost inevitably be a compromise between accuracy and the resources of time and money. Of greatest importance is what do we want the data for in the first place. This will guide us in the level of accuracy that is required of the data.

Question design

Before considering the design of questions we must remind ourselves that we need to decide carefully on the research questions our survey seeks to answer and on the information requirements before drafting our questionnaire questions. Only by following this process will we develop a coherent survey that is useful for management. There are many types of question that can be asked and the exact phrasing of each individual question is critical to gaining meaningful answers.

Question types

There are many ways in which we can ask questions to collect data. Different question formats will collect different types of data. Let us look at the different types of question that can be asked and consider the type of data that each question type will yield.

Pre-coded questions

Pre-coded questions are those in which interviewees are required to tick pre-coded boxes. Let us look at an example:

How did you get to the site today?	car	☐
(you may tick more than one box)	motorbike	☐
	bicycle	☐
	foot	☐
	public transport	☐
	coach	☐
	minibus	☐
	other	☐

Pre-coded questions are very good at collecting data where the range of answers is well known. For example, in the above question there are only so many ways in which a visitor can get to a site. Pre-coded questions are easy and quick to analyse which makes them useful. They are particularly good at finding out the following types of information.

> *Information about the interviewee*: age, gender, place of residence, economic status, ethnic grouping, frequency of visit and group size.
> *Information about use made of the site by the interviewee*: activities carried out on site, the facilities used, the length of stay, the mode of travel to the site, the purpose of visit and where the interviewee found out about the site.

It is important when asking pre-coded questions to decide whether interviewees should be able to tick more than one box and clearly state this for each question. This will avoid the situation where some interviewees for a particular question tick only one box whilst others tick multiple boxes. It is also important to have a box for 'other' answers, in order to cater for responses you may not have considered. Sometimes 'other' is just a tick box, whilst at other times you may wish to find out what 'other' is. This can be carried out by providing a text box to fill in after the category, 'other', so that new codes can be drawn up after the survey has finished for any new categories.

When drawing up pre-coded questions it is important to consider if your survey can be compared with any other. If this is the case, it is necessary to find out what pre-coded questions have been used in the other surveys and to use the same questions and answer categories. Providing a sound representative sample is surveyed, the two surveys can then be directly compared. The same applies if a survey is being repeated on the same site to find out details about trends.

Open questions

Open-ended questions are used when the possible responses from an interviewee are not known, or where we wish to explore complex issues in greater depth than would be possible from pre-coded questions. In open-ended questions interviewees are free to make their own responses in relation to questions. Let us look at an example:

What improvements would you like to see take place on the site?

Open-ended questions are more difficult to analyse than pre-coded questions, as every response will be different. At the end of the survey when an open-ended question is analysed you will have a large list of different responses to make some sort of sense out of. It is normal practice to view this list in its totality and look for areas of commonality within the responses. These can then be amalgamated together under headings. For example, in a very small survey the results of the open question on page 66 may be:

better signposting	need a children's playground
place for refreshments needed	I'd like to know where I am going more
somewhere for children to play	I'd like somewhere to eat and drink
swings and slides	a café
better car park	somewhere safe for children to run around

These responses could be amalgamated and coded as follows:

improvements to signposting – 2 answers
children's play   4 answers
refreshments – 3 answers
car park improvements – 1 answer

Any coding such as this will involve an element of subjective categorisation of the data and can therefore be a source of potential manipulation and bias. Placing answers into categories therefore needs to be carried out with great care.

Attitudinal questions

Very often we are interested in finding out about visitors' attitudes, feelings and opinions. To do this there is a range of question types which will probe into these areas and provide us with more useful information. The following question types all probe attitudes in differing ways.

Ranking

Ranking questions ask the interviewee to rank in order of importance pre-coded categories. The results they provide indicate the priority that visitors give to various issues. An example question may be:

Please rank in order of importance the reasons why you chose to visit this site today. Please rank from 1 being the most important reason to 6 being the least important reason.

easy to get to   ❑
free entry and parking   ❑
children's playground   ❑
visitor centre   ❑
circular walks   ❑
café   ❑

Scaling

Scaling questions ask interviewees to indicate their agreement or disagreement with propositions or statements by ticking a box. For example:

In terms of the reason why you visited the site today, were the following very important, quite important, not very important or not at all important?

	Very important	Quite important	Not very important	Not at all important
easy to get to	❑	❑	❑	❑
free entry and parking	❑	❑	❑	❑
children's playground	❑	❑	❑	❑
visitor centre	❑	❑	❑	❑
circular walks	❑	❑	❑	❑
café	❑	❑	❑	❑

Attitude statements

In these questions interviewees are asked to respond to statements by indicating their strength of feeling towards a statement. For example:

Dogs should be banned from the site.	I agree strongly.	❑
	I agree.	❑
	I have no opinion.	❑
	I disagree.	❑
	I disagree strongly.	❑

Semantic differential

These questions are linear scales with either end of the scale defined by opposite statements. For example:

How do you rate the children's playground? Place an ✗ on the following lines to express the strength of your feelings.

safe	——————————————✗———	unsafe
exciting	————✗—————————	dull
imaginative	——————✗—————	unimaginative

To analyse this type of question, average results need to be calculated for each pairing by measuring where the cross is located on the line relative to one end of the line.

The wording of questions

In drafting questions there are a number of issues that need to be considered in relation to the wording of each specific question. For each question we need to do the following.

Avoid jargon; use words that everyone understands

There are many technical words and abbreviations that the visitor being questioned may not understand. Always simplify the wording as much as possible.

Badly worded: Did you find out about this site from the local TIC?
Better wording: Did you find out about this site from the tourist information centre in Worcester?

In this question many interviewees will not know what a TIC is, and people's perception of what is local will be different.

Badly worded: Which items of infrastructure did you use whilst visiting the site?
Better wording: Whilst on the site did you use any of the following (you may tick more than one box)?

    seat   ☐
    toilet   ☐
    litter bin   ☐
    car park   ☐
    bird hide   ☐

In this question many interviewees may not understand the term 'infrastructure'.

Ask only one question at a time

Each question should only address one issue. If you draft a question that asks interviewees about two related issues, divide the question into two separate questions.

Badly worded: Having visited the site did you find it to be noisy and covered in litter?
Better wording: Having visited the site did you find it to be (you may tick more than one box)?

    very noisy   ☐
    noisy   ☐
    quiet   ☐
    too quiet   ☐
    no viewpoint   ☐

Having visited the site do you consider it to be (you may tick more than one box)?

    free of litter   ☐
    slightly littered   ☐
    badly littered   ☐
    filthy   ☐

This question asked interviewees about two separate issues: noise and litter. The solution is to ask two separate questions.

Avoid asking leading questions

Leading questions are those in which the question leads the interviewee to a particular answer.

Badly worded: The money raised from the pay and display car park is used directly to benefit the conservation of the site. Do you agree with the price of the parking ticket?

Yes   ❑
No   ❑

Better wording: Do you think the price of parking is?

much too expensive   ❑
expensive   ❑
about right   ❑
too cheap   ❑
much too cheap   ❑

In this question the phrasing indicates that it should be considered that paying for parking is a positive thing. Visitors are more likely to respond positively. A better way to phrase the question is to make it more neutral and give the interviewee a series of choices.

Avoid words in questions that can be misinterpreted

Some words or phrases will mean different things to different people.

Badly worded: Do you consider yourself to be a local to the site?
Better wording: How far away from the site do you live?

within 10 miles   ❑
11–20 miles   ❑
more than 20 miles   ❑

In this question the term 'local' will mean different things to different people. It is better to give the interviewee a series of choices. This will cut out the personal interpretation of what the word 'local' means.

Questionnaire layout and carrying out the survey

Questionnaire layout

Having drafted your questions it is necessary to put them into a logical order and design the actual questionnaire form. This needs to be as user friendly as possible. Each questionnaire form needs to start with some 'housekeeping' information and space to record:

- the name of the interviewer
- the time of the interview

- the date of the interview
- the location of the interview
- a unique number/code for each questionnaire form
- non-responses.

It is normal to have a standard introductory phrase before the beginning of the questions that all interviewers read out at the start of every interview. For example:

> Good morning/afternoon. I am carrying out a survey of visitors using this site on behalf of the local council. The survey will ask you about your use of the site and your opinions concerning its management. Can you spare a few minutes to answer some questions?

It is normal practice to make the initial questions of the closed pre-coded type. This will lead the interviewee easily into more complex questions such as open questions and attitudinal questions. It is important to make sure that questions follow a logical sequence and are laid out clearly with a font size that is easy to read. It is helpful to provide plenty of space around the questions to make them easier to read and understand. It is common practice for the categories within pre-coded questions to be placed onto prompt cards. These have the pre-coded answers laid out on them in a large font size, so that they can be shown to the interviewee at the appropriate time. The layout of the questionnaire is particularly important if it is of the self-completed variety such as in a postal questionnaire. In this situation it is important to make sure that there are clear instructions throughout, that tell the person filling in the form exactly what to do.

Pilot testing

Having decided on your sample frame and drafted a questionnaire it is necessary to pilot test it. This means doing a dry run of the survey to check and fine-tune the methodology and the questions, in order to identify any potential problems. This may take several days but is well worth the input of time. It is good practice when pilot testing to have someone observing the pilot interviews, separate from the questioner, so as to observe accurately and make notes about any issues relating to the wording of questions. Having pilot tested and identified any problems with the sampling procedure and the wording of questions, changes can be made and the methodology and questionnaire improved.

Carrying out the survey

Having made changes based upon the pilot study, the survey for real can take place. It is vital that the exact methodology developed for the study is adhered to rigorously. This means that all interviewers need to select interviewees by the same sampling method and that questions need to be asked in the same way. This can only be achieved by carrying out thorough training of all interviewers prior to implementing the survey. Carrying out an observed dry run with all of the interviewers is a very useful exercise and will give all interviewers a chance to practise before carrying out the survey for real. It is also useful to build in a series of spot checks as a means of quality control (i.e. checking if researchers are carrying out the survey as planned). This will identify any discrepancies between researchers in the sampling methods used and the manner in which the questions are asked.

Analysis of data

The use of computers

Questionnaires generate large amounts of data that will require some form of analysis in order to interpret. Imagine a questionnaire survey of 200 interviews that has 25 questions. This will produce a minimum of 5000 individual items of data. To deal with this data we need to use computers. This has become quite easy with specific user friendly computer packages now being available for the production and analysis of questionnaires. Example software includes; SPSS (statistical package for social sciences), SNAP survey software, Quest, The survey system and Pinpoint. The use of such packages will improve considerably the analysis of your data and aid with the presentation of results. As with all software, some time needs to be invested into learning what the software will do for you and how you use it. A trial run 'practice' survey is useful for this. For most of these computer packages you have to design your questionnaire using the software. This can then be printed out and copied for your survey or used as an e-mail questionnaire.

Data input

Having set up a questionnaire template on a computer the data from the completed questionnaires can be entered. This task needs to be carried out with great care, as any typing errors will affect the results. To ensure the data is put into a database as accurately as possible, spot checks are needed to monitor accuracy regularly. In addition, at this input stage the data can be checked for any discrepancies such as out of range values (age 203 years), consistency errors (visited a site with friends, group size of 1) and missing values.

What can we get the computer to calculate for us?

What kind of analysis can we carry out on questionnaire data?

Averages
In the analysis of questionnaires the average we normally calculate is the mean (it could be the mode or median). You can only calculate means from numeric data. Examples of question areas where a mean may be a useful statistic are: age of visitor (where interviewee gives precise age and does not tick an age range box), expenditure or amount of time spent on site.

Totals
One of the significant ways in which computers aid us with the analysis of questionnaires is by calculating how many times a given response was recorded. For example, we can ask the computer to calculate how many times the answer yes was given for a given question and how many times no was given. This is obviously useful in all pre-coded closed questions.

List

For open questions we can get the computer to list all of the recorded responses. Most computer packages then allow for responses to be categorised under new headings to allow further analysis to take place.

Percentages

For any set of data produced by the computer, percentages can be easily calculated. This is one of the main ways in which questionnaire data is presented. For example we may find from a site survey that 30 per cent of visitors questioned were dog walkers.

Cross tabulation

Cross tabulation is where you compare one question with another. For example, you may wish to ask the computer to compare two questions:

> How old are you?
> What activities did you do whilst on the site?

Both of these questions are closed pre-coded questions. The computer will calculate a cross tabulation table (Table 3.5).

Please note that all figures in this table are in percentages by column. Cross tabulation tables normally also include counts within them (i.e. how many visitors under 18 visited the bird hide). This is important information as it can indicate how much confidence can be placed in the data. If the count for any category (for example, under 18s who visit the bird hide), is very low, then the confidence we can have in the data will be low. To have full confidence in data produced by cross tabulation we need a reasonable sample size (see Table 3.4). Therefore if we intend to carry out cross tabulation it may be necessary to consider obtaining a larger sample than would be necessary if questions were analysed in isolation. Cross tabulation will draw more information out of the data collected than if questions are just analysed on their own. It is therefore an important analytical technique. However, it must be used with great care. It is possible to cross tabulate almost every question with every other question and produce a vast amount of tables. Most cross tabulations will be meaningless. Great care must be taken therefore, in deciding what to cross tabulate with what. It is best practice to sit down with the questionnaire form in front of you and draw up a list of the cross tabulations you wish to carry out *before* you start to analyse the data.

Table 3.5 Cross tabulation table of age category against activity carried out whilst on the site

% columns	Circular walk	Looked in visitor centre	Children's playground	Bird hide	Casual walk
Under 18	15	18	64	11	8
18–29	24	25	14	16	31
30–44	31	24	16	17	26
45–64	17	16	3	23	22
Over 65	13	17	2	33	13

Note
All figures are in percentages by column.

Statistical analysis

Before considering what statistical analysis can be carried out on data collected in questionnaires, it is necessary to question how accurately the sample obtained reflects the whole population. In other words how *representative* is the sample? There is no point spending time calculating statistics on data that you are not confident about. Any statistics calculated would imply a degree of accuracy to the data that is not warranted. It must also be remembered that any results that we calculate from questionnaire data cannot be guaranteed 100 per cent accurate as we are only taking a sample from a larger population and that we cannot be sure that the sample is representative of the total population. Any results are therefore inferential in their nature in that they are based upon probabilities.

If you are confident you have obtained a representative sample there is a variety of statistical tests that can be applied to draw more from the data. It is not within the scope of this book to discuss the details of each statistical test. Readers are referred to the references in the bibliography at the end of this chapter for further details. However, the main types of test used are:

Chi-squared testing
This is used to test the relationship between two variables of a nominal nature. Nominal data is that which is made up of categories such as we find in closed pre-coded questions. Chi-squared testing is normally used in questionnaires to test the relationship between variables in cross tabulation tables and to tell us whether the relationship between the variables is significant.

The t-test – comparing two means
This test is used to compare two means to see if there is a significant difference between them. An example of where this may be used is if we wish to compare the spending on the site of people who live within 10 miles of it with that of people who have travelled over 10 miles to reach it. In this case we will compare the mean spend between the two groups to see if there is a significant difference between the two.

Analysis of variance (ANOVA) – one way analysis of variance
This is used to examine the differences between more than two means at the same time. We could use ANOVA for example, if we wished to see if there was a difference in on-site spending for people who lived less than 10 miles away, those who lived 11–20 miles away and those who lived more than 20 miles away. In this case we would have three separate means.

Before using any of these techniques it is important to read about them carefully and to check whether the data you have is suitable for an individual technique. It is also important to understand what the results actually mean.

Types of questionnaire survey

The methods available to carry out questionnaire surveys are many and varied but can be split into those where questions are asked by an *interviewer* and those where a *respondent* reads and completes a questionnaire on their own. The following are some of the possible types of questionnaire survey, that are applicable to recreational site management.

One-to-one on site surveys – these are surveys where an interviewer questions an interviewee on a one-to-one basis, normally while out 'on site'. This type of survey is good for finding out a wide variety of information about people's use of sites and their attitudes towards them. However, the results are limited to those who visit the site. One-to-one surveys generally have a high response rate.

Household surveys – these are surveys conducted in people's homes. The technique could be used for example to find out why people do not visit a site. Households are normally selected at random from lists such as electoral registers or the postal address file. Household surveys generally have a high response rate.

Telephone surveys – conducted over the telephone. For this type of survey you need a resource base of telephone numbers. The technique may be useful for example, to conduct a survey of people who have been issued with fishing permits or are members of a boat club. Telephone surveys generally have a high response rate.

Postal surveys – in this type of survey questionnaires are sent to people through the post. It is then down to the selected respondent to fill in the questionnaire and send it back. Postal questionnaires can be given out by hand for later return by post. Postal surveys normally have a low response rate and results must be treated with care as respondents may not be representative of the whole population being studied.

Self-registration – self-registration surveys rely on people picking up a questionnaire themselves, filling it in and either handing it in or placing it in a box. For example, a questionnaire may be left on the counter of a visitor centre or in a weatherproof box in the middle of the countryside. The problem with self-registration forms is that the people who fill them in are self-selecting and may not be representative of the whole population being studied. The results of such surveys should therefore be treated with care. The response rate is generally low.

Captive surveys – in this type of survey you work on a 'captive' known group such as a school or a group of volunteers. The response rate should be 100 per cent.

Observation surveys

Why carry out observation surveys?

One of the best ways to find out about the visitor to your site is one of the most simple and obvious. That is, to observe. We know a great deal about behaviour, distribution and numbers of animal species just from observation. After all, animals are not known for their ability to answer questionnaires or to take part in focus groups. What sort of information can observation give us? Through observation we can find out about:

- the distribution of visitors around a site
- the numbers of visitors coming to a site
- the behaviour of visitors whilst on a site.

In addition, observation can be used for testing. For example, we may wish to test the effect of placing a new signpost at a path junction. Observation is very good at telling us *what* people do, but it cannot tell us *why* people do what they are observed doing. To discover this, other forms of research are needed such as questionnaires or focus groups or in-depth interviews. Observation as a technique therefore, often runs in tandem with other research techniques.

Observation can be both qualitative and quantitative. Qualitative observation is something we do every day of our lives. As we walk around we observe the world around us, and store in our memory information about what we have seen. As we walk around recreation sites we will be making useful and important observations about what is happening on a site. The importance of just going out and looking at what is going on is much underrated. It does not produce data, but it does help in developing an understanding of the use made of recreation sites. However, observation can be quantitative as well. In quantitative observation, systematic methodologies are developed to observe and record information about site visitors in a systematic manner. This means that data is collected that can be analysed and interpreted. How do we go about gathering data through observation?

Decide what you want to observe

As with questionnaire surveys this will be dictated by the needs of site management. If we remember from Table 3.1 the first step in any survey is to decide the management issue it will address. The research question(s) can then be decided upon and the information requirements identified. Most observation surveys will be concerned with distribution, behaviour or numbers.

How are you going to carry out your observations?

As with questionnaire surveys we need to develop systematic and repeatable methodologies that ensure that the data collected is free from bias and is as accurate as possible. As with questionnaire surveys a sampling frame needs to be developed. As a reminder this means deciding *where* to sample, *who* to sample and *when* to sample.

> *Where to sample* – in deciding where to sample we must first consider the individual site to be observed and what is to be observed. If we are observing the *number* of people using the network of paths on a site we would probably observe people at set points on the path network (often at path junctions) and record the number of people using each path, the type of use (walking, cycling . . .) and the direction of travel. However, if we wish to observe the *distribution* of people across a site then we need to observe across wider areas (people may not stick to paths). For most sites it will not be possible to observe a whole site from one location. The site therefore needs to be divided into zones and observation points decided upon. Some zones may be quite small, others larger. There should be no overlap between observation zones, otherwise site visitors may be recorded more than once. Figure 3.4 shows a fictitious country park and shows the observation points that could be used to observe the use made of the paths and the observation points and zones that could be used to observe the use of the whole site.

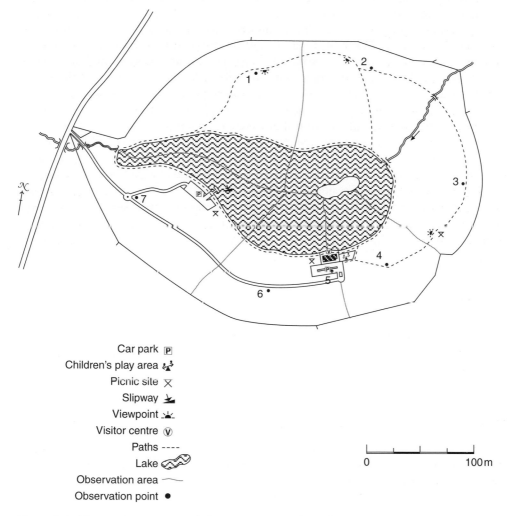

Car park ⓟ
Children's play area 🧒
Picnic site ✕
Slipway ⤓
Viewpoint 👁
Visitor centre ⓥ
Paths ----
Lake ⬭
Observation area ⌒
Observation point ●

0 ———————— 100m

Figure 3.4 Observation points and observation zones for a fictitious country park

Who to sample – in observation there are three approaches to the who question.

1   Observe everyone in an observation zone at discrete points in time (for example on the hour or every five minutes). If all the observers on a site observe their zone at the same point in time then the whole site will be observed at one moment.
2   Observe everyone that passes an observation point or is in an observation zone, over a period of time.
3   Randomly select individual people to observe.

The choice of which of the above techniques to use will depend on what you are seeking to observe and the number of people using the site. If there are large numbers using a site, observation at one point in time may be very difficult unless small zones are created.

When to sample – the guidance for when to sample is the same as for questionnaire surveys. Many of the decisions about when to sample will be dictated by the constraints imposed by budgets. However, every effort should be made to observe over a variety of times that will reflect the true use made of the site at different times of the day and year. If carrying out observations at discrete points in time, a decision will have to be made as to how often observations take place. For example, should they be every five minutes or every hour? This may depend on how busy the site is and what the information will be used for. If you are seeking to find out the numbers of visitors using the site at different times of the day it may be important to observe regularly throughout the day. If however, you are just seeking to find out the activities that are carried out on the site then more widely spaced observation times may be chosen.

How will you record the observations?

To be able to record what is observed, a recording form needs to be created. This will provide space to record details of for example:

- date and time of observation
- name of observer
- location of observation/zone of observation
- number of people observed
- activities of people observed
- location of people observed.

As with questionnaires, a period of pilot testing the methodology needs to be carried out in order that the method can be refined. Similarly, with questionnaires, a period of training is required prior to the actual survey so that all researchers adopt the same methodology.

How will I analyse the data?

Data from observation surveys is easily analysed by placing the information onto a computer spreadsheet or database. Totals, averages, lists, percentages and graphs can then, be easily computed.

Observation is a very useful tool in gaining an understanding of recreation sites. It is less complex than questionnaires to carry out and yields very useful management information. Being simpler it is normally cheaper and is easier to analyse and draw conclusions from.

In-depth interviews

In-depth interviews are a qualitative technique that probes more deeply into issues than questionnaire surveys. In an in-depth interview individuals are selected for interview and then questioned. The format of the interview is much less structured than questionnaire surveys and interviewers are able to question the interviewees about responses. It is normal to have a checklist of questions and question areas that the interviewer will ask, but, unlike the questionnaire surveys, the interviewer can probe into issues raised by particular answers. For example, if an interviewee answers a question stating that she does not find the children's playground very good, the interviewer can then ask why and probe issues associated with that playground more fully. In-depth interviews will normally take at least half an hour to conduct and therefore are normally only carried out on a few people. The information collected is therefore qualitative in its nature. It is normal practice to tape record interviews, as the responses will be too complex to record in written form as the interview progresses. The tape recordings are then transcribed into a written record. Analysis of in-depth interviews consists of comparing the transcripts of different interviews and looking for common threads between the interviews. A good starting point for this is to go back to the original questions and look at each transcript under relevant question headings.

In-depth interviews will not give you statistics or any other form of numerical data but they will provide a greater understanding of the issues. It must always be remembered that due to the small sample sizes involved, in-depth surveys may not be representative of the whole population and so should be treated with some caution. However, they are very useful, since in-depth interviews can be used before designing questionnaire surveys to gain a greater understanding of site issues. This will help in developing question areas and in considering possible responses to pre-coded questions.

Focus groups

Focus groups are similar in principle to in-depth interviews; however they are conducted with a group of people, rather than on a one-to-one basis. As with in-depth interviews, a checklist of questions is used and issues raised by responses, are probed. In focus groups the interviewer plays the role of a facilitator that guides a structured discussion about particular issues. It is the facilitator's role to:

1   establish rapport with the group and set objectives
2   provoke discussion in the relevant areas
3   summarise the group's responses.

The facilitator plays a key role in the success of the focus group and should clearly understand the topic being discussed and have good interpersonal skills.

Participants in a focus group should be allowed to interact with each other and knock issues and ideas around in an informal way. As with in-depth interviews the session is normally tape recorded and transcribed into a written format. The important element of focus groups and in-depth interviews is to select carefully as to who should participate. The size of focus groups is normally between 8 and 12 and so it is not possible to use probability sampling techniques. The most commonly used method is to hold a number of focus groups where each focus group is made up of representatives from particular groups from within the research population. Examples of groupings that could be used for focus group work include:

•   local unemployed youth
•   cyclists

- dog walkers
- local retired
- local children between 12 and 16
- local residents' groups
- holidaymakers
- mothers
- fishermen.

For each focus group the same basic questions will be asked and the group probed about their responses. An approach such as this will reveal the differences of opinion between different groups and will provide considerable insight into visitors' opinions about a recreation site. Analysis of focus groups is the same as dealing with in-depth interviews.

References and further reading

Brunt, P. (1997) *Market Research in Travel and Tourism*, Oxford: Butterworth-Heinemann.

Clegg, F. (1990) *Simple Statistics: A Course Book for the Social Sciences*, Cambridge: Cambridge University Press.

Countryside Commission (1996) *Market Research for Countryside Recreation*, Cheltenham: Countryside Commission.

Countryside Recreation Network (1997) *Do Visitor Services Count? Making Use of Surveys for Countryside Recreation*, Conference proceedings, Cardiff: Countryside Recreation Network.

Dey, I. (1993) *Qualitative Data Analysis: A User-Friendly Guide for Social Scientists*, London: Routledge.

Dytham, C. (1999) *Choosing and Using Statistics: A Biologist's Guide*, Oxford: Blackwell Science Ltd.

Finn, M., Elliott-White, M. and Walton, M. (2000) *Tourism and Leisure Research Methods*, Harlow: Longman.

Gordon, W. (1999) *Good Thinking: A Guide to Qualitative Research*, Henley-on-Thames: Admap Publications.

Kraus, R. and Allen, L. R. (1990) *Research and Evaluation in Recreation, Parks and Leisure Services*, Boston: Allyn and Bacon.

Lindsay, J. M. (1997) *Techniques in Human Geography*, London: Routledge.

Miles, M. B. and Huberman, A. M. (1994) *Qualitative Data Analysis: An Expanded Sourcebook*, London: Sage Publications.

Morgan, D. L. and Knueger, R. A. (1998) *The Focus Group Kit*, London: Sage Publications.

Oppenheim, A. N. (1992) *Questionnaire Design, Interviewing and Attitude Measurement*, London: Pinter.

Rowntree, D. (1981) *Statistics Without Tears, a Primer for Non-mathematicians*, London: Middlesex.

Scottish Natural Heritage (1995) *Visitor Monitoring Training Manual*, Edinburgh: Scottish Natural Heritage.

Seaton, A. V. and Bennett, M. M. (1996) *Marketing Tourism Products*, London: Thompson Business Press.

Smith, S. L. J. (1995) *Tourism Analysis: A Handbook*, Harlow: Longman.

Veal, A. J. (1997) *Research Methods for Leisure and Tourism: A Practical Guide*, London: Pitman Publishing.

4 Making your site more accessible

If the intention for a site is to develop it for the visitor, we must consider how we can make it more accessible. This means making it easier to find out, about, easier to find and easier to get to. This chapter considers the methods available to do all of these.

This chapter is concerned with the techniques that we can use to make country-side recreation sites more accessible. What do we mean by accessible? Dictionary definitions of accessible include: easy to approach or enter, obtainable, the right to enter. Therefore making a site more accessible means that you make it easier to obtain details, approach and enter. We can make sites more accessible in many ways. These can be broken down under the following headings:

- making it easier to find out about a site
- making the site easier to find
- making the site easier to get to.

Before exploring the many techniques that we can use to make our sites more accessible let us consider the ways in which people first find out about them. The many surveys that have been carried out generally show the same trends. Let us look at an example survey.

In 1995 the Peak District National Park carried out a visitor survey of Longden-dale. The survey was conducted over four days and 1716 questionnaires were completed. One of the questions asks visitors what had prompted them to visit Longdendale. The answers are shown in Table 4.1, p. 82.

The reasons that visitors gave for visiting the site can be amalgamated into a number of broad categories.

Been before and enjoyed/suggested by relatives

It can be seen from the responses in Table 4.1 that the main reason people choose to visit the site was because they had been there before. The fact that they have returned implies that they have had an enjoyable experience at the site on a previous occasion and that their needs had then been adequately satisfied. To increase the number of visitors that return after a first visit we need to have a good product that is well managed and meets in full the needs of those visiting it. In addition, consider-able numbers of visitors stated that they came because friends or relatives had suggested the site. Again this suggests a degree of satisfaction from the friends and relatives. After all, how often do we suggest to friends that they to go to a site that

Table 4.1 Factors prompting visitors to visit Longdendale

	August Friday	August Saturday	August Sunday	September Sunday
Been before and enjoyed	51	55	56	56
Driving past	20	16	14	16
Suggested by friends/relatives	15	19	17	9
TV/radio	6	4	3	0
Read in books	4	5	2	2
Brochure/holiday guides	5	2	2	1
Live near	5	6	1	4
Newspapers	2	3	2	4
Leaflet in TIC	5	4	1	4
Road sign	5	2	6	3
Other	10	14	17	13
No answer	0	1	1	0

Source: Peak District National Park (1995).

Note
Percentages add up to more than 100% as people could name more than one reason.

we have been to before and had not enjoyed? Overall these responses demonstrate the importance of providing experiences and service to the visitor so that they have a good time whilst on the site, so much so that they wish to return and will tell friends and relatives all about their visit. There is no better advertising for recreation sites than satisfied customers spreading positive information by word of mouth. However, we must also remember the converse being true. In Chapter 1 we saw how Horowitz (1990) considers that a disgruntled customer will tell eleven people about their experience, whilst a satisfied customer will tell only three. Therefore, as we have seen in Chapter 1, news travels fast and dirt tends to stick. In this survey the two combined categories of 'been before' and 'enjoyed and suggested by friends and relatives' accounts for about 75 per cent of visitors.

Driving past/road sign

Within this survey this is the next most popular response with around about 20 per cent of respondents stating that this was the reason they had visited the site. It is an odd thing to think that many people set off for a day in the countryside not really knowing what they are going to do. However, surveys show this to be the case. To increase the instances of visitors chancing upon countryside recreation sites and making a decision to visit them, we can use several methods to try and entice them. First we can signpost recreation sites from roads. Second we can create entrances that are welcoming and actively seek to encourage the first-time visitor to make the decision to come inside.

TV/radio/newspapers

Compared with the above two categories these were not such important incentives to get people visiting the site. There will be some variation in relation to how much media coverage a site has received and the types of media. Most sites have a low level of coverage by the media and therefore it is not an important element of letting people know about sites. However, some sites gain significant media coverage. National parks for example have a high media profile. Consider how many people have probably visited the North Yorkshire Moors after watching the television series 'Heartbeat' or visited the Yorkshire Dales (specifically Herriot country) after watching 'All Creatures Great and Small'? Whilst these two examples are very high profile television, much useful publicity for recreation sites can be obtained at little expense by the effective use of the media.

Read in a book/brochures/holiday guides/leaflet in tourist information centre

This amalgamated category is concerned with the printed media. In this survey between 10 and 20 per cent of visitors stated that printed media had prompted them to come to the site. The development of leaflets, guidebooks and brochures is therefore an important mechanism in getting people to know about countryside recreation sites, and these days we have to include the Internet as a new, and important tool. Printed media will be important in attracting the first-time visitor who has not had contact with someone who has visited the site before. As such it is particularly important for people on holiday away from their normal place of residence.

Live near

In most surveys of this type, local people who have always known about a site through living in close proximity to it, have always made up a proportion of its visitors.

Surveys of this type are very useful in finding out about how visitors learn about sites. This type of information can then be used in making decisions concerning how they can be made more accessible.

By making a site more accessible we are likely to make it easier to find out about, easier to get to and easier to get into. We are in fact making a site more convenient for the customer. As such, if we increase the accessibility of the site, we are likely to increase the number of visitors. Therefore a decision as to whether to make a site more accessible or not, will depend on a detailed assessment of it and a decision as to whether more people using it is a desirable objective. Let us now look at some of the techniques that we can use if we decide to make our sites more accessible.

Making the site easier to find out about

There are a large number of methods we can use to let people know about countryside recreation sites. Each method will have its own benefits and shortcomings and in choosing which method to use, we need to think carefully about which is the most appropriate for the individual circumstances of a particular site and the target audience we are trying to reach. Very often we will choose to use more than one method.

An effective way to let people know about countryside recreation sites is to place advertisements in newspapers and magazines. In choosing which papers and magazines to advertise in, we need to consider the target audience we wish to reach with our advertisement and then select titles which have a readership that matches it. In deciding this we need to find out for each title:

- the circulation figures (how many are sold)
- what kind of person reads it (will indicate who would see any advert placed)
- the price of advertising (the larger the circulation generally the higher the cost of an advertisement, the larger the advert the higher the cost).

In designing any advertisement we must consider carefully what the site product is, and what visitors' needs may be. We can use this information to try and focus the advert such that potential customers will look at it and feel that the advertised site will fulfil their needs on a particular occasion. All adverts should contain the following information:

- name of the site
- location of site
- opening times
- price of entry (if any)
- details of what is available to do on the site
- logo of the managing authority
- phone number and address for more details
- visual imagery that conveys the feel of the site.

Advertisements are a useful means of connecting with visitors but can be expensive and therefore only suitable for sites that are of a commercial nature. However, we can get details about recreation sites in the media in a much more economical manner. By producing stories and features about recreation sites and sending them to suitable papers and magazines we can often get them into the media for free. Certainly speciality magazines such as those associated with climbing, walking and natural history regularly cover feature items on areas of the countryside and are normally glad of stories to print. Local newspapers including the advertising free sheets are also useful in publicising a site to local people. Regular press releases to local and regional media about things that happen on a site such as events, new features, natural history and volunteer days will all increase its profile at very little cost.

Leaflets

Leaflets are one of the key ways in which we can provide information about recreation sites to outside parties. Indeed, if we go into any tourist information centre, bed and breakfast or tourism facility we will find a large number of leaflets all concerned with promoting sites of different types. Leaflets, although they do cost money to produce, print and distribute can be a cheap means of publicity. They are particularly useful in as much as people can pick up a leaflet and read it at their leisure, for example in their car or at home. Indeed, a real advantage of leaflets is that they can be kept for the information they contain, so that they can be used at a later date. Leaflets can contain lots of images concerning sites in the form of photographs and illustrations that will provide potential visitors with an idea of what it is like, so that they can make decisions about matching their needs to what the site offers. They

Plate 4.1 Example leaflets for countryside sites

also contain a lot of information that is necessary in order for potential visitors to make the decision as to whether to visit the site or not.

To produce a high quality and effective leaflet takes skill and imagination. It is not within the scope of this book to go into the detailed intricacies of design. However, the following issues need to be considered when designing and producing a leaflet:

Price

How much a leaflet costs will depend on many factors. These include:

The quantity printed – the more leaflets that are printed, the less the leaflet will cost per item.

Paper type – there are a large variety of paper types that a leaflet can be printed on. Different colours, finishes and thicknesses all have design functions in leaflets and all of these factors have a price.

Colours – within the printing process each colour that is used requires the production of a new printing plate and a separate printing process. Therefore, the more colours that you choose to use, the higher the cost will be. This ranges up to full colour, which will be the most expensive option. Remember, by choosing carefully the colour of the paper to be printed on, you can add colour to a leaflet.

Paper shape – if you require paper shapes that are different from standard sizes the cutting process involved will add to the leaflet costs.

Folds – each time a leaflet is folded will make it more expensive.

It is therefore important in designing a leaflet to first know how much money you have to produce and print the leaflet. In addition, you need to estimate how many you need to have printed. These two factors will then guide you as to what you can afford. Whilst full colour glossy leaflets are very well presented, high quality and effective leaflets can be produced at a much lower cost with a bit of imagination and good design.

Leaflet design

How a leaflet looks will affect how attractive it is to make people put the effort into picking it up. A leaflet's detailed design will influence how easy the information contained within it can be reached. Designing an effective leaflet is a very skilled process and should be left to graphic artists trained in the intricacies of the design process. However, whilst graphic artists will be the best people to carry out leaflet design, the person producing the leaflet must have in mind what he or she wants it to look like in the broadest sense. This can then be used to brief the graphic artist. The following factors need to be considered when designing leaflets:

Shape and size and fold pattern – if you start to gather a collection of leaflets (a good thing to do as you can use other people's leaflets for ideas and good practice), you will find that they come in a wide variety of shapes, sizes and fold patterns. There is no one right choice. Each will be suitable for a different purpose.

One consideration that needs to be made is how and where the leaflet is going to be displayed. Most leaflets are distributed through tourist information centres where they are displayed in purpose built leaflet dispensers. These generally take leaflets that are based upon A4 paper folded in three. As such the front covers of the leaflets are 210mm by 100mm. Leaflets of different shapes and sizes are more difficult to display effectively. Generally you should avoid large cumbersome leaflets with many folds, as these are difficult to use, particularly outdoors. As a general rule the simpler a leaflet is, the more effective it will be.

Fonts – size and type – choosing the right font style and size is of great importance in influencing how easy a leaflet is to use. There is a huge variety of fonts that can be used. Each will convey a different image. As a general rule, choose simple font styles and do not try to get too fancy. It is very bad practice to mix up too many font styles, so keep it simple. As for font size make it at least 12 point and 14 if possible. Fourteen point is considered to be a suitable size for people with some visual impairment.

Photographs and illustrations – the saying goes that 'a picture paints a thousand words' and this is very true for leaflets. The selection of appropriate photographs and illustrations is an essential element of leaflet design. Photographs and illustrations should convey accurately what the site is like and illustrate its key features. Above all the photographs should contain people, so as to connect directly with the reader.

Colours – the colours used in a leaflet should be carefully thought out. They will have a profound effect on how a leaflet looks. Full colour leaflets look very professional but do come at a cost. Bold colours draw attention if used carefully but can be overpowering if used badly. More subdued colours can be effective and subtler but care must be taken to ensure there is good contrast between the colour of the text and the background.

Layout – the physical layout of text, photographs, maps and titles will significantly affect the effectiveness of a leaflet. We must consider what the eye does when it first looks at a leaflet. It looks for clues as to where to start looking and generally starts by looking at the top left of the page (where most pages start)! It will be drawn to bold colours, photographs and illustrations. The actual layout of the leaflet will therefore guide your eye around the page. Badly laid out leaflets without any logical sequence, will be difficult to follow whereas well laid out leaflets will be easy to use.

Maps – most leaflets will contain a map of one sort or another. First there are maps that show where the site is and the main routes to get to it. These are normally located on the back cover and need to be accurate, simple to use and of an appropriate scale for the site. Such maps are normally based upon the road networks and clearly labelled road numbers and navigation features such as towns, villages, churches and public houses will help visitors to find the site. Second, there are maps of the site itself. These should be simple and should aim to show the reader the site features and act as a guide that can be taken around. Most leaflet maps are of a plan style (as if looking vertically down from an aeroplane) similar in style to Ordnance Survey maps. These can take a certain degree of spatial awareness to understand. Better practice is to use overhead oblique maps, which are as if you are looking downwards out of an aeroplane window (not vertically down but at an angle). In overhead oblique maps, artists represent

Plate 4.2 An example of an overhead oblique site map

the features of the site such as buildings, lakes, playgrounds and car parks in a manner that is recognisable on the ground. That is, symbols are not used to represent features but that the features are represented by true to life drawings of the feature as if you were seeing it sideways out of an aeroplane window. An example of an overhead oblique map can be seen in Plate 4.2.

Front and back covers – the front cover of a leaflet is of the utmost importance in ensuring that a leaflet is picked up. It needs to actively grab the attention and say, 'Come on, come over here and pick me up.' A clear simple title is important and this should be at the top of the leaflet so that it can be seen when it is stacked in a leaflet rack. An attention catching photograph or illustration is also important. Primary colours are very effective in grabbing attention. The back cover normally contains details of where the site is, opening times, admission charges and contact numbers.

Information contained in a leaflet

Leaflets are all different in their design and style. However, most leaflets contain very much the same kind of information. This is:

- name of the site
- location of site
- how to get to the site by car/public transport or other means

- admission charges
- opening times
- site features and possible activities
- information for disabled visitors
- details of refreshments, shops, etc.
- any logo and name of managing agency.

It is also good practice in certain localities to translate leaflets into other languages. In Wales it is important that leaflets are produced in Welsh, but other languages such as French, Spanish, Japanese or even Urdu may be appropriate so as to include all potential customers.

Distribution

Having produced a leaflet it is necessary to distribute it. In deciding where to distribute a leaflet we must reflect again on *who* its target audience is and distribute accordingly. One of the key decisions that needs to be made is over what area a leaflet will be distributed. Will it just be within the local area or will distribution be wider? The types of places in which we can display leaflets include:

- tourist information centres
- hotels, bed and breakfasts and other accommodation
- public houses
- shops
- tourist sites
- bus and railway stations
- other countryside recreation sites.

Having distributed our leaflets we need to develop a system for replacing them when stocks run low. This can be done by making a regular inspection of sites displaying the leaflets, by phoning around and asking about stocks or by having a card in the leaflet dispenser that can be used to re-order new stock when it reaches a certain level.

Posters

The production of posters that can be displayed on walls and in shop windows is another means by which sites can be promoted. These need to catch people's attention visually and show through the use of photographs and illustrations the site and its key attractions. These can be distributed to the same locations as leaflets.

Guidebooks

Guidebooks are normally produced by individuals and publishers separate from site managers. As such they are difficult to influence or contribute to. Often the first time you know that your site is in a guidebook is when it has been published. However, local authorities or countryside agencies can produce their own guidebooks, booklets or maps to countryside sites within areas or regions. These can be important sources of information about countryside sites and their facilities and attractions. This sort of information does not always have to be in book format. For example, most national parks produce a yearly free newspaper that provides information about sites within their boundaries as well as information on such things as accommodation, public transport, natural history, heritage and events. These papers are normally subsidised through selling advertising in them.

Tourist information centres (TICs)

These are key places that visitors new to an area can go to find out about what there is to do in there. These are found in most towns particularly in areas that have large visitor numbers. They act as central locations in which information about local attractions can be gathered and distributed. They are always well stocked with leaflets and posters and normally also sell maps and guidebooks to the area. As such they are essential places for distributing any promotional material concerning countryside sites. Tourist information centres also contain staff that are trained in dealing with the public's enquiries and will carry out such functions as booking accommodation. It is a good idea to invite these key people to view your site and talk to them about what it offers to the public. After all, these staff will talk to a considerable number of visitors over a season and the greater their knowledge, the more effective they will be in helping the public make informed choices about where to go.

Plate 4.3 Inside a Tourist Information Centre with staff helping the public with an enquiry

The Internet

The Internet is an increasingly important means of dispersing information. It is therefore important to develop a good user friendly web page that will provide quality information to anyone that seeks it. There are many good examples of web sites just a few of which are listed below:

Lake District National Park:
http://www.lake-district.gov.uk/

Northumberland County Council Northumberland Visitor Guide:
http://www.northumberland.gov.uk/vg/home.htm

Peak District National Park:
http://www.peakdistrict.org/

Pembrokeshire Coast National Trail:
http://www.pembrokeshirecoast.org.uk/english/enjoynp/pcnptr.htm

Suffolk County Council Countryside Service:
http://www.suffolkcc.gov.uk/countryside/

Making the site easier to find

Having found out about a countryside recreation site through the methods outlined above and having made a decision to visit, visitors will then have to travel to a site. It is very helpful to these visitors if the site is clearly signposted and made easy to find. This is particularly important for first-time visitors, and in particular for tourists who may not know the area. Clear signposting to the site is required both for motorists and for pedestrians. In addition, it is important to develop obvious and welcoming site entrances. Quality signposts and site entrances not only make it easier to find but will also attract the passer-by who may not know about the site. Earlier in this chapter it was shown that a proportion of site visitors only make the decision to visit as they drive past it. The more effectively a site is signposted and the more site entrances are made interesting and enticing, a greater number of visitors will drop in on the spur of the moment.

White on brown signs

The white on brown tourist signs (see Plate 4.4 for example) were introduced in the mid-1980s to direct motorists to tourist destinations and have since become a familiar feature on our roads. They are designed for the needs of the motorist and are particularly effective as visitors are aware that a white on brown tourist sign means that there is something of interest to stop and see.

How do we go about getting white on brown tourist signs developed for a countryside recreation site? First it is necessary to contact the highways department of the local authority in which a countryside recreation site is located. It will be the highways department that will decide whether permission for brown on white signs will be granted and will advise on design and positioning. A white on brown sign does not need planning permission but will need the permission of the highway

Plate 4.4 A white and brown tourism destination road sign

authority. The decision as to whether to grant permission to place these signs will be based upon a set of criteria drawn up by each authority. Local authorities are able to develop their own criteria but generally will base their decision regarding applications on the following:

> *The type of attraction the site is* – the following types of site are considered suitable for white on brown tourist signs:

- visitor centres
- theme parks
- leisure complexes
- historic buildings
- museums
- parks and gardens
- natural attractions such as beaches and viewpoints
- areas of special interest
- tourist information centres
- leisure drives and cycle routes.

However, just because a site is in one of the above categories does not necessarily mean that permission will be granted. Decisions will be based upon the needs of the environment (the potential effect of a sign on the surrounding environment) and road safety (too many or misleading signs may confuse drivers and lead to accidents).

When is the site open – local authorities may stipulate that permission will only be given to put up signs if a site is open for a minimum period of time during a year.

Is the site publicised in other ways? – local authorities may stipulate that your site needs to be adequately publicised before permission is granted to put up signs.

Does your site meet the standards of your local tourist board? – local authorities may consult the appropriate tourism board for your area to check that your site meets with their own criteria.

Is there sufficient parking on your site? – permission is only likely to be given if your site can demonstrate that it has enough parking spaces to cope with present or anticipated visitor numbers.

Will your signs be bilingual? – in Wales it may be necessary to have all text on a sign bilingual in line with local authority policy in relation to the Welsh language.

How many visitors do you get to your site or do you anticipate getting to your site? – most local authority guidance in relation to tourism signs does not stipulate a minimum usage figure before permission will be granted to place white on brown tourism signs. However, an authority will wish to be sure that there is sufficient usage to justify the placing of signs. In general the higher the visitor figures the wider the area over which the site will be signposted.

What proportion of site visitors are from outside the locality? – if the majority of site visitors are from the local area permission may not be given on the grounds that local people will already know where a site is.

What information will be on the signs? – the use of commercial names is often seen as inappropriate for white on brown tourist signs. This is because it increases the amount of text on a sign and is therefore more distracting for drivers. Descriptions such as 'country park', 'picnic site' or 'viewpoint' are therefore more often used.

Do you require a sign on a motorway? – the criteria for erecting signs on motorways are even tighter than for other road types and will normally require at least 75,000 visitors annually to qualify for permission.

If your application for signs has met the local authority's criteria then they can be designed and erected. The highways department will advise on design, wording and placements and will manufacture and place the signs on your behalf. For this and the maintenance of the sign, the local authority will levy a charge. This may range from a few hundred pounds for a sign for a small-scale destination in a rural location to several thousands of pounds for a motorway sign.

AA/RAC signs

The yellow AA, and the blue RAC road signs are for signposting specific events over short periods of time. Events may be such things as craft fairs, sporting events, music festivals, open gardens or village fairs. To obtain signs for events such as these it is necessary to contact the AA or the RAC who will take care of the design and obtain the required permissions and erect and remove them. For this they will levy a charge.

Plate 4.5 Signpost directing visitors to attractions

Pedestrian signs

Not everybody comes to countryside recreation sites by car. Some people will arrive more sedately on foot or on bike. For these types of visitor, signs different from those used on roads are required. These will be particularly necessary when a recreation site is situated within or adjacent to an urban area. In situations such as this the recreation site can be signposted to walkers and cyclists within a town or city. These signs will be smaller than road signs and may be designed specifically to fit in with local design styles. For example, many towns now use 'heritage' type signs to match with heritage street furniture such as seats, lights, bollards and bins. An example of a typical pedestrian sign in such an area can be seen in Plate 4.5.

What makes a good sign?

The purpose of a sign is to convey information as effectively and accurately as possible to the reader. Great care therefore needs to be exercised in the design and wording of signs. How much a sign will be read depends on the effort required to read it compared with the expectation of reward from reading it. This can be expressed in the following equation:

$$\text{the number of people reading a sign (LOW)} = \frac{\text{expectation of reward (LOW)}}{\text{effort required to read sign (HIGH)}}$$

$$\text{the number of people reading a sign (HIGH)} = \frac{\text{expectation of reward (HIGH)}}{\text{effort required to read sign (LOW)}}$$

Signs should therefore be easy to use and show quickly potential reward. What makes a sign easy to use will depend on the detailed design.

What do we need to consider in designing a sign?

There are a number of issues that must be considered when designing a sign. These include:

Text – it must be remembered when deciding the text of the sign that people reading it may not have much time to study it. This applies in particular to road signs where people may be passing at 60mph, with the radio on, and with children arguing in the back seats. Such drivers will have to notice a sign, read it and understand it in a few seconds. Any text on a sign therefore needs to be cut down to the minimum. Pedestrians will have more time to stop and study signs but will still have a short attention span. Minimum text is therefore best practice. The text should clearly state the name of the destination, or the type of destination the sign is focusing on and may contain information such as distance to the site.

Font – the font that is used (the typeface), will greatly affect how easy a sign is to read. The basic rule is to keep it simple. Avoid fancy typefaces and mixing different typefaces as this decreases comprehension. Typefaces can be divided into serif and sanserif types.

This is a *serif* typeface (Times New Roman) – serif typefaces have horizontal lines at the tops and bottoms of letters that help to lead the eye along a line of text. As such they are often considered to be the best typefaces for large quantities of text such as newspapers and books.

This is a *SANSERIF* typeface (Helvetica) – sanserif typefaces are simple in design and have no horizontal lines at the tops and bottoms. They are considered to be easy to read where there is only a small amount of text such as on signposts.

It is considered good practice to use sanserif typefaces such as Helvetica or Ariel for signposting. Compare the readability of the two signs below, which use different typefaces.

| Knobbly Bottom Country Park | Knobbly Bottom Country Park |

serif typeface   sanserif typeface

Upper case or lower case? – upper case just means capital letters and lower case is small letters. Which should we use on signposts? It is considered best practice to use lower-case lettering. The reason for this, is that our brains are most familiar with reading words and sentences in lower case because that is how we read most words in books and newspapers. We are therefore able to recognise the shapes of words more easily when they are in lower case as we are more familiar with them. This will make it easier to read the text on signs; as it is the shape of words that allows us to read them quickly, not the individual letters that make up a word. Compare the signs below and assess for yourself, which you find the easiest to read.

Knobbly Bottom Country Park	KNOBBLY BOTTOM COUNTRY PARK

serif – lower case   serif – upper case

Knobbly Bottom Country Park	KNOBBLY BOTTOM COUNTRY PARK

sanserif – lower case   sanserif – upper case

Symbols – symbols are used as abbreviations for text. Instantly recognisable symbols can simplify signs and mean that more information can be placed on them. The important aspect to symbols is that they describe graphically what they represent so that they can be instantly interpreted. Symbols can be particularly important for foreign visitors, as you do not need to speak the language of the country to interpret the symbol. For road signs there are an approved set of symbols that can be used. Useful symbols for countryside recreation sites may be:

agricultural museum	cart
battlefield	crossed swords
beach	sandcastle
castle	castle
camping site	wigwam
canal side attraction	canal boat
canoeing	person in a canoe
country park	three people
cycle hire	person on a bike
fishing	fish on a line
National Trust property	oak leaves
nature reserve	duck
picnic area	person on bench by tree
prehistoric site	monolith
refreshments	cup
RSPB bird reserve	RSPB avocet logo
viewpoint	starburst
wildlife park	stag's head
woodland recreation area	trees
youth hostel	tree by hut

Letter size – how large should the letters on a sign be? This will be determined by how far away people will be, when reading a road sign and how fast the driver reading the sign will be travelling. Table 4.2 below, shows the approach speed, the reading distance and the letter height that is required if text is to be read at the speed and distance stated in the table.

Letter spacing – words need space to breathe. It is therefore important to ensure that words on a sign are not crowded together, and have plenty of space around them. Look at the signs below and consider which is the easiest to read.

Words need space to breathe	If you pack your text too close together it makes it difficult to make out the shape of the words

Contrast and background – the contrast between the letters on a sign and the background will influence how effective a sign is. A high degree of contrast will ensure that the letters clearly separate themselves from the background. In addition, to ensure that the sign is noticed in the first place consideration needs to be given to the background that the sign will be seen against. Signs will blend into some backgrounds and not be visible.

Site entrances

First impressions count, the entrance to a countryside recreation site will be for many, the first impression that is gained of a site. It is therefore important to think carefully about its design to ensure that your entrances are obvious, welcoming and provide sufficient information about the site to enable visitors to decide whether to enter or not. What do we need to consider when looking at site entrances?

Table 4.2 Minimum letter height to ensure readability at differing approach speeds and reading distances

Approach speed in km/h	Reading distance in metres	Letter height in mm
80	120	300
80	90	225
50	60	150
30	45	115
15	30	75
15	23	56
0	15	38
0	11	28
0	8	19

Note
Adapted from Bell 1997: 29.

Entrance signs

It is important that entrances to countryside recreation sites are clearly identifiable. Entrances therefore need to have entrance signs. These have many functions and need careful design. An entrance sign will often contain a variety of information.

- name of site
- name of organisation that manages the site (may be identified by house style of design or logo)
- indication of facilities and attractions within the site
- visual imagery that conveys the nature of the site
- opening and closing times if applicable
- admission charges if applicable.

Above all entrance signs need to be welcoming to the visitor. Indeed many site entrance signs actually use the word 'welcome' on them. Psychologically this is important for visitors, as it lets them know not just that they are permitted to use a site but are *welcome* to use it. This increases visitors' confidence. The last thing visitors want is to feel they are trespassing. It also lets them know that the site is managed and will probably have facilities for them such as toilets and parking. It is also important that entrance signs are large enough to attract attention and are well maintained. The design of these signs can give a real feel for the nature of the site. Entrance signs will normally require planning permission from the relevant local authority. Permission will be based upon public safety and (the signs should not be distracting/confusing for drivers) amenity issues (whether the sign distracts from the environment).

Plate 4.6 An example of a roadside 'attraction' sign

Increasing the amount of information on signs

It is good practice when more than one sign is used to indicate a site, to have the first sign that drivers will see, as simple as possible and with each subsequent sign increase the amount of information given to the driver. An example of this can be seen in Figure 4.1. In this example the first sign just alerts the driver that there is

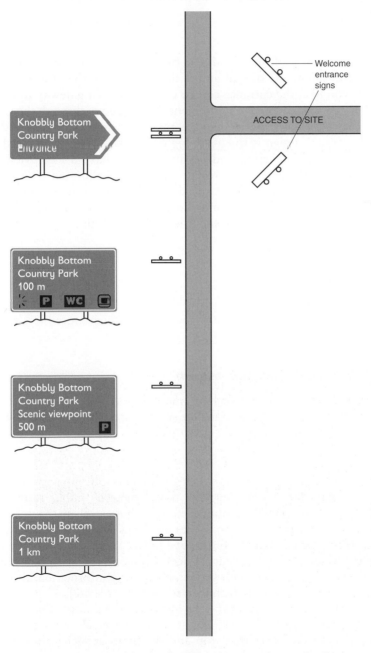

Figure 4.1 Increasing the level of detail on road signs leading up to the entrance of a countryside site

something interesting (a country park) coming up. The second sign adds detail by highlighting that the site has a scenic viewpoint (the site product). The third sign adds further information in symbolic form that there is a scenic viewpoint, parking, toilets and refreshments at the site. The final sign just indicates the location of the entrance. Drip feeding information in this manner allows the driver to take more information in with which to make a decision as to whether to stop there or not.

Entrance design

The entrance sign is only a part of the overall feel of an entrance. The whole layout is important. As with the signs the overall aim is that of making the visitor feel at ease and welcome. If you like, the entrance can be considered as a gateway through which visitors enter a new and different environment. Having gone through the gate, visitors will know that they can have a relaxing time, free from hassle. Another important aspect of entrance design is to ensure highway safety. Sight lines need to be maintained so that vehicles entering and leaving the site have a clear view of oncoming traffic. This is particularly vital where an entrance abuts on to a main highway where vehicles may be travelling at speed. An example of an entrance can be seen in Figure 4.2. Here the entrance resembles a funnel that leads people into the site and also has a gate as security when the site is locked up at night.

Making the site easier to get to

There is rarely anything that managers of countryside recreation sites can do about improving the roads and motorway links to their site. However, there is significant scope to improve public transport links to sites and to make them more bicycle and pedestrian friendly.

Linking your site into the public transport network

The use of the car causes many problems such as congestion, pollution and noise. As custodians of the environment it is important that site managers develop links with the public transport network so that visitors can travel easily to sites by this means. This can be achieved by:

> *Publicising public transport in all site publicity material* – all publicity relating to a site should contain information on how to get there by public transport. Information should where possible contain details of bus numbers, routes, bus times, contact numbers for transport companies and links to railway stations.
> *Liaising with transport companies to improve public transport links to a site* – this may include seeking more frequent services, changing routes so that buses stop at a site, developing linkages with trains and placing information about a site on public transport timetables (which stop to get off for a site).
> *Ensure that bus stops are clearly sited* – the location of bus stops should be as convenient as possible for using the site. Bus stops should be clearly signed and have information about the buses that stop and the times at which they do. If possible, bus stops should provide shelter from the weather and have some form of seating so people can rest while waiting.

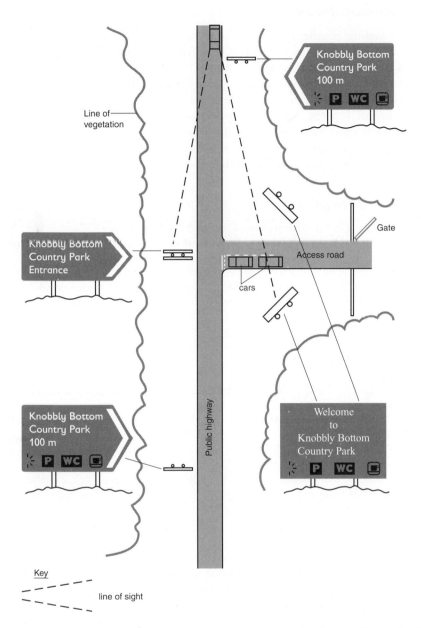

Figure 4.2 Designing a site entrance to ensure road safety and to effectively display entrance signs

Making sites more accessible for walkers

For countryside recreation sites that are situated close to residential areas it is important to develop walking routes into sites from the residential areas. Paths connecting to sites need to be well signposted and easy to use (not full of dog excrement or needing special footwear).

Making sites more accessible for cyclists

Another way of getting people out of cars is to make access to recreation sites by bicycle safer, easier and more enjoyable. It is therefore desirable to make countryside recreation sites as bicycle friendly as possible. This can be done in a number of ways. First it is important to provide places where bicycles can be secured on the site (bike racks). Second, the provision of cycle access routes that link the site to its surrounding residential areas, to other cycle routes and to the national cycle network will make it more accessible to cyclists. Sometimes this will mean segregation so that cyclists and walkers do not use the same path or separating use on a path. It may also mean providing surfacing that is suitable for bicycle use.

References and further reading

Bell, S. (1997) *Design for Outdoor Recreation*, London: E. & F.N. Spon.

Countryside Commission (1981) *Information Signs for the Countryside*, Cheltenham: Countryside Commission.

Countryside Commission (1987) *Public Transport to the Countryside: A Marketing Handbook for Operators and Local Authorities*, Cheltenham: Countryside Commission.

Countryside Commission (1994) *Delivering Countryside Information*, Cheltenham: Countryside Commission.

Countryside Commission (1995) *The Visitor Welcome Initiative*, Cheltenham: Countryside Commission.

Cullingworth, J. B. and Nadin, V. (1997) *Town and Country Planning in the UK*, London: Routledge.

Horowitz, J. (1990) *How to Win Customers: Using Customer Service for a Competitive Edge*, London: Pitman.

Hultsman, J., Cottrell, R. L. and Hultsman, W. Z. (1998) *Planning Parks for People*, PA: Venture Publishing Inc.

Peak National Park (1995) *Longdendale Parking and Visitor Survey*, Bakewell: Peak District National Park.

Sustrans (1994) *Making Ways for the Bicycle: A Guide to Traffic-Free Path Construction*, Bristol: Sustrans.

Web links

Automobile Association (AA) – http://www.theaa.co.uk/

Lake District National Park – http://www.lake-district.gov.uk/

Northumberland County Council Northumberland Visitor Guide –
    http://www.northumberland.gov.uk/vg/home.htm

Peak District National Park – http://www.peakdistrict.org/

Pembrokeshire Coast National Trail –
    http://www.pembrokeshirecoast.org.uk/english/enjoynp/pcnptr.htm

Royal Automobile Association (RAC) – http://www.rac.co.uk/

Suffolk County Council Countryside Service –
    http://www.suffolkcc.gov.uk/countryside/

5   Recreational site infrastructure

The provision, location, style and quality of site infrastructure is a key component of the management of visitors at countryside recreation sites. It also provides an indication of the quality of management and an interface between organisations and visitors. This chapter emphasises the importance of the provision of high quality infrastructure. It will not go into great detail concerning specific infrastructure design, but will concentrate on broader issues that need to be considered, such as function, location, design, image, materials and maintenance.

What is infrastructure?

A dictionary definition of infrastructure is that it is:

> The basic facilities, services, and installations needed for the functioning of a community or society, such as transport and communications systems, water and power lines, and public institutions including schools, post offices, and prisons.

As far as recreational sites are concerned, infrastructure can be defined as the facilities, services and installations that are needed for the functioning of a site. As such the infrastructure of a recreational site is an essential part of its management.

Types of infrastructure seen on countryside recreation sites

There is a wide variety of infrastructure items that can be found within countryside recreation sites. Such items include:

gates	stiles	seats	lighting	bridges
fences	litter bins	paths	signposts	steps
car parks	toilets	waymarkers	walls	bollards
refreshments	cycle racks	picnic tables	information panels	

Selecting what items of infrastructure you need on a site, their exact location and design is an important aspect of countryside recreation site management and requires careful consideration.

What is the function of infrastructure?

Each item of infrastructure has a particular function to carry out. What are the functions of infrastructure on countryside recreation sites?

> *Control of cars* – providing places for cars to park and preventing parking where it is undesirable.
> *Directing visitors* – directing visitors effectively around a site.
> *Control of visitor movement* – stopping visitors going where you *do not* want them to go, and encouraging them to where you *do* want them to go.
> *Providing access through barriers* – allowing people to pass through or over barriers such as fences, walls and streams.
> *Increasing visitor confidence* – to increase visitors' confidence by making them feel welcome and safe to use the site.
> *Making visitors comfortable* – providing visitors with places to rest, toilet facilities and opportunities to eat and drink.
> *Control of litter* – making sure the site is a litter free and pleasant environment.
> *Ensuring visitor safety* – preventing visitors from coming to harm.

Many of these functions are complementary. For example, visitors are often guided around sites by a combination of direction and control through the use of signposts, paths, fences and walls.

In deciding on site infrastructure what do we need to consider?

When considering the infrastructure that is needed on a countryside recreation site a number of issues have to be considered. First, is there a need for a specific item of infrastructure at all? If it is not needed, then it should not be provided. If a certain item of infrastructure is needed, its location, its exact design and materials it should be made from must all be taken into account. In deciding these issues, the nature of the site, the image of the organisation that manages it, and the maintenance, costs and health and safety issues relating to a specific item, all need careful consideration. Table 5.1 illustrates some of the infrastructure tools available and the general issues relating to them.

   The issues relating to *individual* items of infrastructure will be discussed later in this chapter but first let us look at the *general* issues that need to be considered.

Design

Any individual type of infrastructure can come in a wide range of designs. As an example, there is a huge variety of seat types that can be purchased and a wider variety that can be made on site to fit individual site requirements. In selecting a

Table 5.1 The function, type and issues associated with countryside recreation site infrastructure

Issue	Possible infrastructure tools	Infrastructure issues
Control of cars	Car parks, bollards, ditches, banks, fencing, yellow lines	Design Materials Location Maintenance Size Charging Enforcement
Directing visitors	Signposts and waymarkers, orientation panels, information, desire lines, attractions, sight lines	Design Materials Location Information Maintenance
Control of visitor movement	Fences, hedges, barriers, landscaping, information, paths	Design Materials Location Information Maintenance
Access through barriers	Stiles, gates, kissing gates, bridges	Design Materials Location Maintenance
Control of litter	Bins, skips, dog bins	Design Materials Location Maintenance Enforcement
Increasing visitor confidence	Lighting, signs, quality of infrastructure, site information	Design Materials Location Information Maintenance
Making visitors comfortable	Toilets, seats, picnic tables, refreshments	Design Materials Location Maintenance

design for any individual item of infrastructure we must think about a range of issues:

> *The function of the item* – any design must above anything else fulfil the function it is designed for. Therefore a gate should allow easy passage through it by all visitors, open and close with ease and keep stock where it is supposed to be. It is all too easy to design something that looks good but is functionally inadequate.
>
> *Who will be using the item of infrastructure?* – for example, is a gate to be used by horse riders (a bridle gate), walkers (a kissing gate maybe), or by wheelchair users (maybe a kissing gate but of a specific design)?
>
> *The nature of the site* – all countryside recreation sites have a different feel to them. Some are woodland sites, some are in open rocky landscapes, and others

Plate 5.1 A curved stone bench

have a historic feel, whilst others are urban in their nature. It is important to design infrastructure so that it complements the surrounding landscape and does not detract from it. Above all the landscape should remain dominant and any item of infrastructure should fit in with the spirit of the place.

The scale of the item – the size of any item of infrastructure should be in keeping with its surroundings.

The corporate image of the organisation managing the site – site infrastructure will be a visible manifestation of the management of the site. Many organisations develop a design style that reflects the organisation and makes the site instantly recognisable as being managed by a particular organisation. For example, infrastructure on Forestry Commission sites is very distinctive and is uniform across the whole country (see Plate 5.2). You are creating a brand image by creating a corporate style of design. This will be easily recognised by the public who will hopefully link the brand to particular site qualities, much in the way we associate the packaging of Heinz food products with certain qualities of the food within the tins. So for example, the visitor may know from the infrastructure design that the Forestry Commission manages a site and from this we will have a good idea as to the quality of the site product, based upon previous experience.

Creation of local distinctiveness – almost opposite to the development of corporate image is the creation of local distinctiveness. Creating a distinctive design of infrastructure can create a site product that has its own unique image. This may be important for example, in developing a recreational trail such as a

Plate 5.2 Forestry Commission style information sign

regional route. The development of an individual style of locally distinct infrastructure such as stiles, gates and signposts will help the visitor to identify the
route of the trail and will give an indication of its quality. In addition, the creation of distinctive individual items of infrastructure can be used as a means of
creating landmarks that help visitors find their way around a site.

Materials

There is a wide choice of materials available for site infrastructure. For example,
litter bins come in many styles, sizes and materials. Concrete, wood, plastic and
metal are all used. In selecting which material to use for infrastructure, the following
need to be considered:

The nature of the site – it is important to try and use materials that reflect the
nature of the site. Therefore in urban areas the use of concrete, tarmac and
metal may be appropriate and in keeping but would be completely out of place
in a sand dune/beach complex. A basic rule of thumb is to use local products
wherever possible. For example, if a path needs to be surfaced in stone, locally
derived stone should be used so that it fits in as naturally as possible.

The life expectancy of the material – try to use materials that will last as long
as possible. This will save the time and expense of having to repair or replace
items due to failure. If will also help to ensure the safety of visitors. So, for
example, it is normally better to use stone to make the risers on steps, as it will

last longer than wood. Choose materials that last as long as possible and require the minimum of maintenance.

Cost of materials – unfortunately a constant constraint on which materials to use is cost. Different materials all cost different amounts and choice of material may be determined by cost. However, when considering cost the long-term cost of an item is an important factor. So for example, a cheap wooden seat may be initially cheaper but is likely to need replacing much sooner than a more expensive metal seat. In the long term the initial cheap option may be more expensive.

Vandalism – many countryside sites suffer from the blight of vandalism. This will significantly influence the choice of material. For example, wooden bins burn very well and therefore whilst wood might be the most appropriate material for the site, vandalism may mean that metal or concrete bins have to be resorted to. Sometimes you have to be pragmatic.

Quantity and location

For some items of infrastructure the location will be fixed and will require no decision to be made. For example, a stile on a public right of way must be on the right of way and will be where the right of way intersects with a fence or wall. However, other items of infrastructure such as toilets, car parks, signposts, paths, bins and benches require decisions as to their location. In addition, how many signposts or benches do you need on a site? The nature of the site, the users of the site and finance will determine the answers to these questions. Too much furniture close together can make wild areas seem urban and cluttered and significantly detract from the quality of the environment. Keep infrastructure to the minimum required, to provide for and to manage the visitor.

Information

Information is a vital management tool that will help to guide the visitor around a site, increase their confidence and gain the most from a visit. It is such an important area that it is covered in Chapter 9. For this chapter the general issues about information linked to infrastructure will be discussed. The key issues to be considered are:

What information should be provided? – there will be an awful lot of information you *could* provide about a site. What is actually required for any given site to guide the visitor during their stay? Too much information can confuse; too little is of no benefit.

Where should information be provided? – it is likely that there will be a need for information at entrances and car parks to let visitors know the layout of a site, its features and any other useful information required for their visit. Signposts within the site will be needed at path junctions to point the way to site features and provide information on path status. In addition, signposts can give information on such things as distance or estimated time to get to a given point. Waymarkers provide visitors with the confidence that helps them to maintain the correct route.

How should the information be provided? – In Chapter 4 details of good practice in the design of entrance signs were given. The detailed design of sign-posts, the words used, the font style, letter size and the contrast between letters and background all influence the readability of a sign. Great care must therefore be taken in the design of any site signage.

Maintenance

In deciding on the design of an item of infrastructure its maintenance requirements need to be considered. Maintenance costs both time and money, so should be minimised wherever possible. Minimum maintenance is the desired objective. This can be achieved by good design and selecting the right materials. For example, pressure treated wood will last longer than non-treated wood and stone will last longer than wood.

Needs of visitors with disabilities

It has already been stated that design needs to fit with the user of any item of infrastructure. This is particularly true for the needs of people with disabilities. The specialist requirements of people with disabilities are dealt with in Chapter 6.

Health and safety

When considering any item of infrastructure the health and safety needs of visitors in relation to the item is of great importance and should be an automatic consideration.

Specific issues in relation to individual elements of infrastructure

It is the intention of this section to outline the key issues associated with individual types of countryside recreation site infrastructure. Specific design details about individual items of infrastructure are too detailed for a book of this nature and readers should refer to the many excellent texts listed in the references and further reading section at the end of this chapter.

Car parks

Without doubt car parks are one of the most important management tools available to the site manager. There are two key reasons for this. First, on most sites the majority of visitors will arrive by car and will need to park. Second as the first place where people make contact with a site they provide an important communication point for visitors.

> *When do you provide car parks and what size should they be?* – an important decision to be made is whether to provide a car park or not. If you provide no parking for a site you will certainly find that the number of visitors will be small, or people will park in inappropriate places. However, for most sites parking will be required. The number of spaces provided will be one of the

determining factors as to the number of visitors that your site will attract. It is possible to provide enough car parking spaces for even the busiest of summer days but it is also possible to use the size of car parks as a means of controlling visitor numbers. Some sites have even reduced the size of car parks to cut down visitor numbers.

Calculating the number of spaces that are required can only be based upon a sound knowledge of the site and good information about visitor numbers and visitor usage. Designing car parks to meet maximum demand may seem like a sensible approach but will leave car parks that are very empty and potentially unsightly, for most of the year. It is probably best to design around typical levels over the year and accept that there may be overspill in the few really busy days of the year. The use of overspill car parks for busy spells can be planned whereby fields or land adjacent to car parks can be opened up for busy days such as bank holidays. Bell (1997: 4.3) states an equation that can be used as a rough guide for calculating the number of spaces that need to be provided.

$$N = \frac{v \times s}{p \times h}$$

In this equation N = number of spaces required, v = number of day visits, p = average number of people per car, s = average length of stay, and h = average daily period for which the site is in use. This shows that it is not just the number of cars that is important but also how long cars stay. Some car parks, such as that at Pen y Pass at the base of Snowdon, are used by walkers who will be away all day. Others such as near a viewpoint will have a high turnover of cars. If you have the same number of cars entering a car park over a day, you will need a smaller car park if the average length of stay is small, and a larger car park if the average length of stay is high.

Where should car parks be located? – the choice of location for parking is often determined by local conditions such as road layout, attractions, areas of flat ground and the present parking situation. Parking areas and the areas around them are normally the sites' busiest areas and often form their focal point. The location of parking therefore needs to be chosen with care. Placing parking close to facilities and attractions will encourage people to use them whilst if you wish to discourage visitors from areas of your site then placing parking at a distance will discourage use. The nature of the landscape also needs to be considered, as it is good practice to locate car parks where they will have the least visual impact on the landscape. Having decided upon the location of a car park it is necessary to check with the local authority to find out if planning permission will be required, and if it is, apply for and obtain it prior to building.

What aspects of design of car parks should be considered? – having decided on the size and location of parking, the following issues need to be addressed in the design of a parking area:

> *Shape* – should the parking be broken up into small discrete units, be a large open area and what shape should it be? As far as possible try to make the shape fit in with already existing landscape features such as walls, trees and

woodland edges. Another consideration for shape is the creation of a focal point that people will naturally be attracted to when leaving their cars. This can be used as the first stage in directing the visitor to where you wish them to go.

Circulation – should the car park have a circulatory system or should cars be free to go where they wish? This will be dependent on the shape and size of the car park.

Surfacing – should the parking area be surfaced and if so with what? Tarmac will be long lasting and require minimal maintenance but may not reflect the nature of the locality. Unsealed surfacing such as aggregate may be cheaper initially and local stone may fit in better but may require greater maintenance in the long term.

Landscaping – the aim of any design of car park should be to make it as unobtrusive as possible. This occurs by fitting the parking into the natural lines of the landscape. In addition, the area around the car park can be landscaped with trees, shrubs and earth bunds. The aim of such landscaping is to hide the vehicles as much as possible and break up the lines of the parking area.

Types of vehicles – cars may not be the only users of the car park. Provision should be considered for coaches, motorbikes and pedal cycles. In addition, the needs of people with disabilities should be considered.

Disabled parking – disabled people in cars need space adjacent to the car to enable them to enter and exit the vehicle with ease. This should be at least a full door's width so that doors can be fully opened. In addition, spaces designed for disabled people should be located as close as possible to site facilities and the spaces should be clearly identified as parking spaces for the disabled only. The number of spaces within a car park that should be allocated to the disabled is seen in Table 5.2.

In addition to providing special spaces within car parks 'drop off points' can be created for the disabled. These should be as close to facilities as possible.

Should you charge for parking and how much should you charge? – increasingly organisations seek to raise money by charging for parking. This can be done by pay and display machines, honesty boxes or by having a parking attendant selling tickets. Collecting money using pay and display machines takes little

Table 5.2 The number of accessible parking spaces that should be provided for disabled passengers

Total spaces	Suggested accessible spaces
1–25	1
26–50	2
51–75	3
76–100	4
101–150	5

Note
Adapted from Fieldfare Trust 1997: 6.1.

employee input but has a high installation and maintenance cost. A car park attendant can be useful in conveying information to visitors on entry to the site, but is only economic in times of high use. Having a high charge for parking may deter people from stopping and as such can be a management tool. What people are prepared to pay will depend on how long they intend to stay and the perceived value for money of the visit. Visitors may also be prepared to pay more if convinced that the money is used directly towards the upkeep of the site.

Infrastructure to stop parking

There are two aspects to parking control. The first is to provide places for visitors to park in locations where you wish them to park. The second is to stop parking occurring in places where you do not wish them to do so. Parking can be stopped by physical means: bollards, ditches, the placing of rocks and logs, earth bunds, fences and walls. Prevention of parking by the use of yellow lines can only occur on public highways and needs to be carried out and enforced by the relevant local authority.

Bike racks

In order to try and get people to arrive at a site by bicycle, cycle racks should be provided at strategic locations around it.

Paths

People follow paths. It is a lot easier than walking across country. The path network on a site is therefore a vital tool in managing visitors. On most sites the path network will already be established and will consist of public rights of way and routes that have developed either by natural usage, for example, around the edge of a lake, or paths established by managing authorities. These existing paths can still be managed and developed for the visitor but opportunities may also exist for creating new routes. What do we need to think about when considering paths?

> *Creating a path network* – paths generally follow traditional routes as defined by the public rights of way network, link features or follow natural lines. As such, paths often form a network, which can be developed and improved upon. It is good practice to create as much variety within a network as possible. The creation of defined routes of differing lengths, characteristics and difficulty creates interest in a site and provides the visitor with easy to use options depending on interest, time on site and physical ability. To create this flexibility it may be necessary to develop link paths between existing routes.
>
> *Creating interesting paths* – when developing paths on a site it is good practice to try and make them as interesting as possible. With existing paths the route cannot normally be changed so interest can be added along the route. This can be done by creating viewpoints, adding sculpture, landscaping or provision of interpretation. When creating a new path every care should be taken to make the route as interesting as possible. This can be achieved by ensuring the route has variety within it, avoids straight lines and has an air of mystery – an element of 'what's around the next corner' to it.

Creating paths for all visitors – visitors come with a variety of abilities from the fit runner to family groups, the elderly and disabled. Each group has different needs from a path. It is good to cater for the variety of needs by providing routes of differing lengths, surface quality and difficulty.

Routes for cyclists and horse riders – most routes on sites are for walkers. However, cyclists and horse riders may need access within your site. Horses, bikes and walkers do not normally mix very well and conflicts can occur if all are using the same routes. It can be better to think about segregating use by creating separate routes or by segregating use on a path.

Path surfacing – the ideal path is of natural vegetation. However, with use this normally erodes and some form of surfacing will be required. Surfacing can be in the form of aggregates, tarmac, gravel, bark chippings and larger stones pitched together. In deciding which to choose the following should be considered:

> *Cost* – different types of surfacing cost different amounts and cost should be considered in the long term. Some types of surfacing such as bark chippings may initially be cheap, but have a limited lifespan and will require maintenance on a regular basis.
>
> *Maintenance* – differing surface types require differing amounts of maintenance.
>
> *The nature of the site* – tarmac may fit in well in an urban setting but would be out of place in a wilder setting. Surfacing materials should be chosen that fit in with the surroundings. This normally means choosing local materials from local sources.
>
> *Ability to shed water* – surfacing materials should be chosen that either shed water or allow it to drain through. Great care should be taken in the construction of paths to ensure that water is shed from the path surface so as to avoid the ravages of water erosion.
>
> *The needs of visitors with disabilities* – visitors unsteady on their feet require even and level ground that is not slippery even when wet. Wheelchair users find loose surfaces such as gravel or bark chippings difficult to use. Suitable surfaces include concrete, tarmac, stone, brick and paving and mown grass. Visitors with visual disabilities benefit from having paths whose surface colour and texture contrasts with the surroundings.

There is not room within this chapter to describe the individual types of path surfacing, or the intricacies of path drainage. Readers should refer to texts on this subject highlighted in the references and further reading at the end of the chapter.

Path width – how wide should a path be? This may depend upon the use that the path gets. Busy paths should at a minimum be wide enough for two people to walk side by side and hold a conversation. Wider paths may be required if use is particularly high so that groups of people can pass in opposite directions without interfering with each other. Single file paths can be interesting for short sections but make the social aspect of walking difficult. If wheelchairs use a path it will need to be wide enough to allow two chairs past each other or have

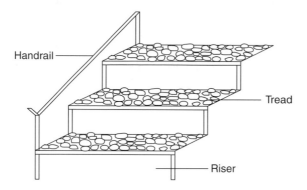

Figure 5.1 Features associated with steps

regular passing places. In addition, we must also ensure that there is a clear walking tunnel so that visually impaired visitors will not hurt themselves. This means ensuring that there is nothing overhanging the path such as branches and signs that may constitute a hazard.

Dealing with gradients – wherever a path goes up or down a slope, decisions have to be made as to how deal with the gradient. The choices are between putting in steps, and having a sloping path. Steps are obstacles for many types of disabled and less mobile people, so should be avoided where possible. However, where the slope is steep, steps may be the only option. Steps consist of risers, (the vertical element), treads (the horizontal element), infill and sometimes handrails (see Figure 5.1).

Ideally steps should have a broad tread and shallow risers and each step should be of the same dimensions. For visually impaired visitors it is useful to change the texture of the path at the top and bottom of the steps as a warning. It is also useful to have the risers and treads of contrasting colours to help the partially sighted to see where the steps are. It is good practice to have handrails beside the steps to provide the less able user with something to pull and balance against. These should be between 40mm and 50mm in diameter and should be rounded to provide the easiest grip.

Gradients should be as shallow as possible. Ideally paths should not run directly up slopes as this increases gradient and creates problems in draining the path. It is better to zig-zag a path across a slope. Where gradients are necessary, try to create 'landings' along the length of the slope so that visitors with disabilities can rest on level ground while ascending the slope. Table 5.3 shows the maximum gradients considered to be suitable for visitors with disabilities in different types of setting, together with the maximum ramp lengths between landings.

Stiles

These provide a means of crossing over fences and hedges, without a gate and without letting stock out of fields. There is a wide variety of stile designs. An example of a standard wooden stile with a balance bar can be seen in Plate 5.3. It is

Table 5.3 Maximum gradients and ramp lengths for different types of countryside setting

Gradient	*Urban/formal landscape* Maximum distance between landings for 750mm vertical climb	*Urban fringe/ managed landscape* Maximum distance between landings for 830mm vertical climb	*Rural/working landscape* Maximum distance between landings for 950mm vertical climb
1:20 (5%)	15.00 metres	16.60 metres	19.00 metres
1:18 (5.5%)	13.50 metres	14.94 metres	17.10 metres
1:16 (6.2%)	12.00 metres	13.28 metres	15.20 metres
1:14 (7%)	10.50 metres	11.62 metres	13.30 metres
1:12 (8.3%)	9.00 metres	9.96 metres	11.40 metres
1:10 (10%)			9.50 metres

Note
Adapted from Fieldfare Trust 1997: 2.1.

good practice to ensure that the treads of a stile are wide and not too high so that less able people can get their legs up onto them. This will normally mean having more than one tread. It is also recommended to have a balance bar so that the walker can balance while crossing the stile. By their design stiles will be an obstacle for some visitors who will be unable to lift their legs high enough, have trouble with balance or are in a wheelchair. It is therefore sensible to use gates instead of stiles where possible to ensure that all visitors are catered for.

Plate 5.3 A wooden stile with balance bars

Gates

The purpose of a gate is to allow walkers, vehicles, bikes or horses through a barrier such as a wall, whilst keeping stock in the fields. There are a number of types of gate:

Field gate – a wide gate that will allow cars, walkers, horses and bikes through.

Bridle gate – a narrow gate wide enough to let horses, walkers and bikes through. Bridle gates can normally be opened on horseback without dismounting.

Kissing gate – a gate that will only allow people through (and help ensure a bit of romance)!

Of fundamental importance to gates is the mechanism for securing them shut. This should be easy for visitors to use and the needs of disabled visitors must be considered. In addition, it is useful to use some mechanism to ensure the gate closes automatically after it has been opened, such as a spring or a weight mechanism. Gates should always be wide enough to allow a wheelchair through and generally come in wood or metal. It should be noted that there are often local designs for gates to be copied as examples of good practice.

Fences, walls and hedges

These have the obvious purpose of preventing people and or stock moving from one area to another. As such they are a form of control. There is a large variety of fence, wall and hedge types which include the following:

Strained fencing – wire and netting strained against wooden posts. Types of wire and netting include stock netting, high tensile wire and rabbit netting. Depending on the fence design and the wire or mesh used, strained fences can control rabbits, sheep, cattle, horses, deer and people.

Post and rail fencing – wooden rails secured to wooden fence posts. It looks more appealing than strained wire but costs more to erect. It is recommended for areas where appearance matters, and is stock proof.

Panel fencing – prefabricated panels attached to posts.

Electric fencing – wire carrying an electric charge, which is useful for the temporary control of stock.

Dry stone wall – very traditional walls made out of stones. Local styles create local distinctiveness.

Hedgerows – made from hedgerow plants such as hawthorn, beech, and blackthorn and often laid in local style. Hedgerows provide a conservation friendly form of stock control.

Making a choice between these will depend on:

- what is to be controlled (visitors, rabbits, horses, sheep, cattle)
- how important appearance is
- budget available (there are considerable differences in the cost of each boundary type)

- local landscape character and tradition
- terrain
- importance of conservation.

Bridges and stepping-stones

These provide a means of getting across watercourses and they come in a variety of sizes from a railway sleeper over a ditch to a complex engineering structure over a river. Bridges often form significant features in the landscape and as such particular care needs to be exerted in their design. They need to be designed to be significantly stronger than required for any load that they are expected to carry and will need regular inspection to ensure they are safe. Stepping-stones are a fun way of crossing a river or stream and add to the sense of adventure for the visitor but will be unsuitable for some disabled visitors, or for rivers where flow varies widely.

Signposts

The purpose of a sign is to make contact with visitors and to provide them with on-site information. As such they help visitors make decisions as to where to go and increase their confidence. They are also a very effective means of directing visitors to where you want them to go. Chapter 3 gives details of good practice in sign design.

What information should a signpost carry?

- *Destination information* – where a route leads to (village, site feature, toilets, visitor centre . . .).
- *Distance/time information* – the distance to the feature highlighted on the sign or an estimated time to get there.
- *Designation of path* – if the path is a legal public right of way its status should be indicated. A coloured arrow is often used for this with a yellow arrow indicating a footpath, a blue arrow a bridleway, a red arrow a byway open to all traffic (BOAT) and a white arrow a permissive path. Sometimes symbols are used instead of arrows with a walking man indicating a footpath and a horse and rider a bridleway.
- *Particular route information* – often a recreation trail may be indicated by the use of a particular symbol, name or a colour code.
- *Warnings* – often we need to warn the public about an issue such as a cliff or the dangers of digging tunnels in a sand dune.
- *Site rules* – often signs are used to inform the visitor about site rules such as no cycling, parking restrictions or speed humps.

As stated in Chapter 3, it is good practice to use symbols as much as possible to replace text. This makes the sign easier to use and can be used by people who cannot read English.

Signposts should always be located at places where the visitor has to make a decision as to where to go. This will normally be at junctions between paths or at places where the visitor needs to be warned about a particular issue. These locations within sites can be termed 'decision nodes'.

Plate 5.4 A signpost that provides the name of the route, destination information, distance and a symbol that shows the route is a National Trail (a white acorn)

Plate 5.5 Short fingerposts with path type and destination

Often on sites, signposts are erected in a piecemeal fashion over time, based upon perceived need. Whilst this is often adequate, it is sometimes useful to go back to basics and look at a whole site to decide where to place signposts and waymarkers and what information they should contain. This can be carried out by a process called decision node mapping. For this you use a large-scale map of your site and systematically walk all routes on the site from all entrances. You then mark onto the map every place where a decision needs to be made as to where to go (see Figure 5.2 as an example). These can be marked onto the maps as circles that can be numbered for identification purposes and are your decision nodes. Each decision node can then be looked at systematically and the individual signpost requirements for each node decided upon giving way to a signposting and waymarking plan. This can be done in tabular form, an example of which can be seen in Table 5.4. At each decision point the following issues need to be decided:

- What sort of sign is required?
- How many signs are required and in what direction should they point?
- Where exactly should the sign be placed?
- What information should be on the sign?

It is important when carrying this out that routes are walked in all directions, as junctions look different depending on the angle they have been approached from.

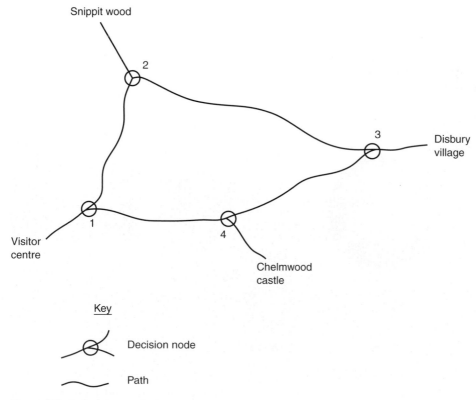

Figure 5.2 A decision node map

Table 5.4 Signage plan based upon decision node map (Figure 5.2)

Decision node	Angles for signs and locations of signposts	Information to be placed on signs
1	130° 2 / 75° / 1 / 3	1 Visitor centre 300m 2 Snippit wood 1.5km 3 Disbury village 2.5km Chelmwood castle 1km
2	1 / 90° / 140° / 2	1 Visitor centre 1.3km 2 Snippit wood 200m 3 Disbury village 2.4km
3	3 / 150° / 60° / 1 / 2 / 3	1 Visitor centre 0.8km 2 Disbury village 2.1km 3 Chelmwood castle 500m
4	1 / 40° 160° 3 / 2	1 Visitor centre 1.4km Chelmwood castle 1.1km 2 Snippit wood 1.2km 3 Disbury village 1.4km

Waymarkers

These are really small signs that are used between larger signs to give visitors the confidence that they are still on the correct route. They are smaller than signposts (normally a plastic disc mounted onto a post or fence) and although they do not make such an impact on the landscape they do reinforce information provided by larger signposts. They normally contain less information than a signpost and are restricted to path designation (as above) and the logo or colour code of the path being waymarked. Plate 5.6 shows examples of waymarker discs.

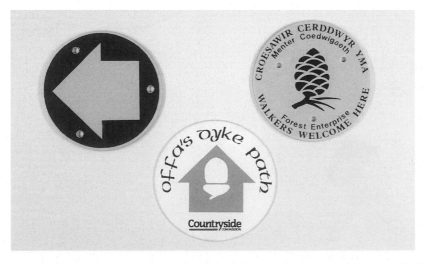

Plate 5.6 Example waymarker discs, that can be used on paths and trails, to provide reassurance to visitors that they are on the correct route

Orientation panels

The function of an orientation panel is to give the visitor an overview of the site and its features. Orientation panels are normally located at entrances, car parks, viewpoints and at visitor centres. It is helpful to place them at points where people naturally stop, for example after a kissing gate. What should be on an orientation panel?

- *Name of site* – helps to develop a site identity in visitors' minds.
- *Name or logo of organisation running the site* – helps to develop a brand identity.
- *Annotated map of the site* – this should be the main feature of the panel and could be a plan, map or, better still, an overhead oblique (as discussed in the section on leaflets in Chapter 4). Above all the map should be easy to use and should contain a 'you are here' arrow to help the visitor gain initial orientation.
- *Description of key site features such as walking routes and castles* – this helps the visitor gain a better understanding of what is present on the site. The use of photographs or pictures helps by making site features visual.
- *Opening times* – and any other information that would assist the visitor's stay.

Great care needs to be taken in the design of orientation panels, as they are core information that will help visitors gain the most from their visit. They need to be simple but informative, interesting and eye-catching. They also need to be weatherproof.

Plate 5.7 An orientation panel featuring a large scale map

Litter bins

The purpose of a litter bin is to provide a convenient receptacle in which the public can deposit their litter. Litter bins come in a variety of shapes and sizes. If litter bins are required then the following design issues need to be considered.

> *The number and size of bins* – this will be determined by local site conditions, such as the number of visitors, proximity to refreshment points, the frequency of emptying and the number of bins placed. If a large number of bins are used then smaller individual bins may be adequate. Alternatively, a site litter strategy may be to only have litter bins in car parks, in which case larger bins or even skips may be required. It must be remembered that the more bins you have, the more bins there are to empty. It is wise to make bins bigger than you expect to need, as visitors often deposit larger than expected litter loads into them. Even if a bin is obviously full, people will still use it. This normally ends up being blown around creating a litter problem. An example of this can be seen in Plate 5.8.

Plate 5.8 An overflowing litter bin creates rubbish

Shape of bin – bins come in a huge variety of shapes. Choose a shape to fit in with the area surrounding the bin. Bins should be visible (people need to see and use them) but not detract from the environment.

Material the bin is made from – bins come in a variety of materials. Choose a material that is appropriate to the surrounding environment. It is not unknown for people to set fire to bins, so consideration may need to be made as to the scale of vandalism on a site and the flammability of the bin. Plastic and metal may fit into urban and managed environments whilst wood may be more appropriate to more rural locations.

Dealing with wind – wind will quickly pick up any loose litter and blow it around creating a litter problem. It is good practice therefore not to use open topped bins but to use bins either with a lid or are designed with wind in mind.

Dealing with vermin – vermin such as rats, stray cats and birds will seek out bins as sources of easy meals. Any bin should be protected from vermin by ensuring that they cannot get at the inner bin bag or get directly at the litter from the top. A metal cage around the bin bag will normally stop vermin from below, whilst a lid will be required to discourage birds.

Ease of emptying – bins require frequent emptying. It is important therefore to ensure that they are easy to empty and located at points where they are accessible. A bin where you have to walk ten minutes to get to will not be emptied as frequently as it should and so will probably create a litter problem.

Stubble plates – visitors who smoke are often deterred from putting cigarettes or matches into bins because they are scared of setting them on fire. A plate attached to the bin on which they can stub out their cigarettes may therefore decrease cigarette litter.

Many sites have now adopted a policy of removing litter bins entirely. This may sound crazy – surely you need litter bins for people to put their litter in! However, it is known that sites that have gone for a no bin policy often become less littered. This is because without a receptacle to place their litter in, people take it home. However, if there was a litter bin present they would use it irrespective of whether it was full or not. How many times have you seen people adding their rubbish to an already overflowing bin? This overflowing rubbish then gets blown around and spread by birds. In this scenario a litter bin has actually created a littering situation. Bins work but they do need to be emptied frequently. If this cannot be done, it may be better to have no bins at all. The time that was spent emptying the bins can then be spent collecting litter from the ground. Research shows that the less litter there is on a site the fewer people that will drop litter. Many sites with a no bin policy, provide skips or other receptacles at car parks for people to place their litter into as they leave.

Dog bins

People like to walk their dogs in the countryside and we all know what dogs have to do! Dog mess is unpleasant and is often a cause for much complaint particularly in areas where people regularly walk their dogs. One solution is to provide dog bins into which owners can deposit the offensive items. Dog bins often come with plastic bag dispensers that can be used for picking up the mess and disposing of it.

Plate 5.9 An example of a 'beehive style' wooden litter bin, containing one bin liner

Seats and benches

These provide people with resting points and are important items for elderly visitors and visitors with a physically disability. Points to consider include:

> *Frequency of placement and distance between* – if seats are being placed along a route with the less able visitor in mind then they need to be frequent and not too far apart. It is suggested (Fieldfare Trust 1997: 4.1) that seats should be no more than one hundred metres apart. Often seats or benches are placed at locations where the visitor may just wish to stop and admire the view, in which case they

can be placed *ad hoc* according to local site needs. In places where there are high concentrations of visitors, such as along a lakeside then a large number of seats and benches may be required.

Position – where possible place seats in positions where there is something interesting to see and where there is shelter. It is also good to provide seating at the tops and bottoms of slopes so that the visitor can rest. Provide space next to seats and benches so that wheelchair bound visitors can be beside able-bodied companions.

Design – seats and benches come in a variety of designs and materials. These range from metal 'heritage' type seats to those cut from a fallen log with a chainsaw. Choose a design that will fit into the surroundings and is functional for the intended user. Heel space under the seat should be provided to make it easier for the less able visitor to stand up. This is aided by the use of armrests so that the visitors can lever themselves out of the chair. It is useful to have a back-rest.

Picnic tables

These provide places for the visitor to sit and have something to eat and drink. Most picnic tables come in a conventional wooden design but it is possible to be more creative. It is good practice to provide somewhere around the table that a wheelchair can gain access to. Picnic tables should be located at areas of interest where the visitor will naturally wish to stop and around car parks. They can also be placed close to shops where food and drink can be purchased to increase the turnover of these establishments.

Toilets

Toilets are a complex item of infrastructure that need planning permission and design by an architect. It is beyond the scope of this book to go into too much technical detail about toilet design but the following broad issues should be considered:

Location – the location of toilets will be dependent on many individual site issues. Most sites will only have one set of toilets so choice of location is important. Normally toilets are located in places of visitor concentration such as next to car parks or at visitor centres. As most visitors will need to use the toilet sometime on a visit they can be used to attract people to particular points on the site.

Size – guidelines govern the number of urinals, WCs and hand basins needed for differing numbers of visitors. Consult with architects for details.

Sewage disposal – how are all the waste products generated within toilets going to be disposed of? Are there sewage mains close by that can be used or is some form of septic tank system going to be needed?

Cleaning – toilets require regular cleaning and checks to ensure toilet paper is present and all is correct. Who will do this? Will it be a task for site rangers, will you use local cleaners or employ contractors?

Opening times – will the toilets be open twenty-four hours a day or will they be closed at night?

Disabled access – special design is required for the disabled visitor. Good practice is to have a unisex disabled toilet separate from the ladies and gents, so that a companion can assist a disabled visitor if required.

Psychological control

The visitor can frequently be influenced in their behaviour and movement, not only by physical means, but also through the use of psychological control. This means influencing visitors in subtle ways through an understanding of what makes them react in certain ways. When effective, visitors will not realise they have been influenced. The following can be considered in trying to exert psychological control.

The visitor will always take the easy option – how can this be implemented as a visitor management tool? Here are some examples:

- Visitors will naturally try to take the shortest route from A to B. These routes are known as 'desire lines'. By considering these and planning for them they can be used advantageously. To fight against them is hard work.
- If you wish to keep visitors on a path, make sure the path is easier to walk on than the area on either side of the path. This can be done by carefully placing rocks or logs, planted vegetation beside the path or leaving the grass alongside the path uncut.
- If you wish to deter people from using a path keep it muddy and rutted and make sure an alternative path is in good condition.

The interesting or the unusual will naturally attract visitors – this can be used in a positive way by placing interesting or unusual items carefully so that visitors are drawn to them and thus leading them down routes you wish them to take. Here are a few examples:

- Create a viewpoint by cutting back vegetation.
- Place an item of sculpture to draw visitors towards it.
- Place an interpretive or orientation panel in a car park to encourage visitors to take a particular direction.
- Cut back the vegetation to reveal a distant feature such as a folly or a playground.
- Create an arch or gateway into an area to suggest that there is something interesting on the other side.

With careful design the visitor can be channelled in a particular direction – this is largely achieved by creating 'funnels' that guide visitors in a certain direction. Fences, walls, vegetation or earth banks can create the funnel. Figure 5.3 shows an example of a funnel in action.

It can be seen that in this example the mouth of the funnel has been 'baited' with an orientation panel. This will lure the visitor to the neck of the funnel down which they will pass. Let us consider what is likely to happen to visitors when they park their cars in this car park. They will get out of the car, look around for clues as to

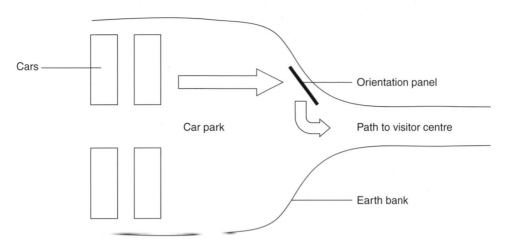

Figure 5.3 A 'baited' funnel

what they should do and in which direction they should travel. The orientation panel will attract their attention and they will naturally walk towards it. The panel will have a map with a 'you are here' arrow and will show that close to the car park is a visitor centre. From the orientation panel this can be seen, so the visitor is drawn towards it. This process of drawing people into making decisions to go in certain directions can be very effective and careful placing of items of interest and infrastructure makes it happen.

Next time you visit a recreation site consider what it is that makes you decide to take particular paths or routes. It is normally a combination of information, careful placement of infrastructure, attractions and careful site design that influence you, often without you being aware of it. By being aware of these psychological controls we can learn how to influence the visitor.

References and further reading

Agate, E. (1996) *Footpaths: A Practical Handbook*, Doncaster: BTCV Enterprises Ltd.

Bell, S. (1997) *Design for Outdoor Recreation*, London: E. & F.N. Spon.

Bicycle Association (1996) *Cycle-friendly Infrastructure: Guidelines for Planning and Design*, Godalming: Cyclists' Touring Club.

Countryside Commission (1971) *Surfaces for Rural Car Parks*, Cheltenham: Countryside Commission.

Countryside Commission (1981) *Information Signs for the Countryside*, Cheltenham: Countryside Commission.

Countryside Commission (1985) *Technical Report 4: Restoring Vegetation at Informal Car Parks*, Cheltenham: Countryside Commission.

Countryside Commission (1997) *Lighting in the Countryside: Towards Good Practice*, Cheltenham: Countryside Commission.

Countryside Commission for Scotland (1985) *Lavatories in the Countryside: A Design Guide*, Battleby: Countryside Commission for Scotland.

Countryside Commission for Scotland (1989) *Footbridges in the Countryside: Design and Construction*, Battleby: Countryside Commission for Scotland.

Davies, P., Loxham, J. and Huggon, G. (1996) *Repairing Upland Path Erosion: A Best Practice Guide*, Lake District National Park Authority, National Trust, English Nature.

Department of the Environment Transport and the Regions (1999) *Environmental Protection Act: Code of Practice on Litter and Refuse*, London: The Stationery Office.

Fieldfare Trust (1997) *BT Countryside for All: A Good Practical Guide to Disabled People's Access in the Countryside*, Sheffield: The Fieldfare Trust.

Hultsman, J., Cottrell, R. and Hultsman, W. (1998) *Planning Parks for People*, PA: Venture Publishing, Inc.

Scottish Natural Heritage (1982) *Information Sheets and Catalogue Vol. 1*, Battleby: Scottish Natural Heritage.

Scottish Natural Heritage (1982) *Information Sheets and Catalogue Vol. 2*, Battleby: Scottish Natural Heritage.

Scottish Natural Heritage (2000) *Car Parks in the Countryside: A Practical Guide to Planning, Design and Construction*, Battleby: Scottish Natural Heritage.

Sustrans (1994) *Making Ways for the Bicycle: A Guide to Traffic-Free Path Construction*, Bristol: Sustrans Ltd.

Sustrans (1996) *The National Cycle Network: Guidelines and Practical Details*, Bristol: Ove Arup & Partners.

The Paths for All Partnership (2000) *Signpost Guidance*, Alloa: Paths for All Partnership.

Trapp, S., Gross, M. and Zimmerman, R. (1994) *Signs, Trails and Wayside Exhibits*, Wisconsin: UW-SP Foundation Press Inc.

6　Access for all

The pleasure to be gained from recreation in the countryside should be available for all. However, many areas of the countryside are 'out of bounds' to some sectors of society due to the nature of the topography, the way sites are managed or because of cultural differences. This chapter considers the issues associated with trying to provide 'access for all' and in particular, considers the implications of the Disability Discrimination Act (1995) on the management of recreation sites. After outlining the difficulties some visitors have in getting to countryside sites, it suggests a structured approach to site development to take account of the needs of people with disabilities and others who find access to the countryside difficult.

Disabled access is just good access

Access to the countryside should be the right of every citizen. However, not all sectors of society are able to enjoy access to the countryside in equal measure. Who is it that has difficulty using the countryside and what are the problems they face that makes access difficult for them? Table 6.1 shows a breakdown of groups who find access to the countryside difficult and the potential barriers they face.

It can be seen from Table 6.1 that access to the countryside is often restricted for people with various forms of disability, the elderly and ethnic communities. This chapter will look at these groups and consider ways in which access for them can be improved. Let us look first at issues associated with visitors with disabilities.

What types of disability are there?

The Disability Discrimination Act (1995) describes a disabled person as: 'anyone with a physical or mental impairment which has a substantial and long term adverse effect on their ability to carry out normal day-to-day activities'.

According to the Labour Force Survey conducted by the Department of Education and Employment (DfEE 2000) disabled people account for nearly a fifth of the working population in Great Britain. This means that 6.5 million people have a current long-term disability or health problem that has a substantial and adverse impact on their day-to-day lives, or limits the work they can do. The level of disability also increases with age: only 12 per cent of those aged 20–29 years have a current long-term disability or health problem compared with 31 per cent of those

Table 6.1 Groups facing barriers to using the countryside and the nature of the potential barriers

Group facing barriers	The potential barriers
People with physical disabilities	• Physical access problems such as stiles, gates, bridges, etc. • Steep, rough or uneven paths • Distances • Shelter/rest points • Access to information • Confidence
People with visual impairments	• Rough or uneven paths • Access to information • Obstructions • Route finding • Confidence
People with hearing impairments	• Communication • Interaction with others • Confidence
People with learning difficulties	• Access to information • Understanding • Confidence
The elderly	• Physical access problems such as stiles, gates, bridges, etc. • Steep, rough or uneven paths • Distances • Shelter/rest points • Confidence
Black and ethnic communities	• Awareness • Language • Culture • Confidence

Note
Adapted from Countryside Recreation Network 1998: 74.

aged 50–59. With such large numbers of people having disabilities, it would clearly be wrong not to make provision for them in the countryside.

What types of disability fit within this definition, and how does it affect their ability to have access and to use the countryside?

Ambulant disabled

These are people with mobility problems who are unable to walk large distances and may be unsteady on their feet. It will include people with:

• heart/respiratory problems
• arthritis/rheumatism
• paralysis
• amputees
• advancing years (the elderly).

Difficulties encountered by this group and their needs include:

Difficulties	Needs
walking long distances	short walks
prolonged exertion	firm and even ground
unsteady on feet	gates
uneven/rough ground	resting points/shelter
steps/gradients	hand rails on steps and gradients
stiles	information

Wheelchair users

These people are restricted in their use of the countryside to locations suitable for wheelchairs. Difficulties encountered by this group and their needs include:

Difficulties	Needs
rough ground	even and level ground
muddy ground	low gradients
paths with a slope across them	reserved parking spaces
kerbs	passing places on paths
steep gradients/steps	gates
gravel/shingle paths	resting places on slopes
stiles/narrow gates/some kissing gates	ramps at kerbs
constrictions in path width	information on site access
standard toilets	specifically designed toilets

In considering visitors in wheelchairs it must be remembered that their eye level is lower. This will affect their ability to see items such as signposts and interpretation points.

Visually impaired

A visual impairment is generally defined as an eyesight problem that cannot be corrected by wearing glasses or contact lenses, or by surgery. Some people are totally blind and have no sight at all whilst others are partially blind and have some limited vision. According to the Royal National Institute for the Blind there were 348,005 registered blind or partially sighted people in the UK in 1997 (source RNIB 2000). Only 4 per cent of visually impaired people see nothing at all, and eight out of ten are over 60 years of age. Difficulties encountered by this group and their needs include:

Difficulties	Needs
getting around – cannot see where they are going or read signs or site information	unobstructed routes
	textured walking surfaces
	colour contrast on paths and steps
obstacles – infrastructure such as litter bins and lampposts can be a real hazard	lighting
	helpers
	information in Braille
communications	information in large print
confidence	information on facilities and resources

Hearing disability

People with a hearing disability have a range of hearing ability. Not all are totally deaf.

- mild deafness – difficulty in following speech, mainly in noisy situations.
- moderate deafness – difficulty following speech without a hearing aid.
- severe deafness – considerable reliance on lip reading, even with a hearing aid. If deaf from early in life their preferred language may be sign language.
- profound deafness – little or no hearing, lip read and may use sign language.

The Royal National Institute for the Deaf (2001), estimates that in the UK in 1996, 8.7 million people were deaf or hard of hearing of which 673,000 were severely or profoundly deaf. What difficulties do deaf visitors have in using the countryside? Difficulties encountered by this group and their needs include:

Difficulties	Needs
communication – hearing and speaking	staff trained in the needs of the Deaf
understanding	information
confidence	

One of the biggest problems for people with hearing difficulties is that they do not have an obvious handicap and unless told, it is often difficult to tell if someone is deaf.

Mentally handicapped/learning difficulties/mental illness

There are a wide variety of conditions and levels of ability in this group. Some members of this group will be totally dependent on other people for their welfare whereas others will have some degree of independence. Difficulties encountered by this group and their specific needs include:

Difficulties	*Needs*
communication	help and support
understanding	encouragement
confidence	confidence building

The elderly

Being old is not a disability. However, as people get older an increasing proportion suffer from a variety of handicaps. This could be deteriorating hearing or eyesight, rheumatism, mobility problems, heart conditions or strokes. Often the elderly suffer from more than one condition. As such the handicaps suffered by the elderly include all of those already described and their difficulties and needs can be drawn from these sections.

All of the above groups have been and often still are, discriminated against in the way in which facilities and information are provided about the countryside. The Disability Discrimination Act (1995) was drafted to ensure that the disabled are not discriminated against. What are the implications of the Act for managers of countryside sites and what are the difficulties of implementing it?

The Disability Discrimination Act 1995

The Disability Discrimination Act (1995) makes it unlawful to discriminate against disabled people in employment, access to goods, services, transport and education.

Managing agencies of countryside sites of all forms will count as service providers.

For service providers it is unlawful to discriminate against disabled people by:

- refusing to provide a service without justification
- providing a service to a lesser standard without justification
- providing a service on worse terms without justification
- failing to make reasonable adjustments to the way services are provided for disabled people.

And, from 2004:

- failing to make reasonable adjustments to the physical features of service premises, to overcome physical barriers to access.

Under the above what will count as discrimination under the Act? Table 6.2 provides a useful summary of what will and what will not constitute discrimination for a service provider.

The Disability Discrimination Act therefore gives the manager of countryside sites some issues to consider.

Table 6.2 As a service provider are you discriminating against disabled people in relation to the Disability Discrimination Act (1995)?

Step	Question	Possible answers	
Step 1	Does the service user meet the DDA's definition of disability? • Is a physical or mental impairment involved? • Does the impairment have a substantial adverse effect? • Does the impairment have a long-term effect? • Does the impairment affect normal day-to-day activities?	*If yes* Go to step 2	*If no* It is not unlawful discrimination on the grounds of disability
Step 2	Is the service exempt from the DDA (education and some services related to it, transport and private clubs)	*If yes* It is not unlawful discrimination on the grounds of disability	*If no* Go to step 3
Step 3	• Has the disabled person received less favourable treatment, and/or • Has there been a failure to make a reasonable adjustment?	*If yes to either or both* Go to step 4	*If no to both* It is not unlawful discrimination on the grounds of disability
Step 4	• Can the service provider justify the treatment, and/or • Is the failure to make a reasonable adjustment justifiable?	*If yes to both* It is not unlawful discrimination on the grounds of disability	*If no to either or both* It may be unlawful discrimination and there may be grounds for action

Source: Disability Rights Commission 2000.

Does all *of the countryside have to be made accessible to people with disabilities?*

It is clearly not feasible to make *all* of the countryside accessible for people with disabilities. For example, it would be a mammoth and not necessarily desirable task to create wheelchair access to all of the mountain tops and ridges of the Lake District. Indeed, disabled people do not want, or expect this to happen. Many enjoy the adventure of getting away from managed areas to the limits of their abilities in the same way as their able-bodied friends. However, in many areas access can be significantly improved. In many cases providing disabled access to the countryside is just providing good access. If a wheelchair can use a path then so can a pram or an elderly relative unsteady on their feet.

How do we decide where access can be improved to provide access for disabled people and what standards do we need to apply to ensure this access provides for the needs of the disabled? To help us with these decisions the Fieldfare Trust in partnership with British Telecom have produced an excellent guide to planning countryside access for disabled people. The guide, *BT Countryside for All* (1997) provides guidance on what standards of accessibility are appropriate for different types of countryside and suggests a structured approach to planning for access for the disabled. The approach developed within this document has been endorsed by a wide variety of groups associated with disability. As such, following the guidelines should ensure that suitable access is created and that you are upholding the law as defined within the Disability Discrimination Act. The following summary is taken directly from *BT Countryside for All* (1997). It is certainly worth obtaining a copy of this document to refer to the detail contained within it.

Standards of accessibility

Differing types of countryside require different standards of provision for disabled people. For example, it could be expected that a much higher level of provision be delivered in a countryside site in, or adjacent to, a town or city compared with wild mountain countryside in the Highlands of Scotland. The standards of accessibility therefore compare four categories of countryside with the standards that should be aimed at in terms of providing access for people with disabilities. The categories are:

> *Urban and formal landscapes* – for example, countryside areas with a lot of artificial features.
> *Urban fringe and managed landscapes* – for example, countryside areas near towns or managed recreation sites.
> *Rural and working landscapes* – for example, farmland and woodland with public rights of way.
> *Open country, semi-wild and wild land* – for example, mountains, moorlands and out-of-the-way countryside.

The standards of provision required for these locations can be seen in Table 6.3. It can be seen from this table that each of the categories of countryside have minimum standards laid down for such issues as path surface, path width, maximum gradient and passing places. Greater details concerning the categories of countryside can be found in *BT Countryside for All* (1997).

How do we use these standards in improving access?

First we have to consider which category of countryside the site being considered falls within. Is it open countryside, a rural and working landscape, urban fringe or an urban or formal landscape? You can then carry out a detailed *access audit*. In an access audit you check your site to assess whether your paths and trails provide suitable access for people with disabilities. To do this you need a large-scale map of your site. The paths and trails on a site can then be walked and the following assessed and recorded:

- *Path surfaces* – size and amount of loose material on the path
- *Path widths* – wide enough for passing, including wheelchair users, visually impaired with long canes or with guide dogs

Table 6.3 BT Countryside for All accessibility standards

	Urban and formal landscapes	Urban fringe and managed landscapes	Rural and working landscapes	Open country, semi-wild and wild land
Path surfaces	Hard, firm and smooth surface with very few loose stones and none bigger than 5mm	Hard and firm, surface with very few loose stones and none bigger than 10mm	Hard and firm with some loose stones and chippings not covering the whole surface. The stones should be no bigger than 10mm	
Path widths	1200mm	1200mm	1000mm	
Width restrictions	At least 815mm for no more than 300mm along path	At least 815mm for no more than 300mm along path	At least 815mm for no more than 300mm along path	
	1000mm for no more than 1600mm along path	1000mm for no more than 1600mm along path	915mm for no more than 1600mm along path	People expect to make their own way, not have this environment changed to provide access
Barriers	There should be no steps, stiles, and no fences, hedges or walls to restrict access			
Maximum distance between passing places	50m	100m	150m	If paths are provided in this setting, they should meet the standard for the rural and working landscape
Maximum distance between rest areas	100m	200m	300m	
Maximum steepness of ramps	1:12	1:12	1:10	
Maximum height rise between landings on ramps steeper than 1:20	750mm (for example landings should be every 9m along ramps of 1:12)	830mm	950mm	
Maximum slope across path	1:50	1:45	1:35	
Maximum step levels	5mm	10mm	15mm	
Surface breaks (grids, boardwalks)	The largest break in the surface of the path should be no more than 12mm measured along the line of the path			
Clear walking tunnels	1200mm wide × 2100mm high	1200mm wide × 2100mm high	1000mm wide × 2100mm high	

Source: *BT Countryside for All* 1997: 8.

- *Restricted width sections* – such as gates
- *Barriers* – stiles, steps, etc.
- *Passing places* – important for wheelchair users
- *Resting places* – such as seats and benches and places where wheelchairs can pull off the path
- *Steepness of path* – what are the gradients of the paths?
- *Height rise on ramps between landings* – what is the distance people have to travel on slopes before being able to take a rest on a flat area?
- *Slope across path* – what is the slope across the path?
- *Step levels* – are there any rises on the path such as steps, potholes, slabs and kerbs?
- *Surface breaks* – changes in path surface can be difficult for wheelchair users and people susceptible to tripping or using canes or sticks
- *Clear walking tunnels* – is there any risk from overhanging branches and so forth?

To help you with these assessments you need:

- a map
- a form for recording the information
- a tape measure
- a gradient gauge – to measure the gradient
- a 12mm diameter stick – to check where walking canes may get stuck
- 5mm and 10mm mesh – to assess surface material.

The *Access for All* guide includes samples of accessibility assessment forms.

What do we do after carrying out an audit?

Having carried out an audit you then need to compare your findings against the accessibility standards for the countryside category your site fits into (see Table 6.3). You can then assess whether you already meet the standards. If you do not, you can decide what improvements would be reasonable to improve access. If any one of the areas in your audit does not meet the standards then your path or trail is not up to standard and you need to decide what you will do about it. Will you:

a   plan and carry out improvements to bring it up to or above the standard?
    or
b   decide not to achieve the standard and justify the reason why?

It was seen earlier in the chapter that the Disability Discrimination Act (1995) makes it unlawful to discriminate against disabled people by:

- refusing to provide a service without justification
- providing a service to a lesser standard without justification
- providing a service on worse terms without justification
- failing to make reasonable adjustments to the way services are provided for disabled people.

The above four statements contain the phrases 'without justification' and 'reasonable'. It may be considered that it may not be reasonable to change a path or trail to a correct standard if (Fieldfare Trust 1997: 22):

- It costs too much.
- It spoils the landscape.
- It has an effect on the ecology of the area.
- It creates safety risks.
- It spoils things for other people using it.

If any of these are considered reasons why a path or trail cannot be brought up to a required standard the reasons for not doing so need to be recorded with full justification. The real test of what is reasonable is whether those responsible for providing the paths or trails can show that they have done everything possible to reach the standard. Wherever possible everything should be done to create 'access for all'.

Involving people with disabilities in the process

BT Countryside for All (1997) provides considerable guidance on designing paths and associated infrastructure with disabled visitors in mind. However, whilst this guidance is very useful there is no substitute for involving people with disabilities in the decision-making process about what improvements to make. After all, they will know better than anyone about their particular needs. It is going back to marketing principles again, creating products to fit the needs of the consumer. In this case the consumers will be people with disabilities.

How do we involve people with disabilities? First we have to identify potential sources of help. Are there any local people or groups who would be willing to take part in the process? Contact with national organisations (listed at the end of the chapter) who represent different sectors of disability may put you in touch with appropriate individuals or groups at a local level. Having found help, explain what you are trying to achieve so that everyone is working to the same objectives. Discussions can be in the form of formal committees such as site committees or access groups, through site visits, or through developing action groups to address a particular issue. Whatever method of communication is chosen, endeavour to *involve* people, rather than just consult with them. By developing closer contacts with people with disabilities you will improve services and facilities considerably, and just as importantly develop friendships and partnerships that will change the approach you have to developing your site services and facilities.

Access issues relating to people with disabilities

When contemplating improvements to site access the needs of disabled visitors should be an automatic consideration. What can be done practically to improve access? *BT Countryside for All* (1997) provides some excellent detailed guidance as to the design of a variety of countryside furniture with people with disabilities in mind. This goes into far more depth than can be covered within this book and reference to this is strongly recommended. In Chapter 5 the functions and design of items of infrastructure (such as gates, seats, car parks and bins) were considered. The needs of people with disabilities should be an automatic part of considering any site issues. As such, the design of suitable infrastructure for people with disabilities was considered in Chapter 5.

Provision of information

People with disabilities need information on where they can go in the countryside. To develop confidence and encourage visits, a greater level of detail is needed about sites than for able-bodied visitors. This information can be publicity material that encourages disabled people to visit a site, or it can be on-site information that provides detail about a site once a visitor has arrived. Many local authorities and national parks now produce leaflets and booklets that provide detailed information for disabled visitors. For people with visual disabilities it may be necessary to provide information in Braille. The kind of information that is required is:

- location and names of sites (a map is useful)
- facilities available on the site to assist the disabled visitor
- availability of toilets
- suitability of paths for wheelchairs
- details about individual paths
- length and nature of paths
- surface material of paths
- frequency of resting points
- availability of help.

Examples of information for people with disabilities can be seen in Plate 6.1.

Plate 6.1 Information booklets for visitors with disabilities

Ethnic minorities

So far in the chapter we have dealt only with the needs of people with disabilities. However, in Table 6.1 black and other ethnic communities were identified as sectors that face barriers in their usage of the countryside. The potential barriers were considered to be:

- *Awareness* – members of ethnic communities are often not aware of the opportunities that are available for them for recreation in and around where they live. This may stem from a poor knowledge of local geography or lack of information often created by language difficulties.
- *Language* – how much of the information provided to visitors of countryside sites (either publicity material or on-site information) is in languages other than English (or Welsh)? Many people from ethnic minorities have little understanding of these languages and therefore miss out on information that is provided about sites. As such, people from ethnic communities often do not know where to go in the countryside or what is available to them, even if they have a desire to visit.
- *Culture* – for many ethnic communities the concept of the countryside and its value in their lives is very different from the British one. For example, in their home country the countryside may have been a place of work. It may have been prohibited to them or not been regarded as a recreational resource.
- *Confidence* – the confidence to use the countryside is based upon knowledge of it and your rights as an individual regarding access to it. People from ethnic communities will often have a very poor knowledge of these. In addition, surveys have shown that a fear of racism in the countryside prevents some members of ethnic communities from going there.

How can we encourage more visitors from ethnic communities to visit the countryside? There are a number of things we can do. We can:

Encourage the young to visit the countryside – if we can take young people from ethnic communities into the countryside and give them positive experiences they may wish to visit again. In addition, we can develop their knowledge of the countryside, show them what is available and increase their confidence in using it. There are a number of ways in which we can get young people from these communities into the countryside. One method may be through the school system, whereby schools in areas of ethnic communities are encouraged to visit countryside sites and undertake activities. If this can be done on a regular basis, confidence will increase considerably. Another method may be to contact the young people through community groups and to organise countryside days out. These organised days provide gateways into the countryside.

Provide gateways – gateways are entrances and as such provide ways into something. A way into the countryside is often what is required to stimulate people from ethnic communities to visit it. Events and programmes can be organised to act as gateways. These might be such simple activities as a countryside picnic, simple walks, coach tours or site open days. These can be organised by developing communications with representative groups from within ethnic communities. These gateway events can provide an opportunity to develop confidence, increase understanding and provide suitable information so that future visits will be stimulated. Transport may need to be provided, as one obstacle in accessing the countryside is lack of transport.

Provision of information – standard routes of providing information about sites may not be suitable for people from ethnic communities. Language issues may prevent understanding and just as important, ethnic communities may not use the types of places where site information is normally distributed. A different strategy for promotion may therefore be required to reach this particular market. Can leaflets or other sources of information be provided in languages suitable for an identified ethnic grouping? It may be necessary to produce information in Urdu or Hindi for example. In addition, new ways may need to be found to distribute information. The best way to find out how to do this is to talk to members of the community and identify potential mechanisms for distributing information to that community.

Training site staff about 'access for all'

There is no point in considering how to make countryside recreation sites accessible to all, without providing some training in this area for site staff. It is important to develop a culture in which the needs of all are automatically considered when making any decision concerning the running of a site. This culture will not occur overnight but will develop with training and action over a period of time. What should be included in any training programme in this area?

- the needs of people with disabilities and of ethnic communities
- how to carry out access audits
- the implications of the Disability Discrimination Act
- technical details of providing infrastructure that meets the needs of all visitors
- sources of help.

Training of site staff will be considered in more detail in Chapter 8.

References and further reading

Centre for Accessible Environments (1996) *Access by Design: Implementing the Disability Discrimination Act 1995*, London: Centre for Accessible Environments.
Centre for Accessible Environments (1999a) *Access Audits: A Guide and Checklist for Appraising Accessibility of Public Buildings*, London: Centre for Accessible Environments.
Centre for Accessible Environments (1999b) *Designing for Accessibility: An Essential Guide for Public Buildings*, London: Centre for Accessible Environments.
Countryside Commission (1987) *Informal Countryside Recreation for Disabled People: Advisory Series No. 15*, Cheltenham: Countryside Commission.
Field Fare Trust (1997) *BT Countryside for All: Standards and Guidelines; A Good Practice Guide to Disabled People's Access in the Countryside*, Sheffield: Fieldfare Trust.
Countryside Recreation Network (1998) *Making Access for All a Reality*, Cardiff: Countryside Recreation Network.

Web references

Department of Education and Employment (2000) *DfEE disability briefing: February 2000*, DfEE. Online. Available http://www.disability.gov.uk/dissum99.html (3 September 2001).

Field Fare Trust (1997) *BT countryside for all: standards and guidelines; a good practice guide to disabled people's access in the countryside*, Sheffield: Fieldfare Trust. Online. Available http://www.fieldfare.org.uk/ (3 September 2001).

Disability Rights Commission (2000) *Assessment Guide in Relation to Services*. Online. Available http://www.drc-gb.org/drc/RightsAndRequirements/Page113.asp (3 September 2001).

Royal National Institute for the Blind (2000) Office of National Statistics mid-1996. Population estimates, estimates for 1996 of visually impaired people (i.e. registerable) and the number of people registered as blind and partially sighted as at 31 March 1997 in United Kingdom. Online. Available http://www.rnib.org.uk/wesupply/fctsheet/authuk.htm (3 September 2001).

Royal National Institute for the Deaf (2001) Statistics on Deafness. Online. Available http://www.rnid.org.uk/html/factsheet_txts/statistics on_deafness.txt (3 September 2001).

Web links

British Council of Disabled People:	http://www.bcodp.org.uk/
British Deaf Association:	http://www.britishdeafassociation.org.uk/
Centre for Accessible Environments:	http://www.cae.org.uk/
Disability Net:	http://www.disabilitynet.co.uk/index.html
Disability Rights Commission:	http://www.drc-gb.org/drc/default.as
Fieldfare Trust:	http://www.fieldfare.org.uk/
Mencap:	http://www.mencap.org.uk/home.htm
National Federation for the Blind:	http://www.nfb.org/
Radar:	http://www.radar.org.uk/
Royal National Institute for the Blind:	http://www.rnib.org.uk/welcome.htm
Royal National Institute for the Deaf:	http://www.rnid.org.uk/

7   Developing attractions

The development of site attractions may be an important component of site management, particularly if an objective of the site is to increase visitor numbers. The selection and sympathetic development of attractions that meet the needs of the site and the customer is therefore important. This chapter considers the types of attraction that can be developed and outlines the issues associated with them.

Why develop site attractions?

The development of attractions on countryside recreation sites takes time, money and imagination. Why is it necessary and why not just leave a site as it is? Sometimes this may be exactly what we decide to do. For example, for conservation reasons, we may not wish to attract visitors to a site. However, on many sites we may wish to improve the attractions that already exist and develop new ones for the following reasons:

> To *increase visitor numbers* – there are a number of reasons why we may wish to increase the number of visitors to a site. It may be desirable to increase the revenue generated for the site through entrance charges, parking fees, retail outlets and refreshments. This money can then be used for improved management of the site. It may also provide a larger platform to get messages across to the visitor in the form of interpretation and environmental education.
>
> To *increase income of the local economy* – by increasing the number of visitors to a site you will indirectly be supporting the economy of the surrounding area. Visitors to your site may eat in local cafés and public houses, use local garages, shop in local shops and stay in local accommodation. This will generate employment as well as income.
>
> To *attract visitors to certain parts of a site* – it is often desirable to manage visitors by attracting them to certain locations within a site. This may be for conservation reasons, to avoid user/user conflict or to enable the most effective use to be made of limited resources. On many sites a 'honey-potting' approach is used whereby facilities and attractions are grouped together to attract visitors to particular places and to maximise the use of resources.
>
> To *promote health* – it is a desirable objective to provide facilities to help people get more exercise and hopefully become healthier in mind, body and spirit.
>
> To *compete with other recreation sites* – this may be true for the more

commercial countryside recreation site. Recreation sites within your area may develop new attractions that directly compete with those on your site. This may have the affect of decreasing the number of visitors. To compete it may be necessary to repackage existing attractions and/or develop new ones.

To allow new groups of users to gain access to your site – specific attractions can be designed to allow access for groups of users who previously had difficulty using the site. This could occur by improving the site infrastructure for disabled visitors, providing cycling or horse riding routes or developing attractions specifically for children such as adventure playgrounds.

To create educational opportunities – it is sometimes useful to create educational opportunities by developing new attractions. This may be through such means as setting up an interpretive visitor centre, an education facility, some interpretive theatre or an interpretive trail.

To create site features to create focal points – some site attractions such as sculpture, visitor centres or gardens form focal points for visitors and help them navigate their way around a site.

Before you create new site attractions make the most of what you already have

Before deciding to develop new attractions it is necessary to consider what it is that attracts visitors to the site as it stands. This can be formalised through the production of a site features list (as discussed in Chapter 2). Only by producing such a list and considering each product from a marketing perspective (the core product, the tangible features of the product, the intangible features of the product and the product of the product), can we understand the existing site features and therefore be in a position to decide what improvements need to be made and what new attractions need to be created. Examples of site attractions include:

castle	cliffs	children's playground	sculpture
visitor centre	mountain bike trail	walking trails	
bird hides	open-air theatre	watersports	orienteering trail
natural history	river	maze	BMX track

In developing a successful site it is very important to consider what really attracts people to it. This can then be capitalised upon and developed. However, as well as considering the site attractions (the site products) we also need to consider visitors' needs. Remember from Chapter 1, that a product satisfies people, when their needs have been met or exceeded. This is where knowledge of site visitors and their needs is very important (as emphasised in Chapter 3). Equally valuable is developing an understanding of what it is that detracts visitors from the site (i.e. what is it that does not satisfy their needs). By understanding the site features and visitors' needs, existing attractions can be improved or new ones developed that will satisfy them.

In addition to the physical attractions, we also need to consider events and activities that take place on a site. These can be such things as craft fairs, sporting events, music, guided walks, fireworks or battle re-enactments. How successful have these events been in the past and what would need to be done to make them more successful?

Creating new attractions

There are a wide variety of attractions that can be developed on a countryside recreation site. These range from unobtrusive developments such as walks, bird hides and sculpture, through to more entertainment driven features such as pitch and putt, adventure playgrounds and falconry displays. In addition, events can be programmed on sites such as orchestral concerts, firework displays, sporting events and craft fairs.

It is not possible in a chapter of this size to go into all possibilities in-depth. What this chapter will do is outline the possible types of site attraction that can be developed and illustrate the issues involved in their development. The possibilities outlined in no way constitute a definitive list, but seek to illustrate the range of options available to the site manager.

In deciding on what new attractions to develop the following points need to be considered:

> *What are the management objectives of the site?* – this will be crucial in deciding whether new attractions are required and what they should be. Is the site one where there are significant conservation issues such as on a site rich in ornithological interest? In such a case the management objective will be focused on the conservation needs of the site as the primary site objectives and any new developments will have to complement this. On such a site the organisation of events such as music festivals or the development of an orienteering course may be completely inappropriate. However, building bird hides, developing walks and providing interpretative panels and guided walks may be very appropriate. Conversely, some sites will have management objectives that focus more on recreation, interpretation and education. On such sites higher profile attractions such as adventure playgrounds for children, watersports facilities such as canoe and windsurfer hire, and craft fairs may be very appropriate in meeting the site's management objectives.
>
> *What is the nature of the site?* – some sites are large and have a diverse range of topographic, heritage and landscape features. Others are small and uniform in their nature. Some will have woodlands and forests, some water features and others large open spaces. The attractions that are developed on a site need to reflect the conditions of a particular site. So for example, mountain bike trails need significant lengths of track and an interesting and varied topography and as such, are ideally suited to forested areas.
>
> *Existing attractions* – as stated earlier in this chapter the first stage in developing new attractions is to consider what already exists and how existing attractions can be further developed and improved. New features can then be developed that complement the existing provision.
>
> *The nature of your visitor* – who are the visitors to a site and what are their needs? Are the majority of visitors local repeat visitors who come to the site for

informal recreation, or are the majority of your visitors tourists who visit it on an infrequent basis? Do horse riders or mountain bikers use the site and how much is the site used by children and school groups? Remember that in marketing terms we seek to develop products that satisfy the need of the consumer (in this case the visitor). It is therefore essential that we know who the consumers are and what their needs are. It may also be useful to identify who does not visit your site and consider what needs to be done to attract them. The nature of the visitor will therefore influence significantly the attractions that are developed for a site.

The costs of developing a new attraction – resources can be split into the capital start up costs and the ongoing costs of maintenance, staffing and overheads such as heating and electricity. Some site features such as walking trails will cost relatively little to set up and will require only small amounts of staff time, whereas attractions such as visitor centres will have a high capital cost to build and will require the employment of staff. Offset against the costs must be the potential income that can be generated by the new feature.

Only when the above has been considered can nature, scale and location of attractions to be decided.

What sort of attractions can be developed?

Walks and trails

On most sites there will be a network of walks and trails. To turn a particular trail into an attraction, an interesting and logical route needs to be decided upon. Successful trails have some, or all, of the following features:

- start at parking locations
- follow interesting routes
- make use of distinct landscape features such as cliff tops and river banks
- pass through a variety of scenery
- pass interesting features along the way
- good walking surfaces
- are easily followed
- distinct route identity
- pass by pubs and or cafés somewhere along the route
- high quality infrastructure such a stiles, gates, benches and signposts
- appropriate length for likely users
- provide peace and quiet
- have good information about them in the form of leaflets, orientation boards and signposts
- circular in their route such that the trail starts and finishes at the same location.

Walks and trails are often one of the major attractions to a recreation site and as such require careful planning. Routes of differing lengths and difficulty should be developed to provide for the differing needs and aspirations of visitors. As walks are linear features they do not need to be constrained within the boundaries of a site.

Walks can extend beyond the boundaries and be a means of linking a site to the outside world. Quite often, longer routes such as national trails and regional routes will pass through recreation sites.

Disabled access trails

Visitors with disabilities may be a particular target group which site facilities, such as trails, may be designed for. Indeed, under the provisions of the Disability Discrimination Act (1995) there is a duty to provide access for people with disabilities. Different types of trails can be produced for differing types of disability. Examples include sensory trails for the blind, and routes suitable for wheelchair users. In producing high quality trails for the disabled we also provide high quality trails for a wider public.

Cycle routes

Routes for cyclists tend to be linear in their nature and cover a number of miles. As such it is unlikely that a whole cycle route will be contained within a recreation site. Cycle routes are becoming popular, for example, using old railway lines and quiet country roads. These routes often have a large degree of management specifically for recreational purposes and thus could be said to constitute long thin recreation sites! What needs to be considered in developing a cycle route?

- *Location* – ideally linking urban areas with the countryside.
- *Parking facilities* – a lot of people take their bikes to the countryside by car!
- *Continuity* – the route should offer a continuous route.
- *Attractiveness* – like walks, any cycle route should pass through attractive surroundings.
- *Quietness* – cycling is a quiet activity; peace and quiet is an important issue.
- *Traffic free* – cyclists like to be separated from road users. This makes routes

safer for all, particularly families with children and makes the route quieter and less polluted.

- *Length of route* – there should be opportunities to break a cycle ride at regular intervals so that visitors can decide how far they want to cycle.
- *Circular routes* – is it possible to make circular routes that start and finish from the same point?
- *Surfacing* – easy surfaces to ride on.
- *Gradients* – routes should avoid steep gradients.
- *Bike hire* – not everyone has a bike or has a bike with them. This is particularly true in tourist areas.
- *Bike parking facilities* – places to lock bikes to are required at strategic locations.
- *Information* – this will be required in the form of leaflets, route maps, orientation boards and signposts.
- *Quality infrastructure* – gates, seats, picnic benches and signposts.
- *Links to pubs and other sources of refreshment* – somewhere to eat and drink.

Web case studies

Cycle trails in the Peak District: http://www.dclally.demon.co.uk/index.htm
Derwent walk country park and Derwenthaugh Park:
    http://www.gateshead.gov.uk/leisserv/dertrails.htm
Forest of Dean cycle ways: http://www.chepstow.co.uk/fod-cycling.htm
Tarka trail: http://www.tarka-country.co.uk/tarkaproject/recinfra.html
Tehidy country park cycle trails:
    http://www.chycor.co.uk/holidays/cycling...y/tehidy-cp.htm

Mountain bike trails

Mountain biking is an increasingly popular activity. Mountain bikers travel a long way to find high quality routes that challenge their technique and stamina. Mountain bikers come in a variety of shapes, ages and abilities and it is therefore important to provide trails of different lengths and provide challenges for the expert and the novice. In developing mountain bike trails all of the considerations outlined above for cycle routes should be addressed as well as the following more specialist issues:

- *Unsurfaced tracks* – mountain bikers like off-road adventure.
- *Rugged topography* – steep climbs and descents make riding more interesting and challenging.
- *Bike washing facilities* – somewhere to clean the mud off.
- *Variety of technical challenges* – features that test the rider's skill.

Case study – Coed y Brenin mountain biking

Managing authority: the Forestry Commission.

Environment: mature conifer plantations in an upland setting in Mid-Wales.

Nature for development: a network of graded mountain bike trails of different lengths and difficulties created within the forest. Routes range from expert routes of 35km to a fun route of 11km. Each route is named to create a unique identity. Two of the trails carry sponsorship from Karrimor and Red Bull, with the routes named after the sponsor (the Karrimor trail, and the Red Bull trail).

Management: the site is signposted off a main trunk road as a mountain bike centre with brown tourist signs. The hub of the site consists of car parks set amongst the trees and a visitor centre and café. The visitor centre contains information about the mountain bike routes and a free leaflet is distributed. Staff in the centre and café are all keen mountain bikers and offer good advice. All routes start from the centre and all are clearly waymarked using colour coded posts with the difficulty of the route identified at the start. As well as using forest tracks the routes utilise specially developed stages within the forest as challenging sections that require differing amounts of technical ability to ride through. These stages include steep ascents and descents. Short cuts exist for all routes to provide riders with flexibility in difficulty and length of route.

Visitor numbers: increased from around 27,500 in 1996/97 to 110,000 in 1999, following the development of the mountain bike trails. Surveys show that 87 per cent of visitors to the site are mountain bikers.

Expenditure within the local economy: based upon survey work conducted by the Forestry Commission on site, it is estimated that visitors who come to Coed y Brenin spend in the region of £4.60 million within the local economy on such items as accommodation, food and fuel.

Plate 7.1 The start of the Karrimor mountain bike trail, Coed y Brenin, Wales

Horse riding routes

In some locations horse riding is very popular and a site may have a network of bridleways and byways open to all traffic (BOATs) that riders have a legal access right to. However, some sites will be poorly served with such routes and new routes may need to be created. By and large the needs of horse riders are poorly catered for compared with walkers and cyclists and the facilities for them are few and far between. Developing routes and facilities for horse riders may therefore be important. What needs to be considered in the development of riding trails?

*   suitable surfaces for horses
*   provision of bridle gates so that riders do not have to dismount
*   places for the horses to drink
*   places to tie up horses when the rider is dismounted
*   signposting of the trails
*   segregation from other users
*   information on routes.

Sporting facilities

There are a wide variety of sports that can take place on countryside recreation sites and each sport will require different facilities, resources and management. Table 7.1 shows the potential sports, their facilities and the resource requirements and illustrates the variety of possibilities that are open to the site manager.

For all sporting facilities the following points need to be considered before a decision is made to develop:

*   *Is there a demand on the site for the sport?* – will there be enough customers for your proposed sporting facility?
*   *Who will manage the facility?* – will the management of facilities be placed in the hands of a club such as a sailing club or a golf club?
*   *How much will it cost to develop?* – what are the capital requirements in the development of the facility?
*   *What are the maintenance implications and what will maintenance cost?* – how

Table 7.1 Possible sports that can be carried out on a countryside recreation site, and the facilities and resources that they require

Sporting activity	Facilities required	Resource requirements
Archery	Safe location, targets, bows	Suitable location, equipment, supervision
Ball games: football, rugby, cricket, hockey, tennis	Pitches, changing facilities, clubhouse, all-weather viewing facilities, equipment	Flat well drained land, grass cutting, nets, white lines, equipment, building and maintenance of changing rooms and clubhouse
Climbing	Rock faces or artificial climbing walls, climbing equipment	Guidebooks, equipment, building and maintenance of climbing wall
Fishing	Water bodies such as lakes, rivers or the sea, fish	Re-stocking of fish, monitoring of fishing (bailiff)
Fitness trails/trim trails	Outdoor fitness equipment	Equipment, trail
Golf/pitch and putt/putting	A golf/putting course, golf clubs and balls, clubhouse	Golf course, building and maintenance of course and clubhouse, equipment
Motorcycle trials riding	An old quarry or similar	Suitable location
Orienteering	Maps, marker posts	Map production and printing, maintenance of posts and course
Running or jogging	Suitable routes	Maintenance of routes
Watersports: sailing, windsurfing, canoeing, rowing, jet ski-ing	Water bodies such as lakes, rivers or the sea, secure boat storage, launching facilities, changing rooms, clubhouse	Water body, boats, building and maintenance of facilities

much will it cost to maintain, for example cutting grass on football pitches or maintaining and heating changing facilities?

- *What are the staffing implications?* – how many staff will be required to run the facilities and what will this cost?
- *What income can be generated?* – what are the returns on the investment? How much can be earned for example by charging for fishing permits or from hire of equipment?
- *What are the insurance issues associated with the facility?* – what are the liabilities associated with the sport and how will any insurance premiums be covered?

Only when all of these issues have been considered can a rational decision be made as to whether or not to progress with the development of a sporting facility.

Activities for children

If you can provide activities that will be attractive to children, parents will be very grateful and will come to your site. Parents are constantly searching for activities and facilities that will entertain and stimulate their children. There is a wide variety of attractions that can be developed (indeed you are only limited in your choice by your imagination). New ideas are constantly developing so keep an eye on other recreation sites for ideas. Possible attractions include:

playgrounds   adventure playgrounds   mazes   BMX tracks

tree-top walks   skateboard parks   tobogganing

animal feeding   crazy golf   putting   go karts

children's clubs   crèches   sand pits   roller-blading

Of particular importance in developing attractions for children is the issue of safety. This is of the highest importance and needs to be considered from the point of view of the design of the attraction, the supervision of children using the attraction and the maintenance of the attraction. The relevant safety standards need to be applied and regular inspection and monitoring needs to be carried out.

Sculpture/art

Many recreation sites are now using sculpture and art as a site attraction. The careful placement of works of art within natural settings can be aesthetically rewarding and will certainly generate interest from the public. Items can be placed on a 'sculpture trail' complete with interpretation or located generally around a site such that the visitor is surprised when coming across them. The purposes of art in the countryside can be many, apart from being purely as a visitor attraction. It can be used:

Plate 7.2 An adventure playground for children

- to make an unexceptional landscape more interesting
- to add atmosphere
- as a form of interpretation
- to create local landmarks
- as a community project to help celebrate local distinctiveness.

Differing types of sculpture provoke different feelings. Sculpture made from local materials such as stone and wood, tend to fit into natural landscapes far better than metals and plastics. However, some would argue that the role of art is to provoke emotion and that if a work creates discussion, then it has fulfilled its function. Examples of sculpture in a countryside setting can be seen in Plate 7.3.

Web case studies

Grizedale Forest sculpture park: http://www.parklife.co.uk/grize/gforest.htm
Hebdon Bridge sculpture trail: www.sculpturetrail.org
Photo archive of countryside sculpture:
    http://www.shu.ac.uk/services/lc/slidecol/pubart/other/index.html

Viewpoints

Wherever a site has some areas that are higher than the surroundings there is the potential for creating viewpoints. The public always like places where they can sit or stand and admire or photograph beautiful views. Indeed, on many sites it is the views that attract people to the site in the first place. In many cases the viewpoints are already in place and just need to be enhanced by placing seats and perhaps

Plate 7.3 Sculpture as a 'gateway'

adding an interpretive panel that helps to interpret the view and identify the key features. In other cases trees may obscure the view. Careful thinning at selected places to create viewpoints may be required.

Wildlife features

There is an increasing number of visitors who are interested in seeing natural history close up. The wildlife on a site can therefore be used as an attraction. This should only occur where this will not conflict with the needs of the wildlife. With careful management and an understanding of the conflicts that can occur between the wildlife and the visitor, these can be minimised or eliminated. Indeed, the fact that visitors are coming to see the wildlife can increase the profile and resources available and therefore enhance protection and management. What sort of wildlife attractions can be developed?

- *Bird hides* – places where the visitor can go and observe birds at close quarters without disturbing them
- *Bird feeding stations* – places where birds are fed at a regular time so that the public can get to see them at close range (example: the red kite feeding stations in Mid-Wales)
- *Video links* – to wildlife sites such as osprey nests or seabird colonies on cliffs
- *Captive animals* – captive animals that can be seen at close quarters in a similar fashion to animals in a zoo
- *Arboretums* – collections of trees
- *Butterfly gardens* – gardens planted with wild flowers that attract butterflies
- *Falconry* – displays of flying by birds of prey
- *Telescopes* – to allow visitors to look more closely at the wildlife
- *Interpretation* – to inform the visitor about the on-site wildlife.

Web case studies

Royal Society for the Protection of Birds (RSPB) reserves:
http://www.rspb.org.uk
Wildfowl and Wetlands Trust: http://www.wildfowlandwetlands.org.uk/

Heritage attractions

These are items from the past such as castles, woollen mills, battlegrounds, Iron Age hill forts and old buildings. As such they are items that already exist on a site. It is therefore important when considering the development of attractions on a site to identify the heritage items that it has, and assess their potential for becoming attractions. Heritage items range in size and importance and each will have its own unique issues attached to it. Issues could be the conservation designation placed upon it (scheduled ancient monument/listed building), the condition of the feature, how prone it is to damage and the cost of restoration work.

Heritage features may well form a major attraction of a site and for many sites will be the major attraction. The management of the item is therefore very important. However, whilst the overall heritage value is important in itself, its value will be increased significantly by the use of interpretation.

Interpretation

Interpretation is the process by which the significance of cultural, historic and natural resources is communicated. Chapter 9 of this book looks at information and interpretation, and will discuss in greater detail the function of interpretation and the types of interpretation that can be carried out on a site. It is sufficient to say in this section, that interpretation can enhance the visitor 'pull' of any site attraction as well as becoming an attraction in itself. What forms of interpretation can we have on sites?

visitor centres	interpretive panels	guided walks
guides	interpretive theatre	leaflets
historic re-enactments	tape/slide sequences	video
objects/artefacts	models	demonstrations

Events

Countryside sites are being used increasingly for a variety of events. Why do we organise events at countryside sites?

- to publicise a site and raise its profile
- to introduce people to countryside activities
- to publicise new site features
- to provide public enjoyment
- to generate revenue
- to engender community cohesion
- to develop awareness of site issues.

What kinds of events take place on countryside recreation sites?

open days	new feature launches	music festivals
craft fairs	car boot sales	fireworks displays
game fairs	agricultural shows	steam fairs
sporting events	antique fairs	battle re-enactments

These are only a selection of the possibilities. Events can take a lot of preparation, organising and planning. What needs to be considered when organising an event?

- *Publicity* – how the public will know about an event?
- *Consultation* – with all relevant parties including the police
- *When to have the event* – not at the same time as the FA Cup Final or Wimbledon
- *Location* – avoid sensitive habitats and heritage sites
- *Staffing/volunteers* – how many people will be required to staff the event and what are the training requirements?
- *Finance* – what will it cost to stage the event and what is the expected revenue generated by the event?
- *Signposting* – how will you let the public know where the event is?
- *Parking* – will extra parking be required and how will it be managed?
- *Collection of entry fees* – will there be admission charges, how much will they be and how will the money be collected?
- *Catering* – will catering be required and who will do it?
- *Toilets* – are extra toilets required?
- *Shelter* – are marquees and tents required?
- *Communications* – is a tannoy system required?
- *First aid* – what will be the first aid requirements and how will they be covered?
- *Security* – who will provide site security?
- *Insurance* – what are the insurance implications of holding the event?
- *Health and safety* – what health and safety issues need to be considered?

Some events will be small scale and the level of organisation will be small. Other events such as music festivals will take a great deal of detailed planning and organisation and will take up a lot of staff time.

References and further reading

Bicycle Association (1996) *Cycle-friendly Infrastructure: Guidelines for Planning and Design*, Godalming: Cyclists' Touring Club.

Countryside Commission (1991) *Organising Countryside Events: Advice for Countryside Staff*, Cheltenham: Countryside Commission.

Knudson, D. W., Cable, T. T. and Beck, L. (1995) *Interpretation of Cultural and Natural Heritage Resources*, PA: Venture Publishing Inc.

Lumsdon, L. (1996) *Cycling Opportunities: Making the Most of the National Cycle Network*, Stockport: Simon Holt Marketing Services.

Sports Council for Wales, Countryside Council for Wales (1998) *Sporting and Challenge Events in the Countryside: Guidelines for Organisers*, The Sports Council for Wales.

Sustrans (1994) *Making Ways for the Bicycle: A Guide to Traffic-Free Path Construction*, Bristol: Sustrans Ltd.

8 Customer care

Customer care is about more than saying 'have a nice day'. In the first chapter on marketing, the concept of placing the needs and aspirations of the public at the centre of the countryside recreation planning was discussed. This chapter considers the value of customer care and focuses on how the needs of 'customers' when visiting a site can be met or, better, exceeded. Particular emphasis is placed upon the service element of site management and the importance of well trained site staff.

Have a nice day! – no thank you: the concept of customer care

The perception of the public concerning customer care is associated with the smiling American waitress saying, 'Have a nice day.' Is this really what customer care is? The answer is a very definite no. Whilst being polite and pleasant to customers is important, customer care is a more fundamental issue that needs to be central to the management philosophy of any organisation concerned with interacting with customers. So what is it? Customer care could simply be defined as: meeting the needs of customers.

In Chapter 1, it was identified that when a visitor decides to visit a countryside site, this decision is normally driven by individual or group needs that require satisfying. Customer care is therefore concerned with meeting customers' needs, when they visit a countryside site. The bottom line is that if you meet or exceed visitors' needs, then they are likely to return to your site again. Conversely if their needs are not met, they are unlikely to visit again. Many of the needs of visitors to countryside sites (the customers) will be met by the nature of the site and the product that it offers (topography, views, physical challenges, etc.). However, there are many aspects of site management where good customer care will influence an individual's satisfaction with a site visit. Examples of this include:

- how easy it is, to find the entrance to the site
- how staff communicate with visitors
- how clean the toilets are
- how easy it is, to find your way around the site
- how tidy and litter free the site is
- how customer complaints are dealt with.

What we are dealing with in customer care, is the *service* sector of the site product (one of its intangible components). If we are to gain happy satisfied visitors then we must provide them with service that meets or exceeds their expectations. Some recreation sites will be fairly self-contained and service is only a minor component of visitors' needs, whereas at other sites service will be more important.

Why is customer care important?

The ultimate aim of customer care for countryside recreation sites is to gain happy and satisfied visitors. However, the benefits go much further than this. Good customer care will also provide significant benefits to site staff and to the organisation that manages a site. What are these benefits?

Benefits to the visitor

Visitors' needs are met – if visitors' needs are met or exceeded, it will help to ensure that they enjoy their visit having had them met.

Visitors feel valued – if customers feel that they have been treated well and received a high quality of service, then they feel valued. This is a real feel-good factor that increases their satisfaction with the visit.

Benefits to staff

A happier more satisfied workforce – an organisation that treats customer care seriously will normally use the same philosophy of service to its 'internal customers', that is, its workforce. This will create happier employees. In addition, complaints should decrease and compliments increase. This increases job satisfaction and decreases stress all around.

A sense of pride – a customer care approach to dealing with visitors will create a sense of pride in the service that is being delivered. This increases job satisfaction. Staff will feel that what they do is valued, both by the visitor and the organisation they work for.

Benefits to the organisation

Happy visitors – there are considerable benefits to an organisation from having happy visitors. A happy visitor is likely to return to a site repeatedly and to tell friends about their experience. As word of mouth is one of the most important ways of promoting a recreation site, this is important.

Enhanced reputation – if an organisation develops a name for high quality customer care, then the reputation of that organisation will increase.

Decreasing number of complaints – if high quality customer care becomes core to an organisation, then the number of complaints from the public should decrease.

Happier more motivated staff – a happier more motivated staff will generate happier more satisfied customers. In addition, a happy motivated workforce will have lower absentee rates and staff turnover will decrease.

It can be seen from this that customer care is important and not just for the visitor. The basic philosophy of customer care could be seen as:

happy, motivated and
trained employees   = happy visitors = a happier organisation

Customer care therefore needs to be a philosophy enshrined within the management of a site and not just seen as something carried out by front line staff.

What gives customers a bad impression?

Before the techniques we can use to achieve high quality customer care are described, let us stop and think about what gives customers a bad impression.

Think about the last time you experienced bad customer care. Where were you and what was it that really annoyed you?

It is likely that it was one or more of the following things:

- A service was promised, but not delivered.
- You felt that staff could not be bothered to serve you.
- You were kept waiting.
- Being asked to hold for ages on the phone.
- A complaint being dealt with badly, or not being dealt with at all.
- Feeling that you have paid too much (feeling ripped off).
- Feeling fobbed off – being passed from person to person.
- Rudeness of staff.
- Staff getting your name and details wrong.

Do these sound familiar? If we are to deliver good customer care we need to ensure that they do not happen.

What gives customers a good impression?

Think of the last time that you experienced high quality customer care. Where were you and what was it that gave you a good impression? How did this good customer care make you feel? Often it is simple things done well that leave a good impression. Examples of good customer care include:

- receiving information through the post promptly
- helpful advice on the phone
- provision of free wheelchairs
- provision of helpful information about the level of difficulty of a cycling route
- helping a visitor identify a bird or flower
- developing a system for regularly checking the cleanliness of the toilets
- dealing with a written complaint promptly.

As you can see, some of these examples are concerned with the attitude and approach of staff in communicating with the public. Others are concerned with having robust and efficient systems. In all of the examples, the visitor will have been helped and will have developed positive feelings towards the site and the organisation that runs it.

What are customer care requirements?

What the public requires from good customer care, can be considered under five headings.

- *Reliability* – the ability to perform the promised service dependably and accurately.
- *Responsiveness* – willingness to help people and provide a prompt service.
- *Assurance* – knowledge and courtesy of employees and their ability to inspire trust and confidence.
- *Empathy* – caring individual attention given.
- *Tangibles* – physical facilities, equipment and appearance of staff.

When developing and improving on customer care, all of these headings need to be considered. Customer care is concerned with total service over a whole visit. There is no value in providing good customer care for most of a visit if one item seriously lets you down. All areas of service, over the whole duration of the visit therefore need to be considered. In addition, when considering customer care, it must be remembered that every individual person has different expectations of the service they expect and will accept. Visitor expectations will also differ from site to site. For example, they are likely to expect a higher standard of service on a heavily managed and used site, than on a simpler unmanaged site. This is the same as expecting higher levels of service at a five star hotel, than in a bed and breakfast establishment.

How do we ensure quality customer care?

First we have to embrace customer care as a core function of an organisation. This needs to occur at all levels within an organisation from the top manager to the most junior employee and will come into being through selecting the right staff, training them in customer care, setting up robust systems for dealing with visitor enquiries and complaints, and constantly monitoring and improving the service given to customers. In addition, we need to understand our visitors and what their needs are. Let us look at these components in more detail.

Understanding your visitor

Methods of finding out about site visitors were considered in Chapter 3. One of the main reasons for carrying out visitor surveys is to gain a greater understanding of site visitors and their needs. This will be important in improving customer care on a site. After all if we do not understand what visitors' needs are, how can we expect to provide for them? Visitor surveys can help us identify a number of issues relating to customer care:

- Why do visitors choose to visit the site?
- What are the needs of visitors?
- Are these needs being met?
- What do visitors like about the site?
- What do visitors dislike about the site?
- What are visitors' expectations of the site before they visit it?
- Have these expectations been met?

Through developing an understanding of these kinds of issue, site management can be targeted more accurately to meet the needs of the visitor.

Selection of staff

If we are to gain high quality customer care we need to employ people who have the personal abilities to deal with visitors in a professional manner. It is therefore important when interviewing, to consider candidates' personal qualities in relation to their ability to provide high quality service to the customer. The following are possibly some areas that need to be considered:

- Do they have a genuine smile?
- Are they confident?
- Can they communicate effectively?
- Are they presentable?
- Do they have appropriate skills?
- Are they reliable and trustworthy?
- Can they work under pressure?

Above all, select candidates that are personable and get on with people. Whilst training can develop the skills required to deliver high quality customer care, employing the right people to start with, will make the task considerably easier.

Develop good communication skills

The development of good communication skills is central to customer care. Communication with visitors can be face-to-face, on the telephone, in writing (including e-mail) or through non-verbal language (body language).

Face-to-face

This is where you talk to visitors directly and as such can be in a variety of situations. On a countryside recreation site it may be a warden talking to visitors outside, or staff in a visitor centre answering enquiries. If you are face-to-face you will be communicating with more than just your voice. Your whole body communicates and this is known as body language. Your posture, your eyes and your location relative to the visitor will all communicate messages and attitudes. Indeed, it is believed that body language communicates more strongly than the spoken word! When talking face-to-face the following points are examples of good practice:

- Provide a warm welcome – introduce yourself and ask how you can provide assistance. Be friendly in your outlook – smile (with your mouth and eyes).
- Make positive eye contact – show that you are listening and that you are interested.
- Listen carefully and do not interrupt.
- Try to use people's names (if you know them) in your conversation.
- Avoid using jargon – speak at an appropriate level.
- Do not pretend you know the answers when you do not know them – if you do not know an answer, find it out or find somebody that does.
- Always be sure to represent your organisation – even if you do not believe in a policy you are implementing.

- Avoid threatening postures (such as a pointing finger) – use open and confident body language.
- Do not be afraid of your natural gestures – they reinforce what you are saying.
- Always finish a conversation positively – thank visitors and say goodbye like you would to a friend.

Above all, in face-to-face communication you want to make the visitor feel valued and important and to help them as efficiently and courteously as you can.

Telephone

This is similar to face-to-face communication but without the body language! As such, much of the good practice for face-to-face communication will be similar. However, the following are also important for telephone conversations:

- Answer calls quickly – use an answering machine if you are not in, and check and respond to it frequently.
- When answering a call, state clearly at the beginning who you are and who you work for and ask how you can help.
- Smile when you are talking – it shows in your voice.
- Take notes and read back any details to the caller to check you have written them down correctly.
- If you take messages for other staff members make sure you pass them on quickly and that you have recorded enough detail.
- If you promise to call back make sure you do!

Written

Written communication can be in a variety of forms. These include letters, faxes, memos, press releases and e-mail. Generally, written communication is more formal than verbal and its role is often to communicate precisely and record decisions, information and conversations. Therefore, written communication needs to be precise and accurate. Good practice in written communication includes:

- Use an appropriate form of written communication depending on the information to be conveyed and the recipient (report, internal memo, letter, e-mail).
- Write down any information accurately and check what you have written.
- Make sure grammar and spelling are correct.
- Ensure that the style of writing is appropriate (formal letter, friendly letter, report).
- Always check written work before it is sent.

Dealing with conflict situations

No matter how hard you try, there will always be situations where you have to deal with a conflict. This may be dealing with a dissatisfied visitor or approaching someone on site that is acting inappropriately. Each situation will be different and the severity of the conflict can range from sorting out a misunderstanding to a serious incident requiring police assistance. Conflict situations can be very stressful and upsetting, but if dealt with appropriately negative feelings can be minimised. One major credit card company even considers a complaint to be an opportunity. This is on the grounds that if the complaint is resolved quickly and to the satisfaction of the customer, those customers will think more highly of the company. What should you do in a conflict situation? Let us deal with a complaint situation first:

- Stay calm – do not lose your temper.
- Listen carefully to the complaint and ensure that you understand what the problem is.
- If there is an easy solution get the complainant to agree and instigate immediate action to resolve it.
- If there is no easy solution record the details and tell the complainant what action you intend to take to resolve the problem.
- Make sure action is taken if promised.
- Be sympathetic and thank the complainant for bringing the problem to your attention.
- Stay in your organisational role at all times.
- Do not enter into an argument.

If a conflict is more serious, great care needs to be taken. Of highest priority must be the safety of site visitors and site staff. All of the above points for dealing with a complaint are appropriate. However, you also need to consider the following:

- Summon help – other staff (preferably senior) and/or the police.
- Make sure you understand what the problem is.
- Ensure you have a witness to an incident.
- Keep your distance – avoid physical contact.
- Ensure that site visitors are removed from the area of an incident.
- Make sure you identify who you are and the organisation you work for.
- Explain what the problem is and state clearly what action you wish to occur.
- Try and find common ground that can be agreed upon.
- Observe and record the incident in detail – you may be required to give evidence to the police.
- Do not get personal – stay in your organisational role and do not lose your temper.
- Keep your body language non-threatening.
- Try not to take any remarks personally.

Serious incidents do not often have a simple solution. Often, the best that can occur at the time is to diffuse the situation and calm tempers. The issue to which the conflict relates can then be dealt with later, when people are calmer.

Standards of service

Standards of service are pre-defined standards that are considered to be appropriate for a particular service. Standards may well differ depending upon the location and customers' expectation of the service that they expect. So for example, a very high standard of service will be required in a top-class hotel whereas a lower standard may be acceptable in a corner café. Standards are useful to set, because they define the level of service to be achieved and as such act as benchmarks upon which service can be monitored. What sort of areas can we set standards in?

- cleanliness and frequency of inspection of toilets
- the maximum length of time someone has to wait for food
- the maximum amount of time before a written enquiry or complaint is replied to
- the amount of litter found on the ground
- the minimum standard of dress required by staff.

Obviously there is no purpose in having standards if there is no means of monitoring them and ensuring that they are adhered to. Monitoring customer care will be addressed later in this chapter.

Establish efficient systems

The development and continual improvement of systems that will help you deliver high quality customer care is important. Systems ensure that members of staff know what to do in differing circumstances and what standards they should seek to achieve. Any systems developed need to be as simple as possible and staff need to be trained in their implementation. In addition, it is the role of managers to check the systems are working and that standards are being kept to. What sort of systems are we talking about?

Dealing with complaints – in the previous section we looked at how to deal with complaints. Often these can be dealt with and addressed immediately. Even if the complaint is satisfactorily resolved it is useful to have a system for recording what the problem was, why it occurred and what action was taken. This could be as simple as having a site complaint book in which all complaints are recorded. This can then be reviewed on a regular basis to work out ways in which complaints can be avoided. However, some complaints cannot be dealt with straight away. For these there needs to be a system through which they can be resolved. Possibilities include:

- having a system for recording the complaint and monitoring what action is taken
- deciding who should be responsible for dealing with complaints
- having a procedure for resolving complex or contentious complaints
- setting a standard for the maximum length of time before a letter of complaint is responded to
- having an appeals procedure.

Communication – good customer care will require responding to customer enquiries quickly and ensuring that any issue that may impact upon the visitor is responded to efficiently. To do this, it is often necessary to communicate between different members of staff. The use of radios, mobile phones or pagers will ensure that all staff are contactable to deal with enquiries, or problems as they come up. However, communication is about more than contacting people. Communication between staff is important to allow issues to be discussed, ideas to be raised, messages to be forwarded, policies to be communicated and staff and management to talk to each other. Communication between staff can be in many forms. These include:

- memorandums
- e-mails
- notices
- one-to-one meetings
- staff meetings
- staff workshops
- staff training.

Each of these methods will be appropriate for different purposes. It is important to ensure that there are communication routes by which front line staff can communicate with management, as well as management with staff.

Regular checking of facilities – to ensure that sites are maintained at a high standard, facilities on site need to be checked on a regular basis. This can range from a weekly walk around a site to check for vandalism, to hourly checks of the toilets. Checks can be informal or more systematic. This may mean detailing how often particular facilities are checked and the time at which they should be checked. It may also necessitate the creation of forms that ensure that facilities are checked systematically. For example, if there is a children's playground on the site it will be necessary for health and safety reasons to check it regularly. A checklist of items to be checked and tick boxes and comments sections can be drawn up. This may include issues such as:

- Is the slide securely attached to the ground?
- Is the ladder in a safe condition?
- Is the slide in a safe condition?
- What is the condition of the slide landing?
- Are the safety mats in a safe condition?
- Are there any hazards on the ground around the slide?

At the end of an inspection the form should be dated, signed and filed for future reference. It can then be used in monitoring of standards and as evidence, for example in the event of an accident.

Training

Training is an important element of customer care. Whilst many employees will have good skills in relation to dealing with visitors, extra training will improve these skills. In addition to improving skill levels, the standards expected by the organisation in dealing with visitors can be shared and developed with all employees. It must be remembered that many recreation sites are heavily dependent on volunteers to assist in their running. It is important to ensure that these volunteers are adequately trained as well as the full-time staff. What areas of training are required?

Induction – when new members of staff are employed they need to have initial training called induction. Induction is often poorly carried out by organisations and new employees are frequently thrown in at the deep end and learn the job from trial and error. This is a very hit and miss approach to such an expensive item as a member of staff. It is much better to develop an induction-training package that covers systematically the initial knowledge and skills an employee requires when starting a job. What elements should be in induction training?

- Developing an understanding of the organisation – its mission, history, values, structure, internal communication systems, rules and regulations
- Site orientation – gaining an understanding of the layout of a site, site features and what it is like to visit a site as a visitor
- Communication skills – how to deal with customers on the phone, face-to-face, in writing or by e-mail
- Dealing with difficulties – how do you deal with difficult customers and difficult enquiries?
- Technical skills required to carry out the job – such as setting up a till, site security, machinery, and computers
- Health and safety requirements – fire, accidents, hygiene, and prevention of accidents
- Dress and appearance conduct – what standard of dress and appearance are acceptable?

It is suggested that induction training should be carried out as soon as a new employee starts a new job. Whilst induction training may cover the above it will not get to any real depth and further training will be required periodically.

Ongoing training – induction will be the first stage of customer care training. However, it is only the first stage. The customer care skills outlined at the induction stage need to be refreshed and developed to higher levels, on a regular basis. There will never be a time when staff are fully trained. There is always something new to learn and skills to develop and strengthen. What forms of training are there?

- formal, externally run courses (courses run external to the organisation)
- formal, internally run courses (courses run within an organisation)
- conferences
- on the job training
- job swops.

All of these are very valuable. Training is not a luxury item. It is an essential part of ensuring that high quality customer care is delivered and that countryside recreation sites are run and managed to the highest possible standards. As such it needs to be considered as an integral part of site management and needs to have a sufficient budget set aside for it to be effective.

Make continual improvements

To have a high quality of customer care we need to continually adjust and improve the service we deliver to visitors. Before we can do this we need to have mechanisms to consider where to make adjustments and improvements. What mechanisms can we use to consider how to improve customer care?

Monitoring standards – earlier in this chapter we considered the setting of standards of service and suggested that to be effective these need to be monitored. To make this happen it is useful to have performance targets for service, which can be objectively measured. An example of this may be having a performance indicator for litter as 'no more than ten items of litter on the ground within a given area'. Performance indicators are not possible in all areas. For example, it is difficult to quantify how friendly a member of staff is. In such cases, standards may need to be assessed more creatively, for example by the use of welcome audits (see below).

Surveys – asking customers what they think about the customer care they have received on a recreation site, is important. After all customer care is all about the customer! In Chapter 3, we considered in detail, methods of finding out about the visitor. The main methods that can be used to find out more about what customers think are:

- face-to-face questionnaire surveys
- self-completion questionnaires (for example a questionnaire form left in a visitor centre or refreshment area, for visitors to fill in)
- focus groups
- telephone surveys (providing you have contact phone numbers)
- observation.

If you remember, surveys can be quantitative (collecting numeric data) or qualitative (non-numeric). For customer care qualitative surveys may be particularly important as they provide feedback on feeling and attitudes.

Suggestion boxes – the use of suggestion boxes provides a simple mechanism by which visitors can help to improve customer care. These involve providing a small, easy to fill in form, upon which visitors can write down their suggestions for improving the site or the service offered by its staff. Pens need to be provided as well as a box to deposit the suggestions. Suggestion boxes are best located where visitors stop for a period of time such as at a refreshment area. The box needs to be emptied on a regular basis and a team of staff review the suggestions, to see if and how they can be implemented. Suggestion boxes need to be designed to be obvious and not hidden in corners.

Staff feedback – staff that deal with visitors will often overhear visitors' comments and will have their own ideas on how to improve customer service. It is therefore useful to hold regular forums in which issues, solutions and ideas can be raised with management and, if appropriate, acted upon.

Monitoring complaints – earlier in this chapter ways of dealing with complaints were considered. It was suggested that some form of monitoring complaints was good practice. This could be in the form of a complaint book or complaint form, which is filled in for every complaint. These can be reviewed periodically and appropriate action taken, to ensure that complaints are minimised.

Welcome audits – in Chapter 2, welcome audits were discussed. Welcome audits are where someone who has not been to the site before visits the site pretending to be a visitor and systematically checks up on aspects of its management. An important element of this may well be the service provided by staff, as well as the quality of the site infrastructure.

The cycle of service – visitors come into contact with components of a site and its staff at different stages during their stay there. Each contact will have an impact upon the visitors' impression of the site and the organisation that manages it. These contacts can be mapped onto paper to enable a full visualisation to occur, to allow 'moments of truth' to be identified. This mapping of site/staff visitor contacts is called a cycle of service. A cycle will start from the first contact about the site and will end when the visitor returns home. A typical cycle of service for a countryside recreation site can be seen below.

For every episode included in the diagram, details of the nature of the interaction between the visitor and the site or site staff need to be considered. This is because every small episode that occurs on a visit will impact upon the visitor's perception of the quality of the product, the service and the organisation. By considering a cycle of service we can consider exactly what happens to visitors during all aspects of their visit and identify areas of weakness where improvements can be made. It is therefore a useful tool in improving customer care.

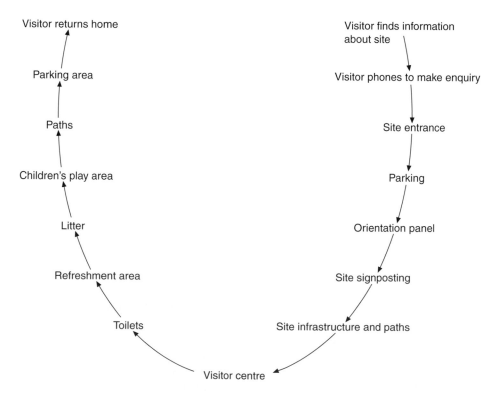

Figure 8.1 A cycle of service for a visit to a countryside site

References and further reading

Countryside Recreation Network (1993) *Customer Care in the Countryside*, Cardiff: Countryside Recreation Network.

Christopher, M. (1992) *The Customer Service Planner*, Oxford: Butterworth-Heinemann.

O'Sullivan, E. (1991) *Marketing for Parks, Recreation and Leisure*, PA: Venture Publishing Inc.

Payne, A., Christopher, M., Clark, M. and Peck, H. (1995) *Relationship Marketing for Competitive Advantage: Winning and Keeping Customers*, Oxford: Butterworth-Heinemann.

Seaton, A. V. and Bennett, M. M. (1996) *Marketing Tourism Products: Concepts, Issues, Cases*, London: International Thompson Business Press.

Ward, J., Higson, P. and Campbell, W. (1994) *Advanced Leisure and Tourism*, Cheltenham: Stanley Thornes (Publishers) Ltd.

Youell, R. (2000) *Travel and Tourism*, Harlow: Longman.

9 Information and interpretation

High quality information, both on and off site, is needed to enable visitors to make informed decisions. Interpretation helps visitors to understand and enjoy a site, makes them aware of the importance of site features and can be used to influence behaviour. Information and interpretation, forms an interface between the managing organisation and the visitor, and as such, needs to be of high quality. This chapter considers the provision of information and interpretation and highlights good practice in its planning and delivery.

Information

In providing people with information we are giving them the facts, figures and knowledge to make informed decisions. For example, providing details about the routes of walks on a site, (such as length of walk, difficulty, features of walk, disabled access) allows the visitor to make an informed choice about where to go. These details are items of information. What sort of information can we provide about recreation sites?

- opening times
- bus times
- entrance charges
- directions
- distance
- details of attractions and facilities
- facilities for the disabled
- details of events
- accommodation
- the bird species seen on a site that day.

Information is a powerful tool in the management of countryside recreation sites. It can be used to influence:

> *Where* people go – by providing information we can influence the sites that people go to, or the locations within sites that people go to.
> *When* people go – by letting people know about opening times, or the timing of events.

How people get to a site – provision of clear information on how to get to it by car, public transport or bike.

What they do when they get to the site – what are the attractions of the site and how do they get to them?

Who goes to a site – information can be targeted at particular market segments.

Above all the provision of information increases visitors' confidence and makes them feel in control of what they are doing. Information can be provided in many forms. Successful information has two key features.

It is easily accessible – when a visitor feels they need some information to help them to make a decision, it is available without them having to work too hard to find it such as having a timetable at a bus stop or a footpath sign at a junction.

It is easy to use – the information provided needs to be unambiguous and user friendly such as ensuring signposts are well designed or timetables are laid out as simply and clearly as possible.

What methods are at our disposal to provide visitors with information? There are a wide variety of ways of providing information. The choice of which to use depends on budget, purpose of the information and target audience. The following are some examples:

- leaflets
- guides/publications/books
- posters
- advertising
- signs
- computers – touch screen/Internet
- town crier
- sandwich board
- the media
- tourist information centres/visitor centres
- displays/panels
- maps
- person-to-person contact.

Details of these methods, and good practice in their implementation, have already been covered in previous chapters (Chapters 4 and 5).

Interpretation

What is interpretation?

The father of interpretation Freeman Tilden, defined interpretation as: 'An educational activity which aims to reveal meanings and relationships through the use of original objects, by firsthand experience, and by illustrative media, rather than simply communicate factual information' (Tilden 1957: 8).

There are three important words in this definition, they are *reveal*, *meanings* and *relationships*. This is very different from information, which uses facts and figures to inform the visitor. Tilden stated: 'Information, as such is not interpretation. Interpretation is revelation based upon information. But they are entirely different things. However all interpretation contains information' (Tilden 1957: 18).

Interpretation aims to develop understanding and as Tilden puts it, reveal meanings and relationships. This is done by using the skills of an interpreter, who uses a range of techniques and media to get the job done. More recent definitions of interpretation define it with a greater focus on the potential outputs. For example, the Association of Heritage Interpretation, defines interpretation as: 'The process of communicating to people the significance of a place or object so that they may enjoy it more, understand their heritage and environment better, and develop a positive attitude to conservation' (Association of Heritage Interpretation 2001).

This definition whilst having much in common with Tilden's, emphasises significance, enjoyment, understanding and positive attitude. These are very outcome based and imply that interpretation has specific outcomes that it will seek to achieve.

Interpretation then, is a communication process whereby meanings, relationships and understanding are developed, rather than merely providing information. It aims to get to the deeper truth behind facts, figures, objects and locations and develop a sense of wonder. In addition, it may seek to achieve outcomes such as enhancing visitor enjoyment, changing attitudes and influencing behaviour. Good interpretation should provide the WOW factor. It should provoke and challenge, educate and inform, and seek to develop a better understanding, empathy and attitude for our surroundings and our heritage. With good interpretation a castle becomes someone's home, a bird's nest a work of art and craftsmanship and a single rock an amazing piece of environmental history.

Example of interpretation that only contains information

WOODLANDS

The woodland you see before you is at least two hundred years old. It contains oak, sycamore, ash and holly trees. Fifteen species of birds live in the wood including robin, redstart and pied flycatcher. The wood is also important for insects with one hundred and eighty species recorded.

The same site explained using good interpretive practice

WHY IS THIS WOOD IMPORTANT?

This amazing old wood is home to many interesting and uncommon animals, plants and insects. Being old it has had time for different species to take up residence there. Ancient woods like this are becoming uncommon, as agriculture and development have caused woodlands to be chopped down. For plants and animals this is like someone knocking your house down. Help us to look after this special site by staying on paths and not picking the flowers.

Why interpret?

Interpretation takes time and money to develop. Why should countryside recreation sites invest in it? Let us look at what the possible outcomes can be for interpretation. In other words what can interpretation achieve? The following are some of the key areas that interpretation can address:

Goals for the visitor

Interpretation should aim to impact upon the visitor by:

- providing recreation and enhancing enjoyment
- heightening awareness and understanding of the natural and cultural environment
- inspiring and adding perspective to people's lives.

For the visitor therefore, interpretation is about improving the enjoyment and satisfaction they get from their visit, increasing their awareness and understanding and enhancing the quality of their lives. It must be remembered that visitors come to sites for enjoyment. We must therefore endeavour to stimulate them, not 'educate' them.

Goals for the site

Interpretation can be used as a tool for site management by:

- fostering the proper use of the site
- developing advocates for the site.

Tilden wrote: 'Through interpretation – understanding, through understanding – appreciation, through appreciation – protection' (Tilden 1957: 38).

This is very much the philosophy of interpretation as it relates to a site. If we can get visitors to understand why a place is special they will appreciate it more. If they appreciate it more, they are likely to change their behaviour in relation to it and protect it. Interpretation can therefore be used as a management tool to change visitor behaviour. For example, visitors are more likely to stay on a boardwalk across a bog if they understand why the bog is special and the damage they are likely to cause if they walk on its surface. In addition, by fostering an appreciation for a site we are more likely to develop site advocates who may become voluntary wardens, become friends of a site, become involved in the management or just keep an eye on the site as they walk their dog.

Goals for the managing organisation

Interpretation can be a very useful tool in furthering organisational objectives. It can do this by:

- increasing the visitor's knowledge of who manages a site
- developing visitors' understanding and support for the managing agencies' role, management objectives and policies.

On many sites interpretation is one of the main ways for an organisation to make contact with the visitor. It is common to see logos on interpretation and very often design will conform to an organisational house style. Interpretation may also carry messages about the function of the organisation and what it stands for. As such, interpretation can be seen as propaganda for an organisation and indeed it frequently is. Organisations through interpretation often seek to develop a positive image in the public's eye.

Having defined what interpretation is and what it seeks to achieve, let us now consider how you go about ensuring that interpretation is effective.

What makes interpretation effective?

If we are to make interpretation effective we must ensure that we understand what makes one item of interpretation work and another not. What are the key concepts responsible for making interpretation effective? There are three critical elements that have a big impact on making interpretation work. These are: provoke, relate, reveal.

Interpretation should provoke

If you want to grab someone's attention – provoke them. It is bound to catch their interest. Interpretation should endeavour to make people think and challenge their knowledge, beliefs and understanding. The use of questions is a good method of provocation. So for example, you could imagine an interpretive panel that has as its title: 'How a glacier shaped this valley'.

Whilst this looks fine on the surface, it does nothing to provoke. A better title may be: 'Why is a glacier like a file?'

This title does not say as much about what the panel is about as the first, but seeks to provoke curiosity. It is put in the form of a riddle and people are always curious to find the answer to a riddle. It will provoke them to read the story that follows which will explain how a glacier erodes and shapes a landscape. If you like, the provocative question acts as a baited hook that you hope the visitor will bite. Having grabbed attention, you can then tell a story. Provocation is not just something you use at the start of interpretation. It can be used throughout interpretive text or during a verbal presentation. In interpretation provocation is important.

Interpretation should relate

Everything we learn is based upon what we already know. Our past experiences and knowledge of the world, form the building blocks upon which new knowledge is built. It is important therefore, to *relate* new subject matter to what people will already know. We must remember when interpreting to the general public, that their knowledge of science or history may be very thin and will certainly vary from person to person. However, there will be shared knowledge of a more basic kind that we can tap into. In the example above, a glacier was likened to a file. This *relates* to what people will already know. People will have an understanding of what a file is, what it does and how it works. The file is an analogy for the more complex processes at work when a glacier erodes its bed. A link can then be made in people's minds between the action of a glacier and that of a file. Whenever we

Plate 9.1 Interpretation should relate

interpret, we must endeavour to relate what we say to what the audience will already know.

Interpretation should reveal

Having been provoked, and examined related knowledge, we need to reveal the answer! The revelation in interpretation should be the 'Oh yes, now I understand' section. If people have to do a little bit of work to obtain the revelation, this is to their advantage. So for example, having been provoked with the title 'Why is a glacier like a file?' and related it to the analogy of a file, the story of how a glacier erodes can be told revealing the answer.

As well as these three cornerstones of interpretation, there are many other issues to consider in making sure that your interpretation works in achieving its initial aims. Let us consider these one by one.

> *Only interpret what you can see* – this goes back to the issue of making sure that interpretation relates. If you cannot see what you are trying to interpret, it is going to be very difficult for the visitor to relate to what you are saying.
>
> *Interpretation should be fun* – people do not go out into the countryside to be educated! People go out to have a good time. If we wish visitors to invest their time in reading some interpretation or listening to a guide, it is important that they will get some enjoyment from it. If you like, they need a reward for the effort they are putting in. You can be sure that if there is no quick reward, they will withdraw from the interpretation and find something more interesting to

Plate 9.2 Interpretation should reveal

do! In addition, people learn better when they are enjoying the experience. In the business it is called recreational learning.

Interpretation should be used sparingly – one of the difficulties for interpretation, is knowing what to interpret. You cannot interpret everything on a site! Before deciding on developing some interpretation, always ask what the purpose of it is and if it is really needed. Too much interpretation on a site can lead to visitors switching off from it. Decide what you wish to interpret, be sure why you are doing it and do not overdo it!

Keep it short and sweet – research shows again and again that people looking at interpretive panels have short attention spans. If you write too much or talk too long, the visitor will switch off. Keep it short! For example, it is suggested that one hundred is the maximum number of words you should have on an interpretive panel.

Good design attracts attention – if an item of interpretation is well designed graphically then it will attract attention. Remember first impressions count. Visitors will make a very quick decision upon viewing an item of interpretation, as to whether they are going to invest their time in looking at it. If you get the design wrong, you will have lost them before you start. Good design will demand visitors' attention.

A picture paints a thousand words – good graphics and photographs will be easier for the visitor to understand than text. A good graphic for example, of what a ruined castle would have looked like when it was at its prime, will be far more effective than trying to describe it. Plate 9.3 shows some of the things that

Plate 9.3 An interpretation panel that shows through pictures the use that elephants make of their trunks

elephants use their trunks for and shows how images can be used as powerful aids to interpretation. Even if we are using the spoken word as our interpretive medium we can paint word pictures to help visitors gain understanding.

Variety improves effectiveness – too much of the same becomes monotonous and boring and will lead visitors to 'switch off'. Try to use a variety of interpretive media to keep it fresh and interesting. Research shows that people learn best when using a variety of senses. Interpretation should therefore seek to engage as many senses as possible. In particular, people learn most when actively engaged in doing something. The development of interactive items of interpretation is therefore good practice.

The thrill of discovery – discovery makes learning fun. This links to revelation again. We all like finding things out and discovering new things. Man is naturally inquisitive and discovery is part of this process. Discovery could occur by having a question answered or by making the visitor do some work to obtain an answer. Interactive exhibits are very effective in this way. For example, by posing a question on the door of a kitchen cupboard, such as: 'What food do you think you would find in a Victorian kitchen cupboard?', provokes the visitor into thinking and being inquisitive about what the answer might be. The visitor can then open the cupboard door and discover it. This is more rewarding than just reading.

Knowing the usefulness of the knowledge makes learning more effective – if someone told you they had a method of picking the numbers for the lottery that gave you an absolute certainty of winning the jackpot, you would listen intently. If visitors are given the reason why the knowledge the interpretation seeks to give them is important, they will gain more from it. For example, an interpretive panel on a bog may be designed to keep visitors on wooden boardwalks to avoid damage to the sphagnum moss. The text may read:

> *Do you know that you can damage the bog?*
>
> A single footprint on the bog can take twenty years to disappear! Imagine the damage that many feet can do. Help us to look after this amazing place by walking only on the wooden boardwalks provided.

In this example, visitors are told about the damage that walking on the bog can do before being requested not to do it. Note that the text provokes, relates and reveals.

You cannot beat being there – first hand experience is far more stimulating than looking at photographs and videos in a visitor centre. Interpretation is likely to be at its most powerful when the visitor is directly in contact with the subject matter being interpreted. The best place to interpret woodland is in woodland; the best place to interpret the way of life of a Viking is in a reconstructed Viking settlement.

Organised interpretation is more effective than unorganised – interpretation needs to be organised. That is, it needs to be focused and presented in a logical order. To do this you need to organise it carefully. Let us now look at how this can be done.

Organising your interpretation

In order to organise interpretation we need to consider: topics, themes, stories.
Let us consider each of these in turn.

Topics

One of the biggest problems that we face when undertaking any interpretation is deciding what to interpret. For example, in a woodland, there are hundreds of possibilities ranging from the management of the habitat to the birds that live in it, from insect camouflage to the life history of fungi. Choosing a topic or several topics to interpret helps us to organise the subject matter that we wish to interpret. So for example, if we are carrying out some interpretation about a woodland, we may decide that the topic we wish to interpret is 'the management of the woodland'. Our topic therefore is: management of the woodland.

We may have decided this by first looking at a range of potential topics and thinking about what it is that we think is important for the visitor to know about the woodland. This can then be narrowed down to a topic. A topic is therefore the subject matter to be interpreted.

Themes

A theme is the specific message we wish to tell about a topic. So for example, the topic in the above section was 'the management of the woodland'. Even with a topic such as this, there are many possible stories to tell. We therefore use the development of theme statements to help us organise what it is about the management of the woodland, that we wish to communicate. If you like, we are deciding what the *message* is we wish to get across with the interpretation. We normally write a theme down as a full statement that is in sentence form. For the topic 'management of the woodland' we may decide the theme should be: 'Woodland glades are created to increase the number of butterflies'.

The theme statement is the message you would like people to remember after they have used the interpretation. For the same topic we could also have the themes:

Theme: bird boxes are placed in trees to provide homes for pied flycatchers.
Theme: rhododendron is cut down because if left, it will eventually destroy the woodland.
Theme: sheep are excluded from the woodland because they eat the young trees and woodland plants.

The theme statement helps you to consider and organise the message that you wish visitors to go away with. When they leave, visitors will remember broad messages from interpretation and not the detail. It is therefore important when interpreting, to develop clear messages and writing clear theme statements helps in this process. In this example, when visitors leave the woods we want them to understand that glades have been created to increase the number of butterflies.

Themes can come in a number of levels. First we may develop an overall theme for a site. This is the principal message we wish visitors to go away with, having visited our site. This can then be broken down into smaller sub-themes, each of which reflects the overall theme and collectively delivers the overall theme. So for the woodland, we can organise the message of our interpretation thus:

Topic   Management of the woodlands.
Site theme   The woodland is managed for the benefit of the plants and animals that live within it.
Sub-themes   Bird boxes are placed in trees to provide homes for pied flycatchers.
               Rhododendron is cut down, because if left it will eventually destroy the woodland.
               Sheep are excluded from the woodland because they eat the young trees and woodland plants.
               Glades in the woodland are created to increase the number of butter-flies.

However it may be better to structure the topics and themes in a manner that they can be related directly one to another. Figure 9.1 shows how we could plan some topics and themes for some interpretation of Cardigan Bay (a large bay off the west coast of Wales):

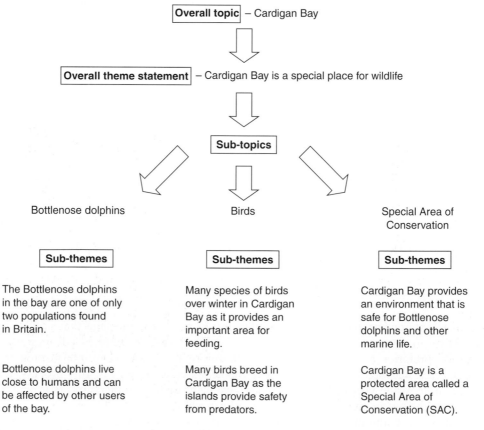

Figure 9.1 Planning topics, themes, sub-topics and sub-themes for interpreting Cardigan Bay

It can be seen from Figure 9.1 that these topic, themes, sub-topics and sub-themes provide a structure for developing for example, a leaflet or a series of interpretive panels. The next stage in developing interpretation, is the development of themes into stories.

Stories

Having developed topics and themes for our interpretation, we now need to tell a story. This is because the format of a story is a very effective form of communication. Every day we encounter stories in a variety of forms, whether reading a novel, watching a soap opera on television or when reading a newspaper. Indeed, we encounter stories from the youngest age. Much of young children's early learning comes in story form. We are therefore very used to absorbing information in this form.

What are the component parts of a story? Well, all stories have a beginning. This sets the scene for the rest of the story. If we do not attract visitors' attention quickly, with a good beginning then we will have lost them before we start. We then move onto the meat of the story in which we move in a logical sequence through what we wish to get across. The story finishes with a good 'out' in which we conclude and sum up what we have been saying. We must remember that interpretive stories must always focus on the themes we have set (the message we wish to get across). You can imagine an interpretive panel for a woodland as telling the following story:

Topic	Management of the woodlands.
Site theme	The woodland is managed for the benefit of the plants and animals that live in it.
Sub-theme	Glades in the woodland are created to increase the number of butterflies.
Story	Sun traps for sunbathing butterflies.

You may have wondered why the trees in front of you have been cut down. The truth is that butterflies like it hot! They need the sunshine to give them enough energy to feed, mate and reproduce. This area of woodland has therefore been cleared of trees to provide them with a sheltered sun trap in which to sunbathe. On a warm summer's day you will see many types of butterfly here.

By using topics, themes and stories we organise our interpretation.

Setting objectives for our interpretation

Earlier on in the chapter we considered the purposes of interpretation. When organising interpretation we must always remember what it is we wish the interpretation to do for us. To help us with this we can develop *interpretive objectives*. An interpretive objective is a statement of what is to be achieved through an item of interpretation. Normally interpretive objectives will be linked to a theme statement and will be measurable. Interpretive objectives come in several forms:

- *Learning objectives*: specific objectives about what we expect the visitor to have learnt having encountered an item of interpretation.
- *Behavioural objectives*: specific objectives about what behavioural changes we expect to occur in the visitor, having encountered an item of interpretation.
- *Emotional objectives*: specific objectives about the emotional changes we expect to occur in the visitor, having encountered an item of interpretation.

For the woodland we have been considering what the interpretive objectives may be:

- *Learning objective*: by the time visitors leave the site the majority will realise that the woodland is managed for the plants and animals that live there.
- *Behavioural objective*: by the time visitors leave the site the majority will know that they should not pick the wild flowers.
- *Emotional objective*: by the time they leave, 50 per cent of visitors will feel that the site is a special place and should be conserved.

Interpretive objectives help us to focus on what we are seeking to achieve and as we will see later, have an important role to play in evaluating if interpretation is effective. We can write interpretive objectives for the overall site theme or for sub-themes.

Writing interpretive text

Writing high quality interpretive text is difficult and is something that needs to be practised and developed. The first question you must ask before starting to write is, 'Are you the right person to write the text?' There may be someone in your organisation more gifted in writing than you or you could even employ a professional writer. Writing interpretive text will become easier and the text will be of higher quality if it follows some basic guidelines.

> *Provoke, relate, and reveal* – all interpretive text should provoke, relate and reveal. This has been discussed earlier in the chapter. It is the foundation of all interpretive text.
>
> *Amount of text* – be brief. You are not writing a novel! If possible keep text to 50 words or less. If text is too long it takes too much effort to read it. This is particularly true if it is all in one block. Being brief is difficult. Mark Twain once wrote to a friend 'I would have written you a shorter letter, but I didn't have the time'. In order to be brief, it is important you are sure what your theme is, and stick to it.
>
> *Age of target group* – always be aware of who you are writing for and write in an appropriate style and for a particular age group. A tabloid newspaper such as the *Sun* has a reading age of 11, whereas the *Independent* has a reading age of 15 or 16. What is it that influences the reading age of text? First the size of sentences is important since short sentences are easier to read than long ones. Second the size of the words used is also significant. Polysyllabic (words of many syllables) words in the text, make it harder to read. If in doubt, keep the words simple and the sentences short.

Use personal words – the use of words like *you*, and *we* can and should be used in interpretive text. It helps in making text relate to the reader and can provoke a response. For example, the sentence 'People in Roman times felt the cold of winter, just like you and me', relates the people in Roman times to people today by the use of the pronouns 'you' and 'me'.

Make a positive start – like the first line of a novel, the first line of interpretive text is important. It should capture and retain attention and give the reader a good idea of the message in the text. If you like, the first line gives the reader the theme. If you get the first line wrong you may have lost the reader before they get to the second line.

Active words – words are the writer's tools and need to be used with precision. The choice of the words can make a big difference as to how readable a piece of text is and what is conveyed by the text. Wherever possible use active words that paint a picture of what you are trying to convey. Think of how many words there are to describe how water moves in rivers and streams: meandering, flowing, babbling, tinkling, roaring, flooding . . .

Each of these conveys their own mental image of what is being described. 'The albatrosses' thin wings help them to soar majestically across the ocean' is so much more descriptive than 'Albatrosses have long narrow wings to help them fly over the oceans'.

Cut jargon – there are many technical words that people with expertise in a particular field use on a regular basis and have considerable meaning for them. Words like 'habitat', 'Neolithic', 'biodiversity' and 'photosynthesis' all have considerable significance to those that know what they mean. However, the visitor may not know what these words mean and if used, will make the text more difficult to understand and as such increase the likelihood that the reader will lose interest. If possible use simpler words that convey the meaning without the necessity for more complex terms.

Having written the first draft of some interpretive text we should now measure it against a checklist:

- Does the text convey the chosen topic and theme?
- Does the text tell a story?
- Does the text provoke, relate and reveal?
- Is the text written appropriately for the intended audience (reading age, likely interest . . .)?
- Is the text too long?
- Does it have a positive start?
- Have you used active words?
- Have you used personal words?
- Have you cut out jargon?
- Could you have conveyed anything in the text better with a diagram or graphics?

Once the text has been checked against these criteria it should be shown to other people (preferably of the target group that the text is intended for) to ensure it is understood and to check if the chosen message is being conveyed.

Finally proof-read the text to check for spelling and grammatical errors.

Designing for interpretation

Design is an important part of interpretation and can influence significantly its effectiveness. The first impression visitors often get of a site or organisation is through information and interpretation. As such, design will be important in conveying the image you wish the public to have of you. In addition to this important first impression, good design is important for the following reasons:

- It will draw attention and hold it.
- It will guide the reader through a sequence of titles, text and graphics in an ordered and sequential manner.
- It will help develop an image for a site and the managing organisation (house style).

As design is so important, before you embark on it, ask yourself if you are the best person to be doing it. Design is not a skill that we all inherit, but is a skill that can be learnt. This section of the chapter will outline some design basics that will assist you in considering design but this will not make you a design expert. It may be a wise decision not to do the design yourself but to use a professional graphic artist instead. However, if you choose this route you still need to brief the graphic artist as to what you require and it is worthwhile drafting some ideas to discuss with them, prior to setting to work.

Design basics

Design is all about understanding what it is that directs the eye to do certain things. Look at Plate 9.4 and consider what your eyes do when looking at it.

Plate 9.4 Good design can lead the reader through an interpretive panel in a sequential manner

It is likely that you will be first drawn to the neck and head of the crane and will follow its neck along to its bill. This points towards the title 'red crowned crane' and it is likely that you will look at this next. The eye may then be drawn to the photos and then sequentially through the text. The simple design of this panel therefore takes you through the contents of the panel in an ordered manner.

It is therefore important in design to have a grasp of what it is that influences what draws the eye and why? There are a number of elements to consider:

- Large photos normally attract the eye more than small ones.
- Dark areas normally attract the eye more than light ones.
- Colour normally draws the eye more than black and white.
- Design elements placed on the outside of the page normally attract the eye ahead of those placed in the centre.

All of the above can be considered to be elements of design that have a 'weighting'. A large photo for example, is considered to have larger weighting than a small one. Good design should try and balance out the weighting of elements across a whole page or panel. This can be done in two ways. First we can make formal designs where the design is more or less symmetrical. Second we can create informal designs. These are not symmetrical but use design to balance the differing weightings of the design elements within the design. An example of informal design can be seen in Plate 9.5. Informal designs are generally considered to be more interesting than formal ones.

Plate 9.5 An example of an informal design

In addition to the weightings of design elements, the following will influence the sequence in which items are viewed. Readers tend to:

- start viewing items from the top left-hand corner and look at the bottom right-hand corner last
- move from illustrations to type
- move from big items to small ones
- move from colour to non-colour
- move from unusual shapes to usual ones.

All of the above information can be of great assistance in planning design and considering the sequencing of interpretation.

Photographs and graphics

Earlier in the chapter, we considered that a picture is worth a thousand words. Good graphics and photographs are an important component of interpretation. They can be used to provide detail of what can be seen (such as birds or flowers), illustrate historical events or show what cannot be seen (for example the inside of a badger's set). Where photographs and graphics are used they should be of high quality and clearly illustrate the subject matter and theme being interpreted. They should always relate to the text and should have a caption to ensure their meaning and relevance is clear. Where possible include people in the photographs or graphics as they help to relate what is being interpreted to the visitor.

Colour and contrast

The use of colour adds interest to design. Colour attracts attention and can give a distinct feel to a design. Bright colours make design lively whilst more pastel colours provide a more relaxed feel. The more colours used the more expensive the interpretation will be, as each colour needs to be printed separately. Impressive effects can be created by using one or two colours on a coloured background (for example coloured paper). Full colour will be the most expensive but will allow colour photographs to be printed. In addition, shades or tones of a colour can be used to add interest even where only one or two colours are used. Choosing colours that both contrast and complement each other is important, in that it makes elements of the design stand out more effectively whilst providing harmony to the design.

Simplicity and unity

The acronym 'KISS', 'Keep It Short and Simple', springs to mind when considering design. Over-elaboration and over-complication makes interpretation more difficult to use and therefore hinders effectiveness. Simple and straightforward designs make interpretation easier to use. Strive for designs that have a distinct unity. This can be achieved for example, by using a similar typeface throughout a design or repeating design elements. Complementary colours also assist in achieving a unified feel to a design.

Selection of interpretive media

It should be noticed that this section comes after planning the topics, themes and stories to be interpreted. This is the way it should be. You can only choose the correct media once you know what you want to interpret and to whom. There is a wide variety of media that can be used as vehicles for interpretation. These can be broken down into a number of categories:

> *Textural* – leaflets, panels, guidebooks, newspapers.
> *Item based* – artefacts, models, reconstructions.
> *Technological* – computers, videos, tape/slide, animatronics.
> *Person- to-person* – guides, theatre, guided walks, re-enactment.

The choice of which media to use will depend on a range of issues. First and foremost we must understand the benefits and drawbacks of each media type. We must then select the correct media to use to get the chosen topic, theme and story across. Issues that need to be considered in making this choice include:

> *Finance* – each media type will cost differing amounts. This can range from the cheap to the very expensive.
> *Location* – the location of the interpretation will influence the media selected. For example, tape/slide sequences may be very appropriate inside a building but will be difficult to use outside.
> *Vandalism* – is the location of the interpretation prone to vandalism?
> *Longevity* – how long will the interpretation last for?
> *Target audience* – what media will suit the target audience? For example, computers may be very good for children but may not be suitable for elderly visitors.
> *Maintenance and reliability* – how reliable are the media and what are the likely maintenance considerations?
> *How interactive is the media* – some media require the visitor to take part in the interpretation, whilst other media involve passive learning.
> *What skills are at your disposal* – some media, such as panels are relatively easy to develop, whereas others will require a high level of skill and knowledge (for example tape/slide sequences).

Having looked at these issues the various types of media at our disposal can be considered and the correct mix of media used to get the chosen message(s) across. Table 9.1 shows a selection of commonly used interpretive media and summarises their benefits and negative aspects of the media.

The media shown in Table 9.1, only reflect some of those more commonly used. Every opportunity should be taken to be creative in thinking about places where interpretation can take place. Why not interpret the water cycle in the toilets, a site map on the café table tops or have a message printed in the bottom of teacups? The opportunities are only limited by our imagination. Unusual forms of interpretation are often interesting and therefore draw people's attention.

Table 9.1 The benefits, negative aspects and requirements of a selection of the media available for interpretation

Interpretive medium	Description of medium	Benefits of the medium	Negative aspects of the medium and requirements
Leaflets	• Text and graphics on printed paper • Sometimes folded	• Cheap • Can be taken away and read • Easily produced • Can be taken with you on walk • Easy to update and replace	• Easily thrown away • Needs distribution system • Limited space on leaflet • Competes with other leaflets • Get soggy when wet
Panels	• Printed text and graphics on mounted panels • Many types of panel material and printing types	• Always on site • Located next to what is being interpreted • Can be read by more than one person • Cheap per unit viewing	• Can be vandalised • Initially costly • Can detract from surroundings • Prone to become dated • Prone to weather
Computers	• Text, graphics, games and quizzes on computer	• Interactive • Liked by children • Lots of information and interpretation can be delivered	• Expensive to program • Reliability of hardware • Can only be used by one person at a time • Not easy to use outside • Ignored by non-computer users
Video/film	• Story told in film or video format	• A medium the public are used to using • Can be viewed by many at the same time • Strong visual imagery	• Expensive to produce to high quality • Not easily used outside • Quality compared with television
Interactive exhibits	• Exhibits that require the visitor to interact with them	• Attract and retain attention • Learning by doing • Stimulate discussion	• Reliability • Can be expensive • Only one person can use at a time
Artefacts	• Objects to be handled, looked at and studied	• Hands on appeal • Stimulates discussion • Low cost • No text involved	• Need to be relevant • Theft • May need interpreting through other media

Table 9.1 continued

Interpretive medium	Description of medium	Benefits of the medium	Negative aspects of the medium and requirements
Re-enactment	• Re-enacting a past event such as a battle	• Visual • No text involved • Dramatic • Involves all senses • Relates past to present	• Takes a lot of organising • May be a one-off event • Requires skilled 'cast'
Reconstruction	• Reconstruction of the past such as an Iron Age settlement	• Visual • No text involved • Dramatic • Involves all senses • Relates past to present	• Needs skill and knowledge • Expensive
Third person/ animators	• Actors role playing people from the past and interacting with visitors	• Visual • Interactive • Dramatic • Relates past to present • Powerful	• Needs skilled actors • Expensive • Needs suitable location
Role play	• Visitors role play history	• Visual • Interactive • Dramatic • Relates past to present • Powerful	• Needs good organisation • Requires props • Needs suitable location
Theatre	• Theatrical events written to convey a message	• Dramatic • Visual • Strong story element • Can be interactive • Captive audience – sitting down	• Needs skilled actors • Needs a good script and direction • Limited audience size • Needs suitable location
Tape, slide, audio visual experiences	• High quality multi-projector slide shows with high quality audio	• Visual • Strong story element • Captive audience – sitting down • Powerful if done well	• Expensive • Requires expertise to produce • No interaction • Reliability
Guides/guided walks	• Person-to-person guiding	• A familiar media • Strong story telling potential • Entertaining • Questions can be asked • Flexible and interactive	• Need guides skilled in communication • Guides need good knowledge of subject • Only reaches a small audience

Evaluating interpretation

Evaluation is a frequently omitted element of interpretation. It is fundamental to the development of effective interpretation and will aid us in a number of ways:

- It can improve the development of interpretation prior to production and during production.
- It will tell us how effective interpretation has been in achieving its objectives.
- It can indicate the reasons why interpretation has not been effective.
- It can provide evidence of the effectiveness of interpretation that can be useful for political and funding purposes (justification for doing it and investing money in it).

Evaluation can therefore occur before interpretation is produced, during production and after production. As such it is an essential component of the interpretive process.

When do we evaluate interpretation?

Most people would consider that evaluation is only carried out to check the effectiveness of what has already been done. Whilst this 'post production' evaluation is valid, there are other opportunities for assessment.

Formative evaluation – it is possible to carry out important evaluation *before* you even write a word of text, or design any item of interpretation. Formative evaluation means finding out what your target audience already knows about the subject matter you are interpreting. This will help you to establish the correct level to pitch the interpretation at. For example, if the topic of your interpretation is the formation of sand dunes, you may wish to find out what people already know about it. It may be that people already have considerable understanding and therefore you may alter what you say or do, to reflect their knowledge.

Developmental evaluation – this occurs during the development of interpretation. If you like, it can be considered as testing interpretation before a final version is produced. This may prevent expensive mistakes. Developmental evaluation can involve the use of mock ups, draft text or draft designs that can be tested on the intended audience prior to final production, to check for effectiveness and to seek ways to improve and fine-tune it.

Summative evaluation – this is evaluation carried out once interpretation has been produced. Its function is to check if its objectives have been achieved. This is where it is important to have interpretive objectives, as these provide a base line against which you can check effectiveness. It could be considered that checking effectiveness 'post production' is valueless because the interpretation has already been produced, like shutting the stable door after the horse has bolted. This is not so. Summative evaluation is an essential first step before planning any new interpretation. After all how can you plan new interpretation without learning first the lessons from past mistakes? It may also be possible to make improvements to already existing interpretation to improve its effectiveness. Summative evaluation and the methods used to undertake it need to be considered at the stage of writing interpretive objectives and need to be incorporated into an interpretive plan.

What methods can we use to evaluate interpretation?

Before deciding on a method to use we need to consider what it is we wish to evaluate. We could evaluate:

- How much an item of interpretation attracts attention.
- How much an item of interpretation retains attention.
- The order in which interpretation is viewed.
- Whether an item of interpretation has achieved the objectives set for it.
- Whether the visitor has enjoyed the interpretation.
- Who views the interpretation (and who does not).

Differing methodologies will be appropriate depending on what you intend to evaluate. What methods are available and what can they evaluate?

Observation – the observation and systematic recording of visitor behaviour in relation to interpretation is a simple and cost efficient method of evaluating interpretation. To carry out observation all you need to do is randomly select visitors to observe (to obtain a representative sample), and record if they stop at an item of interpretation and the length of time that they are stationary. This will provide information on how much an item of interpretation *attracts* attention and how effective it is in *retaining* it. You can also observe and record the order in which the visitor views interpretation, to discover if they follow a sequence or are randomly browsing.

Questionnaires – questionnaires can be used to find out:

- who stops to view an item of interpretation;
- what the visitor has understood from the interpretation;
- whether the visitor enjoyed the interpretation;
- what the visitor liked and disliked about the interpretation.

The methodologies that can be adopted and the types of questions that can be asked have already been covered in Chapter 3. One of the main ways in which questionnaires can be used, is to check whether the interpretive objectives set for an item of interpretation have been achieved. To do this, you select visitors who have already finished viewing the interpretation, and ask them questions that relate to the interpretive objectives set. This will give you a good indication if you are achieving your objectives. However, there are problems with asking questions in this manner, in that visitors may already know the answers to the questions before they viewed the interpretation. If this is true, then the interpretation will have had no effect but the answers to the questionnaire will show that the objectives have been met. To get around this you need to ask the same questions to a randomly selected sample *before* exposure to interpretation and ask the same questions to a different randomly selected sample *afterwards*. By asking questions to people before they view the interpretation, you can establish what they already know and, by comparing this with the after sample the direct effect of the interpretation can be established. The difference between the two samples will indicate what visitors have learnt from the interpretation.

Interpretive planning

The planning of interpretation is essential if a high quality interpretive product is to be developed. As can be seen from the chapter so far, there is much to consider when carrying out interpretation. Dealing with it in a series of logical and sequential stages helps us through the process and keeps us focused on the task at hand. Interpretive planning is essential if messages are to be delivered in a consistent and coherent manner. It is particularly important when planning interpretation over wide areas as it allows planned linkages to occur between different items of interpretation and a consistent design style to be developed. Interpretive planning can come in many different scales from planning an individual item right up to the production of an interpretation plan for a whole country. In most instances an interpretive plan will be made for an individual site which will cover its messages, media and resource issues and develop a prioritised implementation programme. However, the process is the same for an individual item. There are many reasons to plan interpretation. These can be summarised as:

- development of individual, group and organisational consensus around agreed objectives
- developing an understanding of the resources available for interpretation
- development of clear objectives for the interpretation
- development of clear messages
- ensuring the most appropriate media mix is selected
- development of prioritised and costed implementation programmes
- development of evaluation in a planned manner.

The interpretive planning process

To maximise its effectiveness interpretation needs to be planned carefully and in a structured and sequential manner. Figure 9.2 shows the stages involved in interpretive planning.

Let us go briefly through these individual stages. Most of them have already been discussed earlier in the chapter but will be considered here in relation to interpretive planning.

Evaluation

Before planning any new evaluation it is important to review interpretation that is already on a site and check its effectiveness and learn lessons as to how to improve it. Formative evaluation can also take place to establish what the target audience already knows about the subject being interpreted.

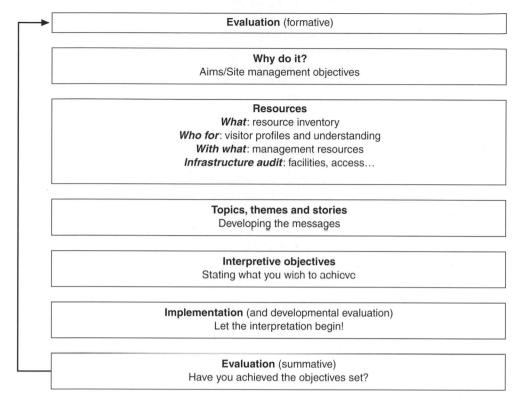

Figure 9.2 The interpretive planning process

Aims of interpretation: *why do it?*

Before planning interpretation it is vital to establish clearly the reasons why it is being done and to establish what it seeks to achieve (the aims of the interpretation). This will normally be linked to the site management objectives, but this is not always the case. The reason for the interpretation and the aims for the interpretive need to be agreed and recorded. Without establishing clearly why you are carrying out interpretation and its aims, it will be unfocused and unlikely to be effective. In addition, unless the aims for the interpretation are clearly established and recorded, it is very difficult to evaluate its success.

Resources

Having established clear aims for the interpretation it is necessary to consider resource issues. This can be broken down into:

> *What: resource inventory* – this is concerned with establishing what the physical and heritage resources are that can be used for the interpretation. It is likely that this will be a list of all possible opportunities on a site for interpretation and may include buildings, habitats, viewpoints, geological features and

archaeological artefacts. Even the inside of a toilet could be considered as an interpretive resource if thought about creatively. By systematically going through possible resources, all opportunities can be considered, not just the obvious.

Who for: visitor profiles and understanding – it is important to know details of who uses a site and establish their knowledge concerning its aspects. This enables interpretation to be planned to meet their needs and to be produced at a level that is not too challenging but is also not too basic. For example, a site may mainly attract enthusiastic bird watchers that already have a reasonable knowledge of ornithology. Interpretation about birds may be aimed at a completely different level for such a site compared with one that is visited mainly by non-bird watchers. Visitor profiles and understanding of visitor knowledge can come from questionnaire surveys or focus group work.

With what: management resources – this is concerned with the finance available to carry out interpretation and the staff resources to make it happen. What budget is allocated to interpretation over the next few years and what skills do the site staff have, to produce interpretation? Assessment of this will be important in deciding on the scale and type of interpretation to be carried out and will establish the best people to be involved in its production. It may be that as the result of this process that a decision is made to get more expert help such as professional writers, designers and graphic artists.

Infrastructure audit – this is an audit of site infrastructure that may be important in interpretation, including consideration of the relative location of different items. Remember it is infrastructure that is largely responsible for directing visitors, and establishing where the car parks, toilets, trails and general site facilities are. All of these will help in deciding where to place interpretive items.

Topics, themes and stories

The need to develop clear topics, themes and stories has been established earlier in the chapter. The important issue in interpretive planning is that these should only be developed once clear aims for the interpretation have been established and when a full resource assessment has been carried out.

How do we do it?

Only when the above planning stages have been completed can we consider the best mix of interpretive media to get across the messages outlined by the topics, themes and stories. Much interpretation goes astray because this is where interpretive planning often starts. This is the wrong approach. Media should only be selected when the aims and topics, themes and stories, have been decided upon. These together with resources will dictate the best mixture of media types to get across effectively, the messages contained within the interpretation.

Interpretive objectives

These have also been discussed earlier. Interpretive objectives can only be established once topics, themes and stories have been organised. They provide a clear link to the aims set at the beginning of the interpretive planning process and help to ensure that the planning of interpretation is on course to reflect the aims set for it.

Implementation

Having gone through all the previous stages in interpretive planning, we now come to the part when the interpretation is actually developed and produced. Within an interpretive plan this stage needs careful thought. The following need to be considered:

- What are the priorities within the plan (what should be produced first, second, etc.)?
- What are the deadlines for production?
- What are the budgetary requirements for implementation?
- Who is responsible for different elements of production?

A programmed, fully costed plan of action is therefore required to ensure that what is planned actually happens. Only now can we let the interpretation begin.

Interpretation can begin following planning of what will be done. This is the exciting bit. Remember that whilst interpretation is being produced, that developmental evaluation can take place and changes made. This will improve the quality of the interpretation.

Evaluation

Having produced the interpretation outlined within the plan the time now arrives to evaluate its success in meeting its objectives (summative evaluation). It is useful at the stage of considering interpretive objectives to think of the methods by which the objectives can be monitored. If the interpretive planning process has been followed and the guidance given within this chapter on producing interpretation has been used then there is no reason why success cannot be assured.

References and further reading

Association for Heritage Interpretation (2001) *Strategic Plan 1999–2002*. Online. Available http://www.heritageinterpretation.org.uk/index.htm

Ham, S. (1992) *Environmental Interpretation: A Practical Guide for People with Big Ideas and Small Budgets*, Colorado: North American Press.

Knudson, D. M., Cable, T. T. and Beck, L. (1995) *Interpretation of Cultural and Natural Resources*, PA: Venture Publishing Inc.

Machlis, G. E. and Field, D. R. (1992) *On Interpretation: Sociology for Interpreters of Natural and Cultural History*, Oregon: Oregon State University Press.

Northamptonshire Countryside Service (1988) *Guidelines for Producing an Interpretive Panel for Community Projects*, Northampton: Northampton Countryside Service.

Piersenné, A. (1999) *Explaining Our World: An Approach to the Art of Environmental Interpretation*, London: E. & F.N. Spon.

Scottish Natural Heritage (1996) *Visitor Centres: A Practical Guide to Planning, Design and Operation*, Battleby: Scottish Natural Heritage.

Serrell, B. (1996) *Exhibit Labels: An Interpretive Approach*, London: Altamira Press.

Tilden, F. (1957) *Interpreting Our Heritage*, Chapel Hill, NC: University of North Carolina Press.

Trapp, S., Gross, M. and Zimmermann, R. (1992) *Signs, Trails, and Wayside Exhibits: Connecting People and Places*, Wisconsin: UW-SP Foundation Press Inc.

Veverka, J. A. (1994) *Interpretive Master Planning*, Montana: Falcon Press Publishing Co. Inc.

Zehr, J., Gross, M. and Zimmerman, R. (1991) *Creating Environmental Publications: A Guide to Writing and Designing for Interpreters and Environmental Educators*, Wisconsin: UW-SP Foundation Press Inc.

10 Dealing with site conflicts

Even with the best management practice, conflicts on countryside recreation sites do occur. These conflicts can be between different users of a site, the site and local communities, recreation and conservation or be associated with crime and vandalism. With the correct approaches such conflicts can be minimised. This chapter reviews the types of possible conflict that can occur and outlines techniques that can be used to resolve conflict.

Types of site conflict

There is a wide variety of conflicts that can occur on countryside recreation sites. If we are to minimise the chances of them occurring or resolve them we must first understand the nature of the conflict. What types of conflict can occur?

User/user conflict – on many sites there are a number of activities that take place using the same space. Often this occurs without problems but sometimes the needs of different user groups conflict with each other. Examples of activities that sometimes conflict include:

horse riders and cyclists	dog walkers and people who do not like dogs
mountain bikers and walkers	canoeists and anglers
waterskiers and dinghy sailors	noisy sports and quiet sports

The nature and severity of the conflict will vary from site to site and will depend upon the amount and nature of the space available, the level of use of a site, the history of use and the individuals associated with the activity.

Vandalism/crime – vandalism and crime can be a severe problem at some countryside recreation sites, particularly those closely associated with urban areas. There can be a range of problems of differing severity. Such crime can be anything from malicious damage, graffiti, car and motorbike crime such as theft and joy riding, through to arson, firearms offences, poaching, drugs, vagrancy and assault. Such problems can be very severe and involve considerable staff time and physical resources to deal with. They are also stressful for staff and create a negative and threatening site image. The problems created by vandalism and crime are difficult to deal with and may need a wide range of measures both physical and social.

Community/site – the fact that countryside recreation sites attract visitors can be a problem for some residents of surrounding communities. One particular problem may be the congestion caused by the visitors' cars speeding through villages and parking on roads and in residents' parking places. Another issue could be the fact that the recreation site may have been imposed on the community by an outside agency and sectors of the population may resent having an area managed without their control, adjacent to where they live.

Conservation/user – there are a wide variety of potential conservation/user conflicts. The nature and severity of these can be difficult to judge and the conflicts are not always obvious, particularly to the user. What types of conflict may occur?

> *Disturbance* – disturbance relates particularly to birds and animals. It occurs when users of a countryside site displace birds or animals by their presence. Examples of disturbance includes climbers disturbing nesting peregrine falcons, walkers disturbing roosting wading birds on mudflats or anglers disturbing wildfowl nesting on river banks. Disturbance can affect the ability of birds or animals to feed, rest and protect their eggs or young.
>
> *Damage* – users may intentionally or more usually unintentionally damage wildlife habitats. Examples of this may be walkers, walking across areas of bog, motorbikes creating ruts on a saltmarsh or scramblers gill walking. Intentional damage may also come from people lighting fires or picking wild flowers.

There has been considerable research carried out on the effects of different recreational activities on wildlife (Scottish Natural Heritage 1994; Sidaway 1990). The general consensus is that recreation has little significant effect on wildlife when compared with other threats, such as agricultural improvement, grazing and acid rain. However, potential conflicts between users and conservation interests needs to be considered and researched on a site-by-site basis, to enable a rational judgement to be made concerning the issues involved. Constant monitoring of the conservation issues on a site should occur to monitor long-term effects of recreation on the fauna and flora.

Dealing with conflict

It can be seen that there is a wide variety of conflicts that can affect countryside recreation sites. To deal with these, there is a range of techniques that can be used either on their own, or in combination. Before deciding which techniques are the most appropriate it is essential that the nature of the conflict is fully understood. This may involve survey work, discussion with the local community, police and site users. The following is not a comprehensive list of techniques but does outline the range of possibilities that are available.

Infrastructure improvements

As was seen in Chapter 5, infrastructure if carefully planned can be used to influence visitor behaviour. As such it can be used to alleviate certain kinds of site conflict such as theft, fire and user/user conflict. Examples of the ways in which infrastructure can be used to alleviate site conflict include:

Vandal proof materials and designs – by carefully designing infrastructure such as bins, seats and gates and selecting appropriate materials, the impact of vandalism can be reduced. For example, metal will be more resistant to vandals than wood and will not burn. In areas where vandalism is a problem, all items of infrastructure will need securing to the ground and must be as hard wearing, flame proof and damage resistant as possible.

Dog bins – the provision of dog bins (to put the dog mess in, not the dogs) may minimise the conflict between dog walkers and those of the population who do not own dogs, and resent stepping in it.

Barbecues – supplying permanent barbecues in suitable locations will decrease the risk of visitors causing fires by using their own in unsuitable locations.

Lighting – the use of lighting can decrease crime by making it more difficult for the perpetrator to hide in the darkness. In addition, it can greatly increase the confidence of users who have to pass through a site in darkness.

Bollards and barriers – these can stop cars and motorbikes from entering into places where you do not wish them to go.

Gates, fences and building security – locking sites at night and ensuring that building have adequate security such as alarms, window locks, blinds and security lights may decrease vandalism and crime on sites.

Close circuit television cameras (CCTV) – in situations where crime is a real problem the use of security cameras may be required. These can be live (cameras that are linked to video recorders or control rooms) or mock-ups of cameras that are not linked to anything (but the thieves do not know this). These deter thieves and can provide evidence for police prosecution. CCTV is particularly useful in car parks that are subject to regular car crime.

Multiple use of paths – this has already been discussed in Chapter 5 and involves sub-dividing a path or bridleway into identifiable strips suitable for walking, cycling or horse riding. This may sort out multiple use issues on a linear path.

Interpretation/education

In Chapter 5, we saw that interpretation can be used as a tool of site management by fostering the proper use of a site and developing site advocates.

Indeed Tilden wrote: 'through interpretation – understanding, through understanding – appreciation, through appreciation – protection' (Tilden 1957: 38).

If we can get visitors to understand why a place is special, they will appreciate it more. If they appreciate it more they are likely to change their behaviour in relation to it and therefore protect it. As such, interpretation can be used as a management tool to change visitors' behaviour. For example, visitors are more likely to stay on a boardwalk across a bog if they understand why the bog is special and the damage they are likely to cause if they walk on the surface of the bog. In addition, by fostering an appreciation of a site, we are more likely to develop site advocates who may become voluntary wardens, friends of a site, involved in the management or just keep an eye on the site as they walk their dog. Interpretation can therefore be seen as a tool that may seek as one of its aims to change visitor behaviour and therefore minimise potential conflicts. On sites where vandalism is prevalent the materials used in the interpretive process need to be chosen with care and be fire, graffiti, scratch and child proof.

The role of education in resolving site conflicts revolves around making links with schools from the surrounding area and engaging positively with the teachers and children. The purpose of this is to develop an understanding in the children as to why a site is special and to engender a feeling of ownership. A child that feels emotionally attached to a site and feels that the site is 'theirs' is much more likely to look after it and exert peer pressure on his or her friends. Getting children directly involved in a site can be useful, for example planting trees or creating a wild flower meadow. Such activities give a sense of ownership, 'Those are my trees – I helped plant them.'

Patrolling

Patrolling involves having members of staff walking around a site on a regular basis to keep an eye on it. It is like being a police officer on the beat. Anyone patrolling must be identifiable as a member of staff, either by having a uniform or some form of identification such as a badge. It is also important to have a means of communication, such as a radio or a mobile phone, so that help can be summoned quickly if needed. Through regular patrolling, problems can be identified quickly and action taken. This might be identifying items that have been vandalised and need immediate action or dealing with individuals or groups on the site who are behaving inappropriately (such as using motorbikes, air rifles or sniffing glue). Skill is required in dealing with such situations and advice on how to handle them has already been given in Chapter 8. It is important in such situations to have a good grasp of the law. A close working relationship with the local police is also essential as they may need to be summoned for assistance where situations cannot be dealt with by site staff. Volunteer wardens and rangers are frequently used for patrolling duties. This can be very effective but volunteers need to be selected with care (not everybody is suitable for this kind of work; they need good communication skills, tact, diplomacy and confidence and you need to be trained carefully in how to deal with different situations in which they may find themselves.

In addition to dealing with problems, patrolling is a very positive way of developing closer contact with members of the local community and other site users. Having wardens and rangers visibly looking after visitors can deal with many of the problems faced by surrounding communities and alleviate some community conflicts.

Bylaws

Countryside recreation sites frequently have bylaws that cover a range of issues that may be considered as nuisances, such as banning dogs from certain areas, camping, excessive noise or public gatherings. Bylaws are developed by local authorities and need to be confirmed by a relevant secretary of state. They cover minor offences and are designed to cater for the individual needs of an area, by preventing a range of actions that may be considered detrimental to the lives of people, animals and plants in the locality. They do not replace criminal law, but supplement it. The penalty for breaking a bylaw is usually a fine as they are regarded as minor offences. Anyone can take an individual to court for breaking a bylaw and this is done by applying for a summons from a local magistrates' court. Site managers can therefore enforce bylaws if they choose to. However, the value of bylaws lies principally with the fact that on sites, they are normally displayed prominently and inform visitors of the standards of behaviour that are expected, and what is not permitted. This makes life easier for site staff, who when confronted with someone breaking a bylaw, can point to the necessary signs. This makes the defence of ignorance harder to justify and will make it easier for site staff to diffuse conflicts. If all else fails and an individual refuses to comply with a bylaw then site managers still have the option of going to a magistrates' court to seek a summons.

Zoning

Zoning is a technique that is frequently used to resolve conflicts caused by the multiple use of the same space, by competing user groups. This involves creating zones that are dedicated for use by one particular user group or another. Zoning can take place over time as well as over space.

> *Time* – this is where different activities are allowed to use an area at different times. For example, on a lake where there is conflict between waterskiers and windsurfers you could allow windsurfing on Mondays, Wednesdays, Fridays and Sundays and waterskiing on Tuesdays, Thursdays and Saturdays. This separates usage, whilst ensuring both user groups have access (but not use it, at the same time).
>
> *Space* – this is where an area is zoned to enable different activities to occur in different places at the same time. So for example, where there is conflict between waterskiers, windsurfers and anglers on a lake, it can be divided by buoys, into separate zones. In each zone, a separate activity is allowed, thus the resource is shared between different user groups (see Figure 10.1).

The purpose of zoning is to create a win-win situation in which all users feel they have gained something. The use of zones is not restricted to active sports. It is

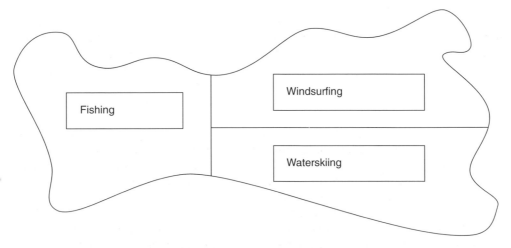

Figure 10.1 Spatial zonation of a lake for different activities

frequently used to deal with other issues, for example dogs. On many recreation sites and in particular in areas where children play, such as playgrounds and beaches, dogs are excluded from some areas, but allowed in others. So for example, dogs may be banned from popular parts of a beach but allowed on the quieter sections. In this way the beach is zoned.

Local involvement

Conflicts between sites and the surrounding communities can frequently be caused by bad communication, lack of understanding and the feeling that the community has no say over the management of a site. All of these concerns can to some extent be resolved, by developing better communications between site managers and site staff and the local communities. This can be through informal channels such as getting local people involved in the site as volunteers, developing links with local schools, giving talks to community groups, holding open days and mixing in with the community. It can also help to develop more formal arrangements. Examples of more formal arrangements include:

> *Site committees* – these are committees of site managers and representatives from the local community. They will have an active involvement in the management of the site and will be a decision-making group.
>
> *Site forums* – these are discussion forums in which site managers can discuss site issues with the local community and or user groups. Whilst they are not decision-making bodies, they do act as a talking shop in which issues can be considered and discussed. The process can help in two ways. First it can be good for site managers to have a forum to listen to the views and attitudes of local people and site users. Second, it helps the local community and user groups to develop an understanding of site issues and develop a relationship with site managers.

Whichever mechanism is used to communicate with the local community, the aim is to get the community to see the site as something of value to them and to feel a sense of ownership of it. If this occurs and local people become actively involved in the site, then it is more likely to be protected and local conflicts will be reduced.

Conflicts between different groups

Some site conflicts will be between different user groups each wanting to use the same space for their particular pastime or between users and conservation or heritage interests. Zoning and the careful use of infrastructure will often resolve such conflicts. However, before such techniques are instigated it is important to get representatives of the different user groups around a table to discuss the nature of the conflict and to consider ways of coming to an amicable resolution. Many sites develop site forums or site user groups and liaison committees, to formalise such discussions. Such groups need to start by identifying the nature of the problem and developing an understanding of the various viewpoints concerning the use of the site and its management. Once the issues involved are clearly understood, areas of common ground can be identified and built upon. From the basis of common ground, management mechanisms based upon consensus decisions can be developed. Through this kind of process all parties will feel that they have an outcome that they are happy with. It will almost certainly require each party to give a little. Meetings need to be carefully chaired to ensure all parties are involved and to direct discussion in a constructive manner. If not handled carefully, positions can polarise and harden.

Sometimes such negotiations fail to achieve results and agreement cannot be reached. In such circumstances arbitration may be required. Arbitration is where a neutral individual agreed by all parties negotiates with them about the issues and possible solutions and makes a decision independently about what will happen. For this to be effective all parties must agree to the process and agree to abide by the decision. Such arbitration can be through voluntary consent or may be in the form of a more formal public enquiry whereby an independent inspector makes a decision.

Voluntary bans

One outcome of such discussions between user groups may be a voluntary ban on certain activities at certain times or in particular places. Many such voluntary bans are already in place on many recreation sites. For example, on a number of climbing crags there is a voluntary ban from climbing particular sections of cliff whilst birds are using it as nesting sites. These voluntary bans on climbing have been negotiated between the British Mountaineering Council and the site managers. Such bans need to be communicated to users and this is normally carried out through news items in magazines, information in guidebooks and on-site information such as signs. Such voluntary arrangements are normally very successful. They work best when the nature of a conflict is obvious and the user groups can readily understand the effect that their using a site will have upon it.

References and further reading

Aitchison, J. W. and Jones, P. L. (1994) *A Sporting Chance for the Countryside: Sport and Recreation in the Welsh Countryside; Case Studies of Good Practice; Report Prepared for the Sports Council for Wales and the Countryside Council for Wales*, Sports Council for Wales.

Parkes, C. (1994) *Law of the Countryside*, Devon: Countryside Management Association.

Scottish Natural Heritage (1994) *Recreation and the Natural Heritage: A Research Review*, Edinburgh: Scottish Natural Heritage.

Scottish National Rural Partnership (1998) *Good Practice in Rural Development: no. 5, Consensus Building*, Edinburgh: Scottish Office.

Sidaway, R. (1990) *Birds and Walkers: A Review of Existing Research on Access to the Countryside and Disturbance to Birds*, London: Ramblers' Association.

Sports Council (1995) *Good Practice in the Planning and Management of Sport and Active Recreation in the Countryside*, London: Sports Council.

Tilden, F. (1957) *Interpreting Our Heritage*, Chapel Hill, NC: University of North Carolina Press.

Web addresses

British Mountaineering Council – http://www.thebmc.co.uk – details of voluntary climbing bans.

11 Health and safety

Looking after the health and safety of site visitors, employees, and volunteers is important. Visitors rightly expect that a visit to the countryside will not end up with a trip to hospital or to a mortuary. Whilst it is impossible to ensure that no accidents will ever happen in the countryside, managing organisations have a duty of care over those who visit, those whom they employ and volunteers. This chapter looks at issues associated with health and safety, outlines the legislation and suggests steps that can be taken to minimise the risk of accidents and to comply with the law.

Why do we need to consider health and safety on recreation sites?

Ensuring the health and safety of employees and visitors on countryside recreation sites is a vital component of managing a site. There are a number of reasons for this. First there is a moral issue in that people are employed to work on sites and visitors are encouraged to use them. There is therefore a moral duty for the organisation that manages a site to take all necessary steps to ensure that the risks of injury or death to people there (visitors or employees) are minimised as far as is practically possible. A second reason is that consideration of the health and safety of employees and visitors is a legal requirement and therefore has to be done. Failure to do so is a criminal offence. Finally health and safety needs to be considered to minimise the risk of litigation. Litigation is where an individual makes claims against an organisation through the courts, for damages and compensation with regard to breaches in the duty of care enshrined in health and safety legislation. Sadly, the culture of litigation that has developed over the last ten years means that fear of litigation forms an increasingly important part of decision making on sites, particularly with regard to health and safety.

Health and safety legislation

The basis of all British health and safety law, is the Health and Safety at Work Act (1974). This sets out the general duties which employers have towards employees and members of the public, and employees have to themselves and to each other. Within this Act duties are qualified by the principle of 'so far as is reasonably practical'. This means that an organisation has a duty to take steps to minimise the risk of accidents. However, it is understood that it is not normally possible to exclude totally the possibility of accidents occurring. What the Health and Safety Executive (the body responsible for overseeing health and safety in Britain) will want to know if investigating an accident, is what steps were taken to minimise risk. They will consider this against the principle of 'so far as is reasonably possible' and make a judgment. There is no complete benchmark of what 'reasonably possible' is, as there are so many different situations in which accidents can occur. Case law (rulings from investigations of accidents in relation to health and safety legislation) will help, as will literature, training and advice from the Health and Safety Executive. One of the difficulties in considering health and safety, is the interpretation of this statement. Failure to comply with the Health and Safety at Work Act is a criminal offence.

The management of Health and Safety at Work Regulations 1992 (the management regulations), specify more explicitly the duties of employers. Regulations are laws, approved by Parliament, and as such have to be adhered to. A core element of these regulations is an obligation for employers to carry out suitable and sufficient assessment of all risks arising from their undertaking and to record the significant findings. This is carried out through risk assessment. Assessment of risk must consider employees and members of the public. Besides risk assessment the regulations state that employers need to (Health and Safety Executive 2001):

- make arrangements for implementing the health and safety measures identified as necessary by the risk assessment
- appoint competent people to help them to implement the arrangements
- set up emergency procedures
- provide clear information and training to employees
- work together with other employers sharing the workplace.

There are a wide range of other health and safety regulations concerning such issues such as reporting of injuries, diseases and dangerous occurrences (RIDDOR – the Reporting of Injuries, Diseases and Dangerous Occurrences Regulations 1995), personal protective equipment (PPE – Personal Protective Equipment at Work regulations 1992) and control of substances hazardous to health (COSHH – Control of Substances Hazardous to Health regulations 1999). It is beyond the scope of this book to go into detail concerning the vast amount of regulations associated with these and other health and safety regulations. For more information refer to the Health and Safety Executive web page detailed at the end of this chapter.

Responsibilities and duties

Under the Health and Safety at Work Act (1974) employers and employees have duties and responsibilities. The Act lists five particular duties of an employer to an employee.

1 The provision and maintenance of plant (equipment) and systems of work that are safe and without risks to health.
2 Arrangements for ensuring safety and absence of risks to health when using, handling, storing and transporting articles and substances.
3 The provision of relevant information, instruction, training and supervision.
4 Maintaining any place of work under the employer's control in a safe condition and without risks to health.

5   The provision and maintenance of a safe working environment without risks to health, and of adequate welfare facilities.

The Act requires that organisations have to prepare, revise and bring to the notice of employees, a written statement of the policy of the organisation in relation to health and safety and the organisation and arrangements for carrying out that policy.

Employees also have legal duties in relation to health and safety. They are charged with a duty to take reasonable care of their own safety and that of others, co-operate with employers on health and safety matters, use work items correctly, report accidents and incidents and inform appropriate people within an organisation of health and safety hazards.

Risk assessment

A requirement of the Management of Health and Safety at Work Regulations 1992 (the management regulations), is to carry out risk assessments. Risk assessment is the systematic and careful examination of everything on a site that could cause harm to people (employees and visitors) and considering if the precautions taken are adequate and comply with the health and safety legislation. An important component of this process is assessing how significant risks are and considering how to minimise them. The Health and Safety Executive suggests five steps that should be taken when assessing risk (Health and Safety Executive 2001a):

Look for and identify hazards – before risk can be assessed all hazards must be identified. A hazard is anything that can cause harm. Hazards can be identified by:

- personal knowledge and experience of managers
- asking employees
- a safety audit where all of a site is considered systematically for hazards
- Health and Safety Executive guidance
- consideration of accident statistics.

By way of illustration, the kinds of hazards that may be identified on a countryside recreation site may be:

water bodies	mine shafts	cliffs
poisonous plants	barbed wire	steps	bridges
badly maintained stiles	cars driving too fast	
contaminated land	electricity pylons	bulls
dangerous substances	machine tools	
children's playgrounds	overhanging branches	

Each site will have its own set of hazards, both natural and artificial, that need to be considered. The main thing is to consider site hazards in a systematic manner to ensure that all hazards are identified.

Decide who might be harmed and how – having identified hazards, who is at risk and what is the nature of the risk? Is it a risk to employees, to specific user groups (such as mountain bikers, anglers or school groups) or to all visitors to a site? What may be the likely severity of an accident caused by the hazard? Will an accident lead to a fatality, serious injury or disease, minor injury or disease or damage to machinery or equipment? A consideration of who will be injured and the severity of injury should an accident occur, will be important in deciding what action to take, to minimise the risk of an accident occurring.

Evaluate the risks and decide if existing precautions are adequate or whether more should be done – risks associated with identified hazards now need to be considered. The risk attached to a hazard is the chance of someone being harmed by it. There are many ways to consider this. Some organisations rate risks on a scale of high, medium and low.

High   would be a very serious injury, which has a high probability of occurring
Medium   would be a very serious injury, which is unlikely to occur, or a lesser injury that is likely to occur
Low   would be where any injury is unlikely and would be slight if it did occur

Ramsey (1996) suggests the following scale:

Likely	occurs repeatedly, even expected	1 in 10
Probable	not surprising, will occur several times	1 in 100
Possible	could occur some time	1 in 1000
Remote	unlikely to occur, though conceivable	1 in 10,000
Improbable	so unlikely that the probability is close to zero	1 in 100,000

Sorting out the chance of an incident occurring (the risk) is difficult, and has to be based upon the best information available at the time. This could be past records of incidents on a site, health and safety statistics or personal experience. Obviously the greater the severity of an incident caused by a hazard and the greater the risk of an incident happening, the greater the imperative is to take action to minimise the risk. It is unlikely that risks can ever be minimised to zero, but action should be taken to ensure that the risks of injury or death to people on the site (visitors, employees or volunteers) are minimised as far as is practically possible.

Having decided upon the nature of the risk, consideration needs to be made as to whether precautions already taken to minimise risk are adequate and whether new action is required to minimise the risk. This may be providing the public with information, fencing off parts of a site considered to present a risk, carrying out regular inspections of trees with branches overhanging a path, providing non-slip surfaces to steps or ensuring a footbridge is inspected on a regular basis.

Record your findings – the regulations require that having carried out a risk assessment, that significant hazards and conclusions need to be recorded. It is a duty of the employer to tell employees about the findings of such a risk assessment. It is good practice to produce an action plan of how identified risks will be minimised, setting out priorities, costs and detailing who will be responsible for achieving the action. Such an action plan can be reviewed on a regular basis and the action that has been taken recorded. Such written records will be important if there is an accident and a health and safety inspector wants to know what precautions have been taken to minimise the risk associated with a hazard.

Review your assessment and revise if necessary – health and safety on sites needs continual review and improvement. It is good practice to review health and safety practices regularly, but it is essential if the nature of hazards on a site, changes, such as the creation of a new cycle trail or the development of a new visitor centre.

Who should be responsible for health and safety on a site?

Employers have a duty under the law to ensure, so far as is reasonably practical, the health and safety of employees and visitors to a site. To ensure this occurs, it is normal for organisations to appoint someone within an organisation as a health and safety officer. This person will be responsible for developing and implementing health and safety policies and ensuring that the organisation discharges its duties in relation to health and safety legislation. Large organisations such as local authorities may well have a full-time health and safety officer, whilst smaller organisations may have someone for whom health and safety is only part of their job. In addition, it is normal to have individual employees allocated responsibility for certain aspects of health and safety provision such as hazardous substances or evacuation of a building in case of fire.

Training

Health and safety is such an important and complex issue that training is required for all individuals who work for an organisation. Indeed, the provision of health and safety training, on recruitment and whenever there are changes which result in an increased risk or different exposure to risk, is a requirement of health and safety legislation. Training must be provided for all people who work at a site and as such volunteers as well as paid employees require training. Training is needed at several levels. First there is the whole concept of health and safety and the legislation and the regulations associated with it. Second there is the aspect of safe practice in the workplace. This may involve training in the use of tools, vehicles, lone working, use of sprays, lifting or use of machinery. First aid is another area where training is required and organisations should train as many of their employees as possible in it.

Gaining more information

The purpose of this chapter is to outline the issues that need to be considered in relation to health and safety. It is not possible to cover all aspects of health and safety explicitly and readers are urged to obtain more detailed information and guidance about specific health and safety issues. The first point of call for this should be the excellent web site of the Health and Safety Executive (the HSE).

References and further reading

Countryside Recreation Network (1996) *Playing Safe: Managing Visitor Safety in the Countryside*, Cardiff: Countryside Recreation Network.

Ramsey, E. (1996) 'Managing the health and safety of visitors', in Countryside Recreation Network, *Playing Safe: Managing Visitor Safety in the Countryside*, Cardiff: Countryside Recreation Network.

Health and Safety Executive (2001) *Health and Safety Regulation: A Short Guide*. Online. Available HTTP: http://www.hse.gov.uk/pubns/hsc13.htm (8 July 2001).

Health and Safety Executive (2001a) *Five Steps to Risk Assessment*. Online. Available HTTP: http://www.hse.gov.uk/pubns/indg163.pdf (8 July 2001).

Potter, D. (1997) *Risk and Safety: the Law and Practice for Adventure Playgrounds*, London: E. & F.N. Spon.

Watkins, G. (1997) *The Health and Safety Handbook*, London: Sweet & Maxwell.

Web sites

Health and Safety Executive: http://www.hse.gov.uk/hsehome.htm

12 Recreation planning

The previous sections of this book have concentrated on marketing, understanding the site and its visitors, and product development. Each of these elements can be looked at on an individual basis but much more is to be gained if a holistic approach is taken to site management. This requires a planning approach and the production of planning documentation. This concluding chapter brings together the previous elements of the book and discusses the need for planning and the process involved in the successful production of a plan.

A management plan is a document written specifically for a site that explains *how* a site is to be managed and *why*. Management planning is the process by which a management plan is produced and put into practice.

There is much confusion about management plans. They are however very straightforward. Management plans are used to decide:

- where we are now
- where we want to be in the future
- how we will get there
- how we know when we have arrived.

Why plan site management?

A comment often heard about management plans is that they are a waste of space and take up time and resources that could be used for actually getting on and carrying out site management. Nothing could be further from the truth.

One of the first important things to understand about management plans, is that it is the process of planning that is important, rather than the plan itself. Without going through a rational planning process, it is difficult to decide how a site should be developed, what needs to be done, how much it will cost and who is going to do the work. Not all recreation sites will need a plan. Some small sites may be too small to warrant the time required to go through the planning process and production of a plan. However, the larger the site and the more complex it is, the greater is the need to plan. What are the key reasons for going through the planning process and producing a management plan?

- to describe the site
- to identify and evaluate site attributes
- to guide future managers and ensure continuity of management

- to formulate site objectives
- to help in setting priorities
- to resolve conflicts of interest
- to bring together people and organisations involved in managing a site
- to help to manage change
- to programme and schedule work (who does what and when)
- to identify resource requirements
- to provide a means of checking on the effectiveness of management (monitoring).

These reasons are not stated in any order of importance and will be different for each site. No two management plans will ever be the same and there is no standard way of producing a management plan. However, there is good practice and a general approach that can be followed and adapted to meet individual site needs. Let us look at the management planning process.

The management planning process

The management planning process can be broken down into a number of component parts (see Figure 12.1 below).

It can be seen from Figure 12.1, that the process is sequential in its nature and broken down into two key areas. First there is the strategic planning of a site. This is followed by the operational planning stage concerned with producing and implementing a work plan, monitoring and finally reviewing the plan. Let us look at all of the planning process in more detail.

Strategic planning

Strategic planning is associated with assessing a site, and based upon an evaluation of site issues developing a vision and policies for site management. This process can therefore be broken down into a number of component parts.

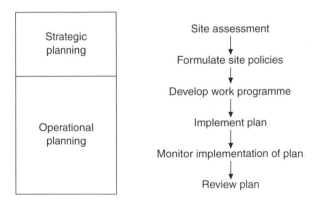

Figure 12.1 The management planning process

Introduction

The introduction will set the scene for the rest of the plan and the planning process. An introduction to a management plan may outline some of the following:

- the purpose of the plan
- the organisation(s) involved in producing and implementing the plan, together with their individual remits
- a map of the area covered by the plan
- the linkages between the plan and other planning documentation such as previous management plans.

An introduction should not be too detailed, but should set the context within which the plan should be viewed.

Assessment of the site

A full assessment of a site will help us to establish the opportunities that the site offers, but will also inform us about the many factors that may constrain what we are able to do. This is very pertinent to the management of recreation sites, in that whilst recreation may be a key objective of a site, other factors such as conservation, landscape, archaeology and community issues, need to be considered. Only by systematically describing a site and evaluating the relative value of different aspects, can we develop a full understanding. The assessment of a site can therefore be broken down into two stages. First there is the description of the site and second the evaluation of the site based upon the description.

1 Description

Before any strategic decisions can be made about a site and its management, it is first vital to describe the site fully. What should be in a description? The description can be broken down into two key areas, the description of the site itself and a description of what is known about site visitors. Headings that can be used in the description of the site can be seen in Table 12.1. This is not an exhaustive list and individual sites may have areas that are not covered by these headings.

It can be seen that these headings reflect areas already covered in detail in Chapter 2. Readers should refer to this for more detail. In putting all of this

Table 12.1 Headings under which site description can be considered

General site details	*Environmental information*	*Recreational information*
• Maps/photographs	• Physical	• Accessibility
• Land ownership	• Biological	• Access within site
• Designations	• Archaeological/historical	• Site features
• Management/staffing	• Landscape	• Site infrastructure
• Community issues	• Land use	• Relationship with surroundings
		• Information audit
		• Welcome audit

information into a plan, always seek to compile the information into as concise a form as possible. So for example, a description of the ornithological interest of the site should outline the importance of a site for birds and describe notable or endangered species and species that have specific management requirements. The description should not be everything that is known about the birds on a site. Species lists should not form part of a plan, but can be listed in appendices. It is also important as part of the description to identify any shortfall in knowledge. Addressing this may then form part of the future work plan.

In terms of describing the visitor to the site and the nature of visitor use, the following information should be considered:

- Who visits the site?
- What motivates people to visit the site?
- What do they do when on the site?
- Where do the visitors come from?
- How did they find out about the site?
- What do they like about the site?
- What do they not like about the site?
- How many people visit the site and when do they come?
- Where are they distributed across the site?
- Are there any trends in the visitor usage of the site?

Again, the description should be a concise summary of the key information that is required to make management decisions and not a description of everything that is known about the visitor. As with the site description, it is important to outline areas where there is no data available. The methods available to find out details of visitor usage have already been outlined in Chapter 3. This chapter should be referred to for more detail.

2 Evaluation

The evaluation of a site will be based upon its description. Evaluation involves a more detailed examination of all of the facts about a site as revealed by the site description. Evaluation involves making judgements about important site elements such as conservation value, visitor use and community issues. Making these judgements may not be easy and there is no hard and fast method of going about it. The use of criteria, against which the site can be compared may make the process more systematic. The Countryside Commission (1998: 28), suggest the following evaluation criteria:

- formal status
- rarity
- fragility/vulnerability
- diversity/variety
- survival/condition
- representativeness/typicality
- physical location and ecological relationships
- documentation, recorded history and cultural associations
- recreation, safety and security

- economic potential
- size/extent.

By comparing these headings against what is known about a site as outlined in the site description, the site will be viewed from a different perspective. It should also help in asking questions about a site that will assist in the next stage of the planning process, that of formulating site policies. It can be useful at this stage to consult with relevant organisations and individuals to obtain a range of views, on what is important about a site. This will make organisations and individuals feel part of the planning process and therefore feel some ownership of the final plan.

Another technique that can be used in evaluating a site is called a SWOT analysis. SWOT, stands for *Strengths, Weaknesses, Opportunities and Threats*. In this technique you view a site or specific site features against each of these four headings. For example, a simple version of a SWOT analysis for a site may be as follows:

Strengths:	location close to town
	good car parks
	circular walks
	viewpoint
	wetland area important for birds
Weaknesses:	deteriorating toilets
	lack of children's facilities
	litter
	lack of public transport
Opportunities:	develop facilities for children
	improve facilities for bird watching
	make site accessible for disabled visitors
Threats:	lack of resources
	competition from neighbouring site
	vegetation succession on wetland area

SWOT analysis will help in the consideration of site issues and will help towards the next stages of planning.

Having carried out an evaluation it needs to be presented in a concise form within the plan. There is no standard way of doing this. However, it should be presented as a structured argument that shows why the conclusions about the site have been reached. This can be arranged under headings such as conservation, archaeology, interpretation, visitors, or under the evaluation criteria headings such as fragility, diversity and economic potential. It can also be in the form of headings relating to important site features such as wetland, castle, woodland and visitor centre. Whichever route is chosen, seek to be concise. A summary of the key findings from the evaluation exercise is a useful end to this section of the planning process.

Vision for the site

Having evaluated a site, a vision can be developed. This will highlight the ideal way that a site should be developed and the purposes that it should seek to achieve. It should be an idealised view of what a site could become and does not have to be based upon the realities of present resources. It must however, be based upon the site assessment and will guide managers and others associated with a site as to what the core purposes of the site should be. The vision for a site is often expressed within a management plan as the aims for the site. An example of a vision expressed as aims could be:

Vision

To make Knobbly Bottom Country Park into a recreational resource of the highest quality whilst conserving the conservation, landscape and archaeological interest of the site.

Site aims

- To increase the number of visitors to the park through the provision of high quality infrastructure and the development of site features.
- To develop the site so that all members of society have access to it.
- To manage and conserve the wetland areas of the site, and in particular undertake management to protect the resident population of marsh fritillary butterflies.
- To preserve the remains of the castle so that visitors may gain access to it.
- To provide visitors with high quality information and interpretation about the site.
- To develop facilities for walking, cycling and mountain biking.

Note that these do not state the specifics of what will be done but give an outline of what the plan seeks to achieve. How these aims will be achieved will be addressed within the operational part of the management plan.

Developing site objectives

Having decided what the vision for the site should be, specific objectives should be decided upon. These state exactly what the plan seeks to achieve within its life-time. They therefore need to be a realistic assessment of what can be achieved and whilst they should mirror the vision statements, they may not necessarily totally realise the vision. This may take longer to achieve than the lifetime of the plan. They are important, in that they can be used as a basis for evaluation of how successful the plan has been. As such, site objectives should be *SMART*: that is, *S*pecific, *M*easurable, *A*chievable, *R*elevant and *T*imetabled. Example site objectives may be:

- by the year 2005 to increase the number of visitors to the site by 20 per cent
- by 2004 to ensure that the site complies with the requirements of the Disability Discrimination Act
- to continually improve the management of the wetland and increase the population of marsh fritillary butterflies

---

- by 2004, ensure that the castle walls have been consolidated and that the public have access to it
- by 2005, to have completely re-signposted the site
- by 2005, to have developed and placed site orientation panels at every entrance and car park
- by 2005, to have undertaken a complete review of site infrastructure and to have carried out improvements
- by 2006 to have developed a low-level family cycle trail around the site
- by 2006 to have produced a site interpretation plan.

Methods

Having assessed a site, decided upon a vision, and set site management objectives, the last stage of strategic planning is to consider the methods that may be used to achieve the objectives. A single method may be outlined or a range considered and from the range an appropriate method decided upon. The methods will be specific to the objective being addressed. For example:

Site objective

By 2005, to have undertaken a complete review of site infrastructure and to have carried out improvements.

Outline prescription

1 Carry out a full site infrastructure audit to assess the nature, location and condition of present site infrastructure.
2 Develop a design guide for site infrastructure that ensures all infrastructure is fit for purpose, suitable for disabled visitors, low maintenance and is of a design, appropriate for the site.
3 Based upon 1 and 2 above, develop a list of maintenance, replacements and additions to site infrastructure.
4 Make the improvements to site infrastructure.
5 Carry out a yearly maintenance audit on all site infrastructure.
6 Carry out a new review in 2006.

Deciding upon the most appropriate methods for delivering the site objectives is the last component of the strategic planning section of management planning. The next phase is to produce an operational plan based upon the strategic plan. If you like you are deciding what you want to do first (the strategic plan) and then considering how you are going to do it (the operational plan).

Operational planning

The operational planning section of management planning can be broken down into the following parts:

* a work programme
* consideration of resource requirements
* monitoring and review.

Whilst these are separate sections they need to be considered together. For example, the work programme will depend on the resources that are available to carry it out. Having completed the strategic planning it is the operational plan that guides the day-to-day management of a site and provides the plan of what will be done, when it will be done, the resources required and who will do it. It is the part of the plan that site managers will refer to most in making day-to-day decisions.

Work programme

A work programme will specify what is to be done, when it is to be done and who will do it. It can be broken down into two areas:

> *Repeated tasks*: regular tasks carried out such as maintenance, grass cutting and litter collection. These will need to be budgeted for and organised on a yearly basis.
> 　　*Projects*: specific projects that can be seen as management tasks on their own, such as the development of a cycle route, erosion control or development of a visitor centre. Projects should be individually costed and scheduled.

There is no standard way of compiling a work programme. However, it is important that all of the essential information is provided to enable day-to-day management to take place. An example of a small section of a work plan can be seen in Figure 12.2.

　　The projects can be built into more detailed yearly work plans. By planning the use of time in this fashion, projects and regular tasks can be organised to fit in with resources (both financial and human), to ensure tasks are spaced out so that they can be achieved realistically.

　　In addition to such time planning, it may be useful to provide greater detail of each project to make what needs to be carried out more explicit. For example:

Develop family cycle trail – project description and work plan

Description of the project
To develop a cycle trail by using the disused railway track bed linked to the canal tow path, to form a circular route of 5 kilometres. The route has no significant gradients and should be developed to appeal to family groups. This will require the railway track to be surfaced to a width of 2m with crushed aggregate topped with dust and the development of two link paths. The trail will require full signposting and an information leaflet about the route needs to be produced.

Length of path that will need aggregate surfacing:	3.5km
Who will do the work:	Contractors
Costs:	
Estimated cost/m = £15	
Estimated cost of surfacing	£52,500
Signposting – estimated 14 signs @ £75/sign	£1050
Cycle gates – 4 needed at £250 each	£1000
Production of a cycle trail leaflet	£1500
Cycle racks	£1000
Estimated cost of project	£57,050
Anticipated source of funding:	
Heritage Lottery Fund and local authority	
When is the work to be done?	
Surfacing of railway track bed	2004/2005
Development of two links between railway and tow path	2005/2006
Signposting and infrastructure	2002/2006
Production of cycle trail leaflet	2006

Producing a more detailed project specification such as this, links to the next section of the operational section of a plan, resource requirements.

Resource requirements

The planning of resource requirements does not always form part of a management plan and may be developed into a separate budgeting document. However, whether part of the plan or not, it is essential to consider in detail the resources that will be required to implement the plan. This is particularly important if you are bidding for finance from outside agencies such as the Heritage Lottery Fund or grant aid from the Countryside Agency, but it is also essential when bidding for money within the normal budgeting rounds within an organisation. In planning the resource requirements for the implementation of a plan, a number of factors have to be taken into consideration. These include:

- how much money is needed
- breakdown of estimated costs into material, labour, plant, etc.
- labour requirements
- where the money will come from
- estimates of income.

Monitoring

Monitoring is concerned with checking you have done, what you planned to do and whether what you have done has had the effects you intended. It should form an essential part of any plan and may be a requirement for grant aid. Monitoring can

Repeated tasks

Project	Who will do the work	Month work to be carried out											
		J	F	M	A	M	J	J	A	S	O	N	D
Grass cutting	Council					▓	▓	▓	▓				
Litter collection	Site staff	▓	▓	▓	▓	▓	▓	▓	▓	▓	▓	▓	▓
Planting flower beds	Council			▓	▓								
Strimming of paths	Contractor					▓	▓	▓					
Top dressing of paths	Contractor		▓	▓	▓								
Mowing hay meadow	Site staff							▓					
Monitor population of marsh fritillary butterflies	Site staff						▓	▓	▓				

Projects

Project	Who will do the work	Year project to be carried out				
		2002	2003	2004	2005	2006
Improve access for disabled visitors	Site staff, volunteers	▓	▓	▓		
Consolidate castle walls and provide public access	Contractors		▓	▓		
Re-signpost the site	Site staff			▓	▓	
Produce interpretive plan	Site staff				▓	▓
Review and improve site infrastructure	Site staff	▓	▓			
Develop family cycle trail	Site staff, contractors and volunteers			▓	▓	▓

Figure 12.2 An example of a work programme split into repeated tasks and projects

be broken down into two sections, the implementation of the work plan (whether it has been carried out and what problems were encountered) and monitoring of the site and its visitors (the effect the work plan has had on the site). It is normal to review the implementation of the work plan on a yearly basis, whilst monitoring of the site and its visitors needs to be carried out in accordance with what needs to be monitored.

The most difficult part about monitoring is deciding what should be monitored. It is not possible to monitor everything and monitoring the wrong things can waste much time and resources. Monitoring of the implementation of the work plan is relatively straightforward and involves a systematic review of what has been carried out for real, against what the plan intended. However, monitoring of the site and its visitors is more problematic. Start off by considering what issues or features really need to be monitored. This should be based largely upon the site evaluation and the objectives set for the site. The next stage is to consider what indicators will give guidance as to the success or failure of a plan in meeting its objectives. Again, it is important to reflect back onto the objectives set for the plan when deciding upon indicators. Methodologies then need to be considered for how to monitor these indicators. Finally an assessment needs to be made of the resources required to carry out the monitoring and this needs to be written into the financial planning section of the plan. It can therefore be seen that monitoring needs to be written into the work plan from the start and not be an afterthought.

Reviewing the plan

When producing a plan, a date for review needs to be set. Any plan will only ever have a limited shelf life and will need to be reviewed to consider any changes or additions that need to be made. Changes may be needed, due to the changing nature of the site, changing objectives of the managing organisation, changes in funding arrangements or new thinking about the management of a particular issue such as a wetland. A review of the plan will consider the whole plan, both the strategic planning section and the operational planning section. In reviewing the strategic section of the plan it is important to consider the changing nature of the site since the last plan and to carry out a new site assessment. Based upon this, a check can be made to see if the objectives set for the site and the site vision is still appropriate, and consider changes. As the work plan of the previous plan will (hopefully) have been completed, a new work plan and financial plan will need to be produced based upon the new site vision and its objectives. It is normal to review a plan after five years but a smaller interval of time is also appropriate. Management planning is a dynamic process that is never completed. One plan will inevitably lead to another plan that will in turn lead to another one. The process will never end but over time the site product should get better and visitors should leave a site more satisfied. After all, that is what it is all about!

References and further reading

Barber, A. (1991) *A Guide to Management Plans for Parks and Open Spaces*, Reading: Institute of Leisure and Amenity Planning.

Countryside Commission (1992) *AONB Management Plans*, Manchester: Countryside Commission.

Countryside Commission (1998) *Site Management Planning: A Guide*, Northampton: Countryside Commission.

Countryside Council for Wales (1996) *A Guide to the Production of Management Plans for Nature Reserves and Protected Areas*, Bangor: Countryside Council for Wales.

Greenhalgh, L. and Worpole, K. (1996) *People, Parks and Cities: A Guide to Current Practice in Urban Parks. A Report for the Department of the Environment*, Norwich: HMSO.

Morgan, G. (1991) *A Strategic Approach to the Planning and Management of Parks and Open Spaces*, Reading: Institute of Leisure and Amenity Planning.

Selman, P. (2000) *Environmental Planning*, London: Sage Publications.

Sutherland, W. J. and Hill, D. A. (1995) *Managing Habitats for Nature Conservation*, Cambridge: Cambridge University Press.

Index

Note: page numbers in *italics* refer to figures or illustrations where these are separated from the textual reference.